INTERPRETING 2 PETER
THROUGH AFRICAN AMERICAN
WOMEN'S MORAL WRITINGS

EARLY CHRISTIANITY AND ITS LITERATURE

Emerson B. Powery, General Editor

Number 32

INTERPRETING 2 PETER THROUGH AFRICAN AMERICAN WOMEN'S MORAL WRITINGS

Shively T. J. Smith

SBL PRESS

 **PRESS**

Atlanta

Copyright © 2023 by Shively T. J. Smith

Library of Congress Control Number: 2023932887

To our daughters.
Every day you remind me that what we see, hear, feel, and know
through our embodiments matter. Thank you for holding me steady.

Contents

Preface

In the fall of 2020, the Society of Biblical Literature curated an unprecedented and courageous moment—we hosted an international virtual panel called "#BlackScholarsMatter: Visions and Struggles, Lessons and Hopes." As a learned society whose founding did not include scholars of African descent and other minoritized peoples, the Society of Biblical Literature paused to listen to their stories and experiences as members, and we reflected on matters of inclusion, diversity, and humane treatment of our diverse, global membership. In the wake of the internationally publicized George Floyd murder, while our guild was home and quarantined like the rest of the world due to the COVID-19 pandemic, we sat with the unsettling reality that our community has unaddressed histories of omission, prejudice, aggression, silencing, and harm. I was a panelist included in that 2020 forum. I sat at the virtual table among a senior generation of African diaspora biblical scholars—Renita Weems, Randall Bailey, Vincent Wimbush, Madipoane Masenya, and Cheryl Anderson.

Many of them were the stuff of legend for me. I had read them as a study abroad student at Oxford University from the bookstore floor in the city center. I could not afford to purchase the books myself, so I sat and read *Stony the Road We Trod* and other books by African Americans such as Frederick Douglass, James Baldwin, and Octavia Butler for a change of venue from my usual place of study, the Radcliffe Camera library. Those books and their recollections reminded me of why I had to persist in my studies. However, I suffered from extreme culture shock and a new awareness of my intersectional identity. Short of my year-long study abroad, my undergraduate studies occurred at the historic Fisk University (Nashville, TN). It is the school of W. E. B. Du Bois, Aaron Douglas, Virginia Broughton, and even Ida B. Wells (for a short time). I did not realize how lonely and silencing the field of critical biblical studies could be outside the classrooms of my college until I found myself in the United Kingdom. A southern African American woman studying exegesis, languages, and patristics in the halls of one of the oldest institutions of higher learning in the Western world—I was an anomaly in many of my seminars and the library. So, I sat on the bookstore floor to remind myself I had predecessors in my story. I was not the only African American student (and international student of color) who aspired to master the interpretive endeavor with its multiple chronological and contextual histories, translations, and epistemologies. I was one among others.

Almost twenty years later, as I participated in the society's #BlackScholarsMatter Symposium, I purposely left the story-telling about the journey of being a scholar-teacher of African diaspora descent in our learned society to those with seniority. I opted, instead, to imagine the determinants for my colleagues, allies, and guild to act as though those cultural sites mattered now. Thus, I took my courageous step and invited our learned society to join me on that bookstore's proverbial floor. What might happen to our collective scholasticism if we avail ourselves of the opportunities provided by two thousand years of contextual interpretive history that is not overly determined by the cultural records and epistemological artifacts of the Roman Empire, the Byzantine Empire, the Reformation, or even the Enlightenment (to name a few)? I invited us to consider the power of leveraging our intellectual skills to learn something new by using a passage from the moral discourse of a nineteenth century African American woman biblical interpreter, Anna Julia Cooper (1858–1964). She was a biblical scholar our learned society did not recognize as an exegete and interpreter of the Bible in her lifetime. However, she finally received such recognition from womanist and feminist biblical scholars over a century later, starting in the early 1990s. Cooper encouraged her readers to practice the "gospel of intelligence," which seeks to serve the disenfranchised, oppressed, and silenced populations of the world through education. In my paper, I tailored Cooper's descriptions of the social responsibilities of educators to serve communities and society for our intellectual community by saying:

> It is the work of our guild—as arbiters and interpreters of not just ancient texts and histories but arbiters and interpreters of knowledge—to articulate the contextual dimensions and biases of our traditional hermeneutical approaches and contemporary hermeneutical developments. Moreover, our collective responsibility is to work at interpreting from new centers of biblical history and literature, new centers of contextual meaning and significance, and new centers of epistemological inquiry and reason, particularly centers that are not our own. It is no longer

merely the task of African diaspora scholars to resource and center our interpretive histories, sources, and epistemologies. Rather it is a shared dilemma and responsibility that should be taken up by the entire field that reframes the hierarchies of knowledge and scholarship historically omitted and disregarded by traditional studies in biblical history, exegesis, theology, and hermeneutics.

Now, over two years later, I am more convinced that it is our collective responsibility to explore, describe, and model new centers of interpretive knowing and history. The feedback I received from colleagues representing diverse social locations, orientations, and cultures worldwide inform my confidence. An intellectual resolve appears to be forming globally. We want to participate in the tasks of our guild differently, with academic study reflecting the totality of our membership. That response encouraged me and encourages me still. This book is my contribution to that endeavor from the site of my research interests in Petrine studies, translation-based exegesis, rhetorical studies, cultural and social history, and African American literature. That which I proposed from the Society of Biblical Literature's virtual table while recalling my floor-reading book experience approximately twenty years earlier, I now do. It is my contribution to our collective scholasticism as we continue to expand our interpretive borders and become the globally engaged learned society represented by our membership and beyond it.

Such an endeavor has been an act of research, resilience, and hope. I am grateful for the intellectual and personal communities that encouraged this project at different stages in its development. My first notion to analyze early Christian literature, in conversation with the literary canon of African American women, occurred during a coteaching experience with Josiah Young at Wesley Theological Seminary (Washington, DC). While facilitating the Introduction to African Diaspora Religious Thought, I found myself in discussions about the interpretive practices and significance of women like Maria Stewart, Anna Julia Cooper, Ida B. Wells, and others. The course was designed for masters-level students, but it set me on a path that gave birth to this project. It transported me to my ethics courses taught by Marica Riggs at Columbia Theological Seminary. To discuss ethics required engaging African American women's literary production and vice versa. In Riggs's courses, ethical theory and black women writers contributed to the same conversation. She equipped me with the beginnings of a model for how to blend translation-based exegesis in early Christian literature with African American women's moral discourses as a singular pursuit. Thank you, Josiah and Marcia, for curating learning communities in which I imagined the sources of knowledge for my exegetical endeavor differently.

Various organizations and institutions have supported my research. The Louisville Institute's (LI) First Book Grant for Scholars of Color provided the research year I needed to conceive and write this book. I am grateful for the kinds of scholarly projects LI continues to support, including mine. I also appreciate the work of The Wabash Center and the directorship of Dr. Nancy Lynne Westfield. Wabash's virtual venues have created platforms for me to explore how my research may serve scholarship and teaching spaces. The editors of SBL Press and of the Early Christianity and its Literature series were wonderful colleagues throughout the process. They made room for my exegesis, sources, and interpretive approach to be counted as a volume in our learned society's scholarly listing. I am particularly thankful for the editorial feedback and time Nicole L. Tilford and Shelly Matthews committed to my project. Furthermore, my institution, Boston University School of Theology, supplied the resources, time, and support I needed at all levels—from deans, faculty, staff, and students—thank you. Boston University's Howard Thurman Center offered me space to escape and focus on preparing the manuscript for publication, and I am grateful.

The life of the mind and the work of a scholar is often imagined to be a lonely path. This book, however, has been accompanied by a great cloud of scholarly witnesses beyond institutions. Thank you to Meghan Henning, Candida Moss, Juan Hernández Jr., Margaret Mitchell, Laura Nasrallah, Rodney Caruthers II, Rob von Thaden, Kimberleigh Jordan, Stephanie Crumpton, Luis Menéndez Antuña, Nicolette Manglos-Weber, Jonathon Cavillo, Filipe Maia, Courtney Goto, Charlene Zuill, and Shonda Jones. Also, I give special thanks to Vernon K. Robbins, who read many iterations of my research and provided multiple feedback forms. I also extend humble gratitude to my research assistants—Zoe Towler, Austin Washington, and Amber Jogie—for their scanning, citation, and review hours. Of course, I am grateful for my first two Fisk University professors who, together, set me on the path of the life of the mind and introduced African American literature and biblical interpretation to me as one conversation: Drs. Karen Collier and Lean'tin Bracks.

Last, I am thankful for my family and all the ways you have accompanied me through this project. Among them, I position my scholarly sister-friend, Dr. Kimberly D. Russaw. Thank you for my daily encouragement. You listened to me read and think aloud while constantly reminding me to "take care of yourself." You were an anchoring presence who cleared the way so I could keep working. I am also humbled by the gift of my family anchors: Wenefer and Tony White; Deborah Washington and Victoria Downs; Gwen and Ed Thomas; Brian and Cheryl Smith; "The Clarks"; Claudine Smith; Frank S. Jackson Sr.; Angela Sims and family; Satira Streeter Corbitt and family; Dana Williams and family; Theresa Thames and Dawn Hand; Christian and Alexandra Rose; Autumn and Joi Wilson, Julia Buckner, Alisa Parker-LaGrone and family; the Flukers; my Lee family; my Belin-Ingram family; my Nebo Christian Ministries church family (Baltimore, MD); and Metropolitan AME church family (Washington, DC). I am most thankful for "The Crew": Brian R. Smith and our daughters. The three of you believed, read, listened, and joked, and you never stopped supporting.

Abbreviations

1 Clem.	1 Clement
1 En.	1 Enoch
2 Clem.	2 Clement
AB	Anchor Bible
ABD	Freeman, David Noel, ed. *Anchor Bible Dictionary.* 6 vols. New York: Doubleday, 1992.
Abr.	Philo, *De Abrahamo*
ABYRL	Anchor Bible Yale Reference Library
AcBib	Academia Biblica
Acts Pet.	Acts of Peter
A.J.	Josephus, *Antiquitates judaicae*
ANF	Roberts, Alexander, and James Donaldson, eds. *The Ante-Nicene Fathers: Translations of the Writings of the Fathers Down to A.D. 325.* 10 vols. New York: Christian Literature Company, 1885–1887.
Ann.	Tacitus, *Annales*
Apoc. Ezek.	Apocryphon of Ezekiel
Apoc. Pet.	Apocalypse of Peter
AYBRL	The Anchor Yale Bible Reference Library
Barn.	Barnabas
BBR	*Bulletin for Biblical Research*
BDAG	Bauer, Walter, William F. Arndt, F. Wilbur Gingrich, and Frederick W. Danker. *Greek-English Lexicon of the New Testament and Other Early Christian Literature.* 3rd ed. Chicago: University of Chicago Press, 2000.
BDF	Blass, F. and A. Debrunner. *A Greek Grammar of the New Testament and Other Early Christian Literature.* Translated and revised by Robert W. Funk. Chicago: University of Chicago Press, 1961.
B.J.	Josephus, *Bellum judaicum*

BibInt	Biblical Interpretation
BSac	*Bibliotheca Sacra*
BSNA	Biblical Scholarship in North America
BZ	*Biblische Zeitschrift*
CBQ	*Catholic Biblical Quarterly*
CEB	Common English Bible
Comm. Rom.	Origen, *Commentarii in Romanos*
ConBNT	Coniectanea Biblica: New Testament Series
ConC	Concordia Commentary
Conf.	Philo, *De confusione linguarum*
CurTM	*Currents in Theology and Mission*
De an.	Aristotle, *Soul*
De or.	Cicero, *De oratore*
Decal.	Philo, *De decalogo*
Deus	Philo, *Quod Deus sit immutabilis*
Digest	A compendium of Roman law drawn together from laws long in force by (eastern) Emperor Justinian in the sixth century
Diogn.	Letter to Diognetus
ECC	Eerdmans Critical Commentary
Ep.	Pliny the Younger, *Letters*; Seneca, *Epistles*
Eph.	Ignatius, *To the Ephesians*
ESEC	Emory Studies in Early Christianity
GPBS	Global Perspectives on Biblical Scholarship
Haer.	Irenaeus, *Adversus haereses* (*Elenchos*)
Her.	Philo, *Quis rerum divinarum heres sit*
Hist. eccl.	Eusebius, *Historia ecclesiastica*
HKNT	Handkommentar zum Neuen Testament
HTR	*Harvard Theological Review*
HvTSt	*Hervormde Teologiese Studies*
ICC	International Critical Commentary
IDB	Buttrick, George A., ed. *The Interpreter's Dictionary of the Bible*. 4 vols. New York: Abingdon, 1962.
IDBSup	Crim, Keith, ed. *Interpreter's Dictionary of the Bible: Supplementary Volume*. Nashville: Abingdon, 1976.
Int	*Interpretation*
Inst.	Quintilian, *Institutio Oratoria*
Ios.	Josephus, *Iosepho*
JBL	*Journal of Biblical Literature*

JFSR	*Journal of Feminist Studies in Religion*
JSJSup	Journal for the Study of Judaism Supplement Series
JSNT	*Journal for the Study of the New Testament*
JSNTSup	Journal for the Study of the New Testament Supplement Series
KJV	King James Version
LBLA	La Biblia de las Américas translation
Leg.	Philo, *Legum allegoriae*
LXX	Septuagint
LCL	Loeb Classical Library
LEC	Library of Early Christianity
Leg.	Athenagoras, *Legatio pro Christianis*
Legat.	Philo, *Legatio ad Gaium*
Liv. Pro.	Lives of the Prophets
LNTS	The Library of New Testament Studies
LSJ	Liddell, Henry George, Robert Scott, and Henry Stuart Jones. *A Greek-English Lexicon.* 9th ed. with revised supplement. Oxford: Clarendon, 1996.
Mart. Pol.	Martyrdom of Polycarp
MELUS	*Multi-Ethnic Literature of the US*
MM	Moulton, J. H. and G. Milligan. *Vocabulary of the Greek New Testament.* Grand Rapids: Baker Academic, 1995 [1914–1929].
Mos.	Philo, *De vita Mosis*
MT	Masoretic Text
NA28	Aland, Barbara, and Kurt Aland, et al., eds. *Novum Testamentum Graece.* 28th rev. ed. Stuttgart: Deutsche Biblegesellschaft, 2012.
NETS	New English Translation of the Septuagint
NIB	*New Interpreters Bible*
NICNT	New International Commentary on the New Testament
NIGTC	New International Greek Testament Commentary
NIV	New International Version
NKJV	New King James Version
Neot	*Neotestamentica*
NRSV	New Revised Standard Version
NRSVue	New Revised Standard Version Updated Edition
NTL	The New Testament Library

NTS	*New Testament Studies*
Prob.	Philo, *Quod omnis probus liber sit*
Pol.	Aristotle, *Politica*
PNTC	Pillar New Testament Commentary
Praem.	Philo, *De praemiis et poenis*
Praescr.	Tertullian, *De praescriptione haereticorum*
Prob.	Philo, *Quod omnis probus liber sit*
RBECS	*Reviews of Biblical and Early Christian Studies*
RBS	Resources for Biblical Studies
Rhet.	Aristotle, *Rhetoric*
Rom.	Ignatius, *To the Romans*
RRA	Rhetoric of Religious Antiquity
RSV	Revised Standard Version
R&T	Religion and Theology
RVR	Reina-Valera Revisión de 1909
Sacr.	Philo, *De sacrificiis Abelis et Caini*
SBLDS	Society of Biblical Literature Dissertation Series
SBLGNT	Holmes Michael, W., ed. *The Greek New Testament SBL Edition*. Atlanta: Society of Biblical Literature, 2010.
SBT	Studies in Biblical Theology
Scorp.	Tertullian, *Scorpiace*
SemeiaSt	Semeia Studies
Sobr.	Philo, *De sobrietate*
SP	Sacra Pagina
Spec.	Philo, *De specialibus legibus*
SREC	Sociorhetorical Explorations Commentaries
SRI	Sociorhetorical Interpretation
Strom.	Clement of Alexandria, *Stromateis*
T. Sim.	Testament of Simeon
T. Zeb.	Testament of Zebulun
TDNT	Kittel, Gerhard, and Gerhard Friedrich, eds. *Theological Dictionary of the New Testament*. Translated by Geoffrey W. Bromiley. 10 vols. Grand Rapids: Eerdmans, 1964–1976.
Theog.	Hesiod, *Theogonia*
UBS4	Aland, Barbara, et al., eds. *The Greek New Testament*. 4th rev. ed. Stuttgart: Deutsche Bibelgesellschaft/ United Bible Societies, 1994.

Virt.	Philo, *De virtutibus*
WBC	Word Biblical Commentary
WUNT	Wissenschaftliche Untersuchungen zum Neuen Testament
ZECNT	Zondervan Exegetical Commentary on the New Testament
ZNW	*Zeitschrift für die Neutestamentliche Wissenschaft*

Part 1
An Approach to the
Interpretation and Translation of 2 Peter

1

Reading 2 Peter through
African American Women's Moral Discourse

Reading the letter of 2 Peter resembles the experience of listening to the baby in a large family share her perspective of the world. At times, the voice and views of the youngest child sound a bit like her siblings and parents, reflecting their common histories and family stories, cultural idioms and traditions, and sensibilities in matters of religion, society, and culture. Other times, the voice of the youngest child is more improvisational and exploratory. She charts new ground and establishes different kinds of relationships to carve out her unique place within the family. Interpreting the letter of 2 Peter is like listening to the youngest child of the Christian Bible intermix the language, stories, and sensibilities of her older family members and contemporaries with her own. Through its rhetorical strategy, the letter conveys its cultural obligations and, in turn, records its own unique viewpoint about the world. In this negotiation between received tradition and unique perspective, 2 Peter participates in the ongoing development of Christian tradition and its exploration of matters related to family accord and opposition, acceptance and censure, conformity and defection.

The Cultural Rhetoric of 2 Peter

Written in approximately 140–160 CE, 2 Peter stands late in a chronology of early Christian literature. Its literary predecessors include 1 Peter, Jude, Paul's letters, the Synoptic traditions (particularly the Gospel of Matthew), the book of Revelation, and the Apocalypse of Peter.[1] As the latest writing ?

---

1. A strong scholarly consensus concludes that 2 Peter postdates the Pauline letters, Jude, 1 Peter, and the Synoptic tradition (notably, the Gospel of Matthew) and circulated during the time between the Roman-Jewish War of 66–73 CE and the Bar

in the canonical tradition, 2 Peter both inherited and innovated within the religious discourses it received. Some of the most image-rich and discordant biblical retellings in the New Testament occur in 2 Peter's three chapters.[2] The letter tells its own renditions of the stories of Pentateuchal figures like Noah, Lot, Balaam, and angels trafficking between heaven and earth.[3] It also recalls prominent traditions and personages from the earliest periods of the Jesus movement.[4] The letter even plays with Greek and Roman theological imaginations by alluding to underworld episodes such as Zeus casting the Titans to a place referenced as Tartarus.[5] Through

---

Kochba revolt of 132–136 CE. Richard J. Bauckham, *Jude, 2 Peter*, WBC 50 (Nashville: Thomas Nelson, 2003), 139–51. I also presuppose that the Apocalypse of Peter and its traditions predate the writing of 2 Peter. I accept the plausibility that 2 Peter used the Apocalypse as a verbal and thematic literary resource alongside other writings from the Second Temple period. See Jörg Frey, "Second Peter in New Perspective," in *2 Peter and the Apocalypse of Peter: Towards a New Perspective*, ed. Jörg Frey, Matthijs den Dulk, and Jan G. van der Watt (Leiden: Brill, 2019), 13; Richard Bauckham, "2 Peter and the Apocalypse of Peter Revisited," in Frey, Dulk, and van der Watt, *2 Peter and the Apocalypse of Peter*, 278; Wolfgang Grünstäudl, *Petrus Alexandrinus: Studien zum historischen und theologischen Ort des Zweiten Petrusbriefes*, WUNT 2/315 (Tübingen: Mohr Siebeck, 2013), 97–144; Attila Jakab, "The Reception of the Apocalypse of Peter in Ancient Christianity," in *The Apocalypse of Peter*, ed. Jan N. Bremmer and István Czachesz, Studies in Early Christian Apocrypha 7 (Leuven: Peeters, 2003), 174–86; Jan N. Bremmer, "Orphic, Roman, Jewish and Christian Tours of Hell: Observations on the Apocalypse of Peter," in *Other Worlds and Their Relation to This World: Early Jewish and Ancient Christian Traditions*, ed. Erik M. M. Eynikel et al., JSJSup 143 (Leiden: Brill, 2010), 305–22.

2. Vernon K. Robbins, *Exploring the Texture of Texts: A Guide to Socio-rhetorical Interpretation* (Valley Forge, PA: Trinity Press International, 1996), 48–50, 58–60.

3. Noahic tradition: 2 Pet 2:5 // Gen 7:13; 8:18; also see 1 Pet 3:20; Heb 11:7; Lot tradition: 2 Pet 2:6–8 // Gen 19:7–29; also see Jude 7; Matt 10:15; Wis 10:6; Luke 17:28; Balaam tradition: 2 Pet 2:15 // Num 22; 31:16; Deut 23:5; Neh 13:2; traditions of the angels: 2 Pet 2:4 // Gen 6:1–4; also see LXX Job 41:24, Jude 6; 2 Pet 2:10–11.

4. Prominent literary traditions occurring in 2 Peter include the transfiguration: 2 Pet 1:16–18 // Matt 17:1–8; Mark 9:2–8; Luke 9:28–36; and Matthew's Sermon on the Mount: 2 Pet 2:22 // Matt 7:6; 2 Pet 2:14 // Matt 5:28. Important figures of the Jesus movement referenced in 2 Peter include: portrayals of Peter and Paul: 2 Pet 1:1, 16–18; 2 Pet 3:15; apostolic witnesses: 2 Pet 1:16–18; 3:2; Jesus: 2 Pet 1:1–2, 8, 11, 14, 16; 2:20; 3:18; God—the Creator: 2 Pet 2:4; 3:5, 12: God—the Divine Parent: 2 Pet 1:17; and the Holy Spirit: 2 Pet 1:21.

5. Tartarus: e.g., 2 Pet 2:4 // Hesiod, *Theog.* 662–97; 729–30. Compare this to more common Jewish-Christian traditions about hell (Gehenna), Hades, or Sheol: hell (Gehenna): Matt 5:22; 10:28; and 23:33; Mark 9:43–47; Hades: Matt 11:23; 16:18;

its epistolary (or "letter") structure, 2 Peter forges a distinct rhetoric that combines the literary traditions from biblical, testamental, and apocalyptic literature.[6] Profiles of heroes, biblical stories, and ancient literary forms and sources are on full display.

The writers of 2 Peter not only show their facility with blending diverse religious stories and their accompanying social scripts, but they also transcend it linguistically.[7] The letter is a virtual niche lexicon of Hellenistic and koine Greek terminologies distinct from the rest of the New Testament. Of its fifty-seven unique terms (*hapax legomena*), such as "Tartarus" (2:4 *tartaroō*) and "false teachers" (2:1, *pseudodidaskalos*), thirty-two are not

---

Luke 10:15; 16:23; Acts 2:27, 31; Rev 1:18; 6:8; 20:13–14; Sheol: Job 11:8; Pss 31:17; 49:15; Prov 15:24; Ezek 31:15–18; 1 Sam 28:14–15. While it is likely these traditions were intermixed as parallel and overlapping, it is striking that, among the writings of the New Testament, 2 Peter is the only text to invoke the tradition of an underworld with reference to Tartarus. For discussions about the syncretistic traditions of hell, see Meghan R. Henning, *Hell Hath No Fury: Gender, Disability, and the Invention of Damned Bodies in Early Christian Literature*, AYBRL (New Haven: Yale University Press, 2021); Henning, *Educating Early Christians through the Rhetoric of Hell: "Weeping and Gnashing of Teeth" as Paideia in Matthew and the Early Church*, WUNT 382 (Tübingen: Mohr Siebeck, 2014).

6. Comparative testament genre writing includes Gen 49; Deut 33; John 13; 1 En. 81.1–82.3; 91. The testamentary shape of 2 Peter corresponds to the farewell discourses of John 13–15, 2 Timothy, and the Testament of the Twelve from the Pseudepigrapha. Similarly, the apocalyptic expectation of the coming (parousia) of Jesus (2 Pet 1:16; 3:4, 12) is reminiscent of the discourses of 1 and 2 Thessalonians (1 Thess 2:19, 3:13, 4:15, 5:23; 2 Thess 2:1, 8–9), 1 and 2 Corinthians (1 Cor 15:23), and particularly the Synoptic tradition of Matthew, the only gospel to deploy the language of the parousia (Matt 24:3, 27, 37, 39). The grammar of parousia is scattered in a few places across the general letters (Jas 5:7–8; 1 John 2:28). For parallels with Revelation, see 2 Pet 1:19 // Rev 2:28; 2 Pet 2:9 // Rev 3:10; 2 Pet 2:15 // Rev 2:14; 2 Pet 3:13 // Rev 21:1.

7. I leverage recent scholarship that acknowledges that letter writing in ancient times was a corporate activity. No letter of early Christianity is the product of a single prodigious literary actor. Instead, scribal traditions and economic expense necessitated a collection of actors endeavoring to communicate and connect. Even when a so-called single author wrote a letter, the authors' community often ratified that correspondence before the intended community received it. See Hans-Josef Klauck and Daniel P. Bailey, *Ancient Letters and the New Testament: A Guide to Context and Exegesis* (Waco, TX: Baylor University Press, 2006); E. Randolph Richards, *Paul and First-Century Letter Writing: Secretaries, Composition, and Collection* (Downers Grove, IL: InterVarsity Press, 2004); and Stanley K. Stowers, *Letter Writing in Greco-Roman Antiquity*, LEC 5 (Philadelphia: Westminster, 1986).

found in the Septuagint (LXX), while eight are taken from Greco-Roman religion and philosophy, and seventeen are found among the early Christian writings of the second century.[8]

Second Peter's rich rhetorical tapestry of traditions and specialized terminology is not merely decorative; rather, it is purposefully employed cultural rhetoric that contributes to a specific culture-making endeavor.[9] Cultural rhetoric is a literary mode of persuasive speech that reflects the collective history, language, and peoplehood of a specific social unit. At the same time, it is more than a conveyor of linguistic, historical, social, and religious location. It exerts culture-making force on its hearers and readers.[10] Cultural rhetoric, in other words, is a discursive practice that creates communities.

---

8. Sampling 2 Peter's particular linguistic record, (1) some of the approximately twenty-five words shared between 2 Pet and LXX include *apopheugō* ("to flee," "to escape," 2 Pet 1:4; 2:18, 20 // Sir 22:22) and *borboros* ("mud," 2 Pet 2:22 // Jer 45:6). And (2) some of the thirty-two terms unique to 2 Peter and absent from the New Testament and the LXX are *egkatoikōn* ("dwell in," 2 Pet 2:8) and *amathēs* ("unlearned," "ignorant," 2 Pet 3:16). Charles Bigg, *Critical and Exegetical Commentary on the Epistles of St. Peter and St. Jude*, ICC (repr., Edinburgh: T&T Clark, 1978), 224–32; Bauckham, *Jude, 2 Peter*, 135–37. Also see James M. Starr, *Sharers in Divine Nature: 2 Peter 1:4 in Its Hellenistic Context*, ConBNT 33 (Stockholm: Almqvist & Wiksell, 2000); Michael J. Gilmour, *The Significance of Parallels between 2 Peter and Other Early Christian Literature*, AcBib 10 (Atlanta: Society of Biblical Literature, 2002).

9. Brian Blount provides a helpful description of sociolinguistics that focuses on how language reflects the social and cultural location of those deploying it and its interactions. He says, "In the New Testament we are dealing not with sociological models or identifiable social communities that correspond with communities in the present, but with texts. We are concerned with language and with how people in different sociological categories use language to interpret texts. It is our contention that in the time of the New Testament, and in the present as well, different people experience language functioning differently. Therefore, if our interpretation of a text is to escape the charge of being mere ideology, it must consider the text sociolinguistically: it must recognize that the language in the text can legitimately have different meanings for persons from distinct sociological and linguistic backgrounds." Brian K. Blount, *Cultural Interpretation: Reorienting New Testament Criticism* (Minneapolis: Fortress, 1995), 6.

10. Culture, in this study, is understood as "a system of patterned values, meanings, and beliefs that give cognitive structure to the world." It provides "a basis for coordinating and controlling human interactions," and it constitutes "a link as the system is transmitted from one generation to the next." Quoted in Vernon K. Robbins, *The Tapestry of Early Christian Discourse: Rhetoric, Society and Ideology* (New

Second Peter uses cultural rhetoric to promote specific social assessments and theological accords (and dissonances). As a late composition of canonical Christian literature, 2 Peter joins a library of writings attempting to formulate early Christian identity, belief, practice, and imagination, the sum total of which I will refer to as "Christianness."[11] The letter's use of various traditions attests that the writers were well-versed in this archive of early Christian writings, but it also shows that the writers were adept at selecting from it to convey their own form of Christianness. The letter is not an early Christian writing that advocates for the pluralism from which it draws materials. In contradistinction to its variegated cultural and literary environment, the letter champions Christian sameness. Tracing the logic of its cultural rhetoric, 2 Peter disrupts pluralism in favor of uniformity.

Of course, 2 Peter's cultural rhetoric does not exist separate from the religious life of its communities and the broader social arrangements of the ancient world. Culture and religion "are mutually related and penetrate each other."[12] And, as Volker Küster states, "religions maintain

---

York: Routledge, 1996), 4. See original sources of Neil J. Smelser, "Culture: Coherent or Incoherent," in *Theory of Culture*, ed. Richard Münch and Neil J. Smelser (Berkeley: University of California Press, 1992), 11, 25; Peter Berger and Thomas Luckmann, *The Social Construction of Reality: A Treatise in the Sociology of Knowledge* (Garden City, NY: Doubleday, 1967).

11. Here I leverage the scholarship of Denise Kimber Buell and her notion of "Christianness." Buell characterizes Christianness by saying, "Early Christians used ethnic reasoning to legitimize various forms of Christianness as the universal, most authentic manifestation of humanity, and it offered Christians both a way to define themselves relative to 'outsiders' and to compete with other 'insiders' to assert the superiority of their varying visions of Christianness." Denise Kimber Buell, *Why This New Race: Ethnic Reasoning in Early Christianity* (New York: Columbia University Press, 2008), 2; Averil Cameron, *Christianity and the Rhetoric of Empire: The Development of Christian Discourse*, Sather Classical Lectures (Berkeley: University of California Press, 1991). As Sung Uk Lim states, "Most importantly, Buell advocates what is called 'ethnic reasoning,' a mode of persuasion that employs terms related to peoplehood in the rhetorical situation of early Christianity to convince readers about what supposedly constitutes being a Christian, that is, Christianness." Sung Uk Lim, "Race and Ethnicity Discourse in Biblical Studies and Beyond," *Journal for the Study of Religions and Ideologies* 15.45 (2016): 130–31. See below for a fuller discussion about Buell and the nomenclature of *Christianness* in this book.

12. Volker Küster, "The Project of an Intercultural Theology," *Swedish Missiological Themes* 93.3 (2005): 419; this and the next quotation are taken from Musa W. Dube, "Intercultural Biblical Interpretations," *Swedish Missiological Themes* 98.3 (2010): 363.

different forms in different cultures. A culture can be multi-religious, and religion can be multi-cultural."[13] To this end, 2 Peter is a religious writing that resources the multireligious texts, concepts, and language of early Christian culture. However, it responds to the multicultural realities of Christianness populating the communities to which it is addressed by advancing *one* cultural stream over others. Second Peter's Christian epistolary form conveys a "social world in the making" and creates that world through casting a particular cultural rhetoric.[14]

Cultural rhetoric may possess aesthetic properties, but it is not only stylized and structured. It may be image-rich, constructing a metaphorical epistemology that structures its readers' cognitive ways of knowing, but it is not only metaphor.[15] Cultural rhetoric is responsive and social.[16] It is fabricated to rehearse the past and current epistemologies of the com-

---

13. Küster, "Project of an Intercultural Theology," 419.

14. In 1975, John Gager introduced the notion of "social world" to critical biblical studies and early Christian history. Gager used anthropological and sociological theoretical models with comparative analysis. To this end, he describes his approach as both theoretical and comparative saying it is "theoretical in the sense that I will make use of explanatory models drawn from the social sciences, and comparative in that much of the evidence for these models is based on studies of non-Christian religious movements" (*Kingdom and Community: The Social World of Early Christianity* [Englewood Cliffs, NJ: Prentice-Hall, 1975], 2).

15. C. Clifton Black provides a foundational overview about the development of rhetorical criticism in New Testament studies, tracing it through three evolutions: (1) a focus on the poetic nature of rhetoric (James Muilenburg and Amos N. Wilder); (2) a focus on rhetoric as classical modes of persuasion (George A. Kennedy, Margaret M. Mitchell, Duane A. Watson); and (3) a focus on rhetoric as a social tool and mode of praxis (Elisabeth Schüssler Fiorenza, Vernon K. Robbins). This monograph's rhetorical approach extends the third iteration of biblical rhetorical criticism while also engaging classical rhetorical forms, particularly exercises in rhetorical composition (*progymnasmata*). C. Clifton Black, "Rhetorical Criticism," in *Hearing the New Testament: Strategies for Interpretation*, ed. Joel B. Green (Grand Rapids: Eerdmans, 1995), 256–77; Margaret M. Mitchell, review of *Rhetorical Criticism of the Bible: A Comprehensive Bibliography with Notes on History and Method*, by Duane F. Watson and Alan J. Hauser, *CBQ* 57 (1995): 615–16; Mitchell, "Rhetorical and New Literary Criticism," in *The Oxford Handbook of Biblical Studies*, ed. Judith M. Lieu and J. W. Rogerson (Oxford: Oxford University Press, 2008), 615–33.

16. Elisabeth Schüssler Fiorenza, *Rhetoric and Ethic: The Politics of Biblical Studies* (Minneapolis: Fortress, 1999). Also see Jonathan Potter, *Representing Reality: Discourse, Rhetoric and Social Construction* (Thousand Oaks, CA: Sage, 1996); Musa W. Dube, "Reading for Decolonization (John 4.1–42)," in *John and Postcolonialism:*

munities it represents, while envisaging the future of those communities both inside and outside their borders.[17] Interpreting the cultural rhetoric of an early Christian text like 2 Peter requires tracing modes of persuasion in discourse that both represent communities and create communities.[18] It is an endeavor that accounts for interactions with other cultural communities and social possibilities, no matter how distant in time, while describing the cultural norms respective literary moments convey.

The ultimate point of examining cultural rhetoric, at least in this volume, is to understand a text's relational and cultural force, implications, and outcomes. Does the rhetoric bring its hearers closer together or further apart? Does it expand the religion's peoplehood, advocating to become more multicultural or even transcultural and therefore transforming believers into an entirely new people (1 Pet 2:9)? Or does it reform the community and the society within which they are located, expelling alternative formulations of the community's tradition (2 Pet 2:21–22)? An examination of cultural rhetoric wants to know, if readers subscribe to a particular religious discourse, what kinds of people are they in behavior, attitude, and collective peoplehood? Driving this study is the question: does 2 Peter's cultural rhetoric cultivate the kind of human relations and attitudes that speak to the values of moral people seeking justice, human flourishing, and openness to others both in the past and today?

Travel, Space, and Power, ed. Musa W. Dube and Jeffrey L. Staley (London: Sheffield Academic, 2002), 51–75.

17. A defining feature in critical studies of African American rhetoric is the role of communities and cultural exchanges. This theme is significant to my analysis of the cultural rhetoric of 2 Peter and other early Christian literature. See Elaine B. Richardson and Ronald L. Jackson II, eds., *African American Rhetoric(s): Interdisciplinary Perspectives* (Carbondale: Southern Illinois University Press, 2007); Richardson and Jackson, eds., *Understanding African American Rhetoric: Classical Origins to Contemporary Innovations* (London: Taylor & Francis, 2003); Molefi Kete Asante, *Language, Communication, and Rhetoric in Black America* (New York: Harper & Row, 1972); Asante, *Race, Rhetoric, and Identity: The Architecton of Soul* (Amherst, NY: Humanity Books, 2005).

18. As Molefi Kete Asante and Rosemary Chai state, interpretation of cultural rhetoric maps the "cultural intersections and communication implications" for community identities and behaviors. Molefi Kete Asante and Rosemary Chai, "Nkrabea and Yuan in Akan and Chinese: Cultural Intersections and Communication Implications in an African and an Asian Society," *Journal of Black Studies* 44.2 (2013): 119–36.

Resourcing African American Women's
Moral Discourse for 2 Peter Interpretation

This book injects new focus and significance into the critical study of 2 Peter by modeling an interpretive approach that leverages the particularities of historically overlooked contexts, specifically nineteenth-century African American women's moral discourse. This is a particularly generative "contact zone" for biblical interpretation.[19] It is where the cultural rhetorics of New Testament texts and contexts collided with the texts, contexts, and people of another period and where interpreters can see what those collisions produced. Examining the writings of nineteenth-century African American women writers provides "descriptive criteria, conceptual categories, and taxonomies" that can support the exegetical endeavor to describe the rhetoric and moral suasion of 2 Peter as culture making.[20]

---

19. I am indebted to the intercultural projects of Musa Dube, Gerald West, Madipoane Masenya, and the scholarship of other continental African biblical scholars. Their insistence that exegesis account for cultural exchanges and the contextually conditioned nature of biblical translation and interpretation remains an essential principle in my scholarship. See Gerald O. West and Musa W. Dube Shomanah, *The Bible in Africa: Transactions, Trajectories, and Trends* (Leiden: Brill, 2000); Madipoane J. Masenya, "African Womanist Hermeneutics: A Suppressed Voice from South Africa Speaks," *JFSR* 11.1 (1995): 149–55. Dube first introduced me to the notion of the cultural "contact zone" between biblical interpretation and cultures: "It seems to me that to map the journey of intercultural biblical interpretation, to trace the collisions it has sustained and the relationships it has created with other cultures, we have to look at the contact-zones and at the borders that the bible (has) crossed ever since it began its journey and infiltration into other cultures (Acts 1:8). In short, while intercultural biblical interpretation is inevitable, we cannot assume intercultural biblical interpretation to be a self-evident process that occurs without conflict. Within the contact-zones of intercultural biblical interpretation, collision underlines and characterizes the tension and the power struggles of the contact-zones. This collision cautions us to interrogate the prevailing existence of the Bible in other cultures" (Dube, "Intercultural Biblical Interpretations," 368). Rather than allowing such interpretive collisions to occur passively without accounting for them, this book intentionally stages and triggers a collision between 2 Peter and nineteenth-century African American women writers to reconsider standard topics in the critical study of the letter.

20. Clarice J. Martin, "Normative Biblical Motifs in African American Women's Moral Discourse: Maria Stewart's Autobiography as a Resource for Nurturing Leadership from the Black Church Tradition," in *The Stones that the Builders Rejected: The Development of Leadership from the Black Church Tradition*, ed. Walter E. Fluker (Harrisburg, PA: Trinity Press International, 1998), 55.

Like the rhetoric of 2 Peter, the rhetoric of nineteenth-century African American women writers is improvisational. These women blended multiple cultural traditions, while testing the abilities of those traditions to accommodate their experiences. To address social and relational dynamics inside and outside their minoritized and stigmatized African American communities, they (re)sourced traditions from the Bible, their African diasporic traditions and history, and Western literary traditions. Their rhetoric is culturally reflective and socially responsive.

The rhetoric of nineteenth-century African American women is carved out of the linguistic contexts of American slaveholding Christianity that separated its citizens into castes.[21] Describing the existential realities of these women and the rhetorical situation out of which they composed their literary responses, Frances Smith Foster, a pioneer in African American women's literary tradition, asserts,

> The extant literature from 1746 to 1892, albeit small in quantity, proves that African American women, like African American men, deliberately chose to participate in the public discourse despite considerable Anglo American resistance to their doing so. They appropriated the English literary tradition to reveal, to interpret, to challenge, and to change perceptions of themselves and the world in which they found themselves.[22]

A sampling of their extant writings recalls the horrors of federally instituted enslavement and the hope of the Civil War victory for liberation and inclusion as full citizens in the homeland of their birth. Nineteenth-century African American women's writings speak to the new disappointment accompanying the premature disinvestiture of Reconstruction efforts and the abandonment of the United States' newly constituted African American citizenry to rogue white supremacist forms of southern "Redemption" justice. White Redemptionist actors took aim at black communities that threatened to become too prominent, too successful, too independent, and *too free.*[23]

---

21. Isabel Wilkerson, *Caste: The Origins of Our Discontents* (New York: Random House, 2020), 41–43, 53.

22. Frances Smith Foster, *Written by Herself: Literary Production by African American Women, 1746–1892* (Bloomington: Indiana University Press, 1993), 16.

23. Another scholar, Katharine Clay Bassard, describes African American women's ways of reading the Bible as "their biblical self-fashionings," which are "rooted in American chattel slavery and its biblical defense." She goes on to make the point that

African American women writing in the nineteenth century addressed the multiple traumas of their community over a hundred-year period, and they championed cultural responses of hope and concrete social transformation. Each writing represents a version of this response in a different genre. Similarly, 2 Peter represents a particular cultural proposal for Christian social arrangement. It participates in almost one hundred years of diverse Christian social responses and communities. It remains to be seen if 2 Peter is responding to traumas inflicted by cultural wars in ancient society and local Christian communities or whether its cultural rhetoric might reflect a strategy for *inflicting* such trauma.

Like 2 Peter, nineteenth-century African American women's writings reflect rhetorical strategy, cultural commitments, and social responses to their contexts. In 1893, Fannie Barrier Williams (1855–1944), an educator and activist for equal race and gender rights, wrote to this effect for the World's Congress of Representative Women:

> American literature needs for its greater variety and its deeper soundings that which will be written into it out of the hearts of these self-emancipating women. The great problems of social reform that are now so engaging the highest intelligence of American women will soon need for their solution the reinforcement of that new intelligence which our women are developing. In short, our women are ambitious to be contributors to all the great moral and intellectual forces that make for the greater weal of our common country.[24]

America's social arrangement classified African American women as the lowest denominator in citizenship, but Williams designates them vital contributors to the common weal of the country. They were civically attentive, scholarly actors who enriched its literary tradition. African American women writers record and critique their social positions by conveying

---

"black women's reading of the Bible was not simply a matter of identification with certain scriptures or biblical characters; instead, they had to first read through a cultural discourse that had already 'othered' them through American chattel slavery" (*Transforming Scriptures: African American Women Writers and the Bible* [Athens: University of Georgia Press, 2010], 7).

24. Fannie Barrier Williams, "The Intellectual Progress of the Colored Woman of the United States since the Emancipation Proclamation" (1893), in *The Portable Nineteenth-Century African American Women Writers*, ed. Hollis Robbins and Henry Louis Gates Jr. (New York: Penguin, 2017), 397–98.

their theological certainty in the full humanity and rightful citizenship of their communities. Their cultural rhetoric championed the actualization of a greater weal that was pluralistic, tolerant, and perpetually fair and equitable. Second Peter, in contrast, spins a cultural rhetoric that champions a community weal that is more intolerant and less hospitable to intracommunal diversity.

Penning a response to the world as they experienced it, nineteenth-century African American women engaged in a specific discursive literary strategy. They challenged the social and theological norms dominating the society that stamped their bodies and those of their community as not only Other but an inferior form of human, American citizen, and Christian. Even as Christians, they found little equity, common inheritance, and shared notions of the "justice of God" (2 Pet 1:1) among their white Christian neighbors. African American women's moral discourse in the nineteenth century addresses "the phenomenology of multiple and interrelated forms of oppression." Their literature—be it essays, opinion editorials, spiritual autobiographies, and transcripts of public addresses— transmit "an ethic that requires liberation from all forms of personal, communal, and systemic domination and oppression."[25] Their writings enjoin African American, Christian communities "to be fully responsive" to their collective calling to function as truly free, civil, and inclusive communities of God in Jesus Christ in the world.[26] Defined by the endeavor to forge a moral discourse attentive to the lived experiences of African Americans, their cultural rhetoric blended "personal piety and sociopolitical advancement of African American people" into "a healthy and durative alliance."[27] Thus, African American women's moral discourse is cultural rhetoric that "traversed the religious and sociopolitical spheres."[28]

As such, African American women writers in the nineteenth century fashioned a similar rhetorical project of culture-creation and social

---

25. Martin, "Normative Biblical Motifs," 50.

26. The quotations from Clarice Martin's essay were in service to her description of the work of theologian Jacquelyn Grant, but they are also an apt description for how the moral discourse of nineteenth-century African American women functioned. See Martin, "Normative Biblical Motifs," 50; cf. Jacquelyn Grant, "Black Theology and the Black Woman," in *Black Theology: A Documentary History, 1966–1979*, ed. Gayraud S. Wilmore and James H. Cone (Maryknoll, NY: Orbis, 1979), 431.

27. Martin, "Normative Biblical Motifs," 48.

28. Martin, "Normative Biblical Motifs," 51.

response to that of 2 Peter. Like 2 Peter's reformist discourse (1:5–10), the women's social response championed internal reform of African American communities, as well as the entire United States (see Anna Julia Cooper). Their rhetorical strategy sought to fortify readers and hearers by expressing expectations about divine action and revolution (see Maria Stewart) similar to 2 Peter's apocalyptic discourse (3:4–14). African American women, writing across the changing tides of the 1800s in the United States, purposed to cultivate internal identity politics that nurtured cohesion and resilience over and against the pressures of a racist, classicist, and sexist society—both inside and outside the black community (see Virginia Broughton, Mary Virginia Cook). Their writings articulate a social response of revolution, as well as a reforming-prophetic message aimed at their African American and diaspora communities (see Ida B. Wells and Sarah Louisa Forten). But they also aimed their message at the entire social order of the American project and the dominating social and political discourse of the time. They pushed back against biblical rhetoric and imagination wielded primarily to exclude and diminish African American peoplehood and citizenship and that used the grammar of the King James Version of the Bible (KJV) as a tool.[29]

Examining the constructive quality of 2 Peter's religious rhetoric *through* the writings of nineteenth-century African American women orators, essayists, preachers, and autobiographers exposes the letter's distinct cultural and social commitments.[30] The writers of 2 Peter composed

---

29. Tracing the history of white American Christianity, particularly the development of evangelical Christian politics in the nineteenth century, historian Frances Fitzgerald notes the distinction between the origins of white American evangelical Christian forms and African American (*The Evangelicals: The Struggle to Shape America* [New York: Simon & Schuster, 2017], 3): "This book is not a taxonomy or attempt to describe the entirety of evangelical life, but rather a history of the white evangelical movements necessary to understand the Christian right and its evangelical opponents that have emerged in recent years. It purposely omits the history of African American churches because theirs is a different story, mainly one of resistance to slavery and segregation, but also of the creation of centers for self-help and community in a hostile world. Some African American denominations identify as evangelical, but because of their history, their religious traditions are not the same as those of white evangelicals. Only long after the success of the civil rights movement did some black churchmen begin to enter the story of the white evangelicals and their internal conflicts."

30. Some writers included in this book who contribute to the genre diversity within the literary canon of African American women in the nineteenth century

the letter as members of their Jesus communities; similarly, each woman wrote as a professed Christian who took "seriously the biblical injunction 'to write the vision and make it plain' (Hab. 2:2)." Like the writers of 2 Peter, nineteenth-century African American women used biblical verses, stories, language, and literary forms as both tools and weapons "to correct, to create, and to confirm their visions of life as it was and as it could become."[31] The disruptive logics running through African American women's writings exhibit modes of persuasion for negotiating communal Christian identity similar to 2 Peter.

If this book is a time machine, then we are refusing to skip over these women on our journey *back* to the world of 2 Peter. We are stopping first at the period of the nineteenth century to broadly assess the strategies of cultural rhetoric and social response produced by Christian African American women. Using their writings attunes contemporary interpreters to 2 Peter's unique rhetorical voice and sensitizes us to its social endeavors to encourage a particular form of Christian community and practice. In amalgamating the numerous examples of Hellenistic language and literature into their creations, the authors of 2 Peter operated similarly to the small and courageous cadre of early African American women writers. In both kinds of literature, the authors are actors involved in redefining the uses of inherited traditions and language. They chose cultural practices and depicted current social realities in ways that served their own purposes. With entrance into their respective literary traditions that address matters of religion, culture, and society, neither tradition "remain[s] as it had been."[32]

Models of Cultural Rhetoric and Response for Reading 2 Peter

As stated above, cultural rhetoric is not created in a vacuum separate from the religious traditions, social arrangements, and the lived experiences of its devotees. Similarly, rhetoric consists of more than intellectual exercises in prose composition and persuasive literary forms of address. To study early Christian writings is to note the force and forms of their rhetorical composition to mold habits of thinking and behavior. Accord-

---

include Ida B. Wells, Sarah Louisa Forten, Jarena Lee, Virginia Broughton, Mary Virginia Cook, Anna Julia Cooper, Zilpha Elaw, and Maria Stewart.

31. Foster, *Written by Herself*, 2.
32. Foster, *Written by Herself*, 22.

ing to the ancient rhetorician Nicolaus the Sophist (ca. 410–after 491 CE), the author of a series of rhetorical lectures, exercises in Greek rhetoric are useful for composing the ethical character of writings, particularly letters: "we often need *ethopoeia* [imitation of an ethical character] when speaking an encomium and in prosecuting and giving counsel. To me, it seems also to exercise us in the style of letter writing since in that there is need of foreseeing the character of those sending letters and those to whom they are sent."[33] Although 2 Peter is a mid-second century letter and Nicolaus is a rhetorical professor from the mid-fifth century, Nicolaus's emphasis on the forming quality of letters is instructive and retrospective. Ancient religious discourse in the form of letters can be a refracting archive.[34] It can reflect multiple angles of perspective between senders and recipients. Those angles can show foresight or hindsight, and they can express critiques or offer propositions for what might be idealized or actionable in the near future.

Early Christian rhetoric in letter form emits a culture-making force. A letter is penned "to encourage its readers to adopt certain social and cultural orientations rather than others."[35] Letter discourse, therefore, shapes its communities' religious lives, persuading them toward particular social conditions and actions. It addresses patterns of interactions and elucidates forms of community principles that occur inside and outside its membership. The letter of 2 Peter is a prime exemplar of such a rhetorical undertaking.[36] However, two models assist in adequately analyzing an

---

33. "Preliminary Exercises Attributed to Hermogenes," 9.20, in George A. Kennedy, ed., *Progymnasmata: Greek Textbooks of Prose Composition and Rhetoric*, WGRW 10 (Atlanta: Society of Biblical Literature, 2003), 166.

34. Vincent L. Wimbush, *Refractions of the Scriptural: Critical Orientation as Transgression*, Routledge Studies in Religion (New York: Routledge, 2016), 2, 10–11.

35. Robbins, *Exploring the Texture of Texts*, 72.

36. E. P. Sanders's notion of a "pattern of religion" proves helpful in understanding dimensions of what I identify as the social rhetoric of 2 Peter as religious discourse. Sanders describes patterns of religion as "the description of how a religion is perceived by its adherents to function … of how getting in and staying in are understood.… It includes the logical beginning-point of the religious life as well as its end, and it includes the steps in between" (E. P. Sanders, *Paul and Palestinian Judaism: A Comparison of Patterns of Religion* [Philadelphia: Augsburg, 1977], 17; cited in Patrick Chatelion Counet, "Pseudepigraphy and the Petrine School: Spirit and Tradition in 1 and 2 Peter and Jude," *HvTSt* 62 [2006]: 404).

early Christian letter like 2 Peter for its culturally conditioned response to situations conceived by its authors.[37]

Examining 2 Peter as an Exemplar of Early Christian Self-Definition, "Christianness"

Culture matters in the interpretive work and reconstruction of early Christian texts and their accompanying modes of suasion (rhetoric).[38] Writings like 2 Peter reflect and speak toward collective cultural identities and practices. These are ancient peoples socialized in cultural communities located in a broader pluralistic society constituted by many *other* cultural communities. Foundational to community cultures are their land attachments (geography), stories of peoplehood and ancestors, religious rituals and social practices, language and dialect, ethnicity and nationhood, conquest and caste, and more. To study Christian origins and its literature is to take strategies of group identity formation in forms of ethnic reasoning, gender identities, religious practices, and literary trends seriously. Frequently, these features are mutable with elastic boundaries. The diverse cultural, social, and theological dimensions of Christianness are a legacy worth tracing in its many versions.

To this end, Denise Kimber Buell argues, early Christian texts express ancient conceptions of racial categories in the endeavor to fashion Christian identities.[39] Critiquing traditional approaches to early Christian writings that distinguish early Christian identity formations from both ancient and modern racialized identities like Jewish, black, and white, Buell argues that early Christian literature exhibits multiple forms of ethnic reasoning:

---

37. Richard Horsley, *Sociology and the Jesus Movement*, 2nd ed. (New York: Crossroad, 1994), 4–5.

38. For discussions about the centrality of cultural and social contexts in the interpretation and exegesis of biblical literature, see Blount, *Cultural Interpretation*; Vincent L. Wimbush, *White Men's Magic: Scripturalization as Slavery* (New York: Oxford University Press, 2012); Musa Dube, *Other Ways of Reading: African Women and the Bible*, GPBS 7 (Atlanta: Society of Biblical Literature, 2001).

39. Denise Kimber Buell, "Rethinking the Relevance of Race for Early Christian Self-Definition," *HTR* 94 (2001): 449–76. A consistent assumption of this book is that 2 Peter approaches the intra-Christian identity as a kind of ethnic/racial identity. Building on Buell's scholarship, this book highlights 2 Peter as a particular iteration in the workings of early Christian literature's racialized culture-making endeavors.

Many early Christian texts depict Christians as members of a race or people, like Jews, so that "race" does not mark the dividing line between Jews and Christians.... A number of early Christian authors find it strategically valuable to speak about Christianness as a racial category, although they formulate it as an inclusive one (as a race one can join). That is, instead of positioning Christianness as not-race, many early Christian texts define their version of Christianity as a race, sometimes in opposition to other rival articulations of Christianness, and sometimes in contrast to non-Christian groups and cultures (including, but not limited to, those defined as "Jews").[40]

Buell asserts that the workings of Christianness create a people. Christianness is a racial category distinct from others by its porous boundaries in which people outside the community, the proverbial non-Christians, are welcome to join. It is not a closed group identity. Her broad analysis of the trends in early Christian writings to cultivate self-definition using ancient forms of ethnic reasoning is provocative. She maps an approach for sketching the varieties of ethnic Christian formulations.

Rather than searching for a linear and singular essence or original form of early Christian formation, Buell advocates for scholarship that "highlights the processes and strategies of negotiation, persuasion, contestation, and contingency that permeate the very production of Christianness."[41] Buell's approach shifts critical analysis from conceiving of early Jesus communities as ancient forms of professional guilds, fraternal/sororal orders, or even diminished forms of peoplehood to conceiving of them as the creations of a new racial category that is malleable. In the hands of authors writing from and toward their diverse cultural communities, Christian identities germinate multiple expressions. Race and ethnicity in ancient and modern forms, therefore, do not recede into the background in the historical analysis of early Christian literature but move to the foreground.

The letter of 2 Peter exemplifies a distinct iteration of Buell's proposition that early Christian ethnic formations were porous and mutable. Instead of projecting identity border crossings in which non-Christians join its ranks as full-racialized Christian members, 2 Peter's cultural rhetoric emphasizes a crossing in the opposite direction. Recognized members can be ousted from the group for nonconformity to a particular expres-

---

40. Buell, "Rethinking the Relevance of Race," 450–51.
41. Buell, "Rethinking the Relevance of Race," 474.

sion of Christian belief and practice. They can cross *out of* the Christian racial community. Leveraging Buell's approach, this project interprets 2 Peter as a literary instance of Christian ethnicity that pushes members out, rather than welcoming newcomers into, the Christian "race." Its rhetoric disseminates both culture-making and culture-destroying effects. Nineteenth-century African American women writers, who express their own formulations of peoplehood and Christianness, offer a sensitizing lens to detect the "version of Christianity as a race" espoused by 2 Peter's cultural pattern.[42]

Using African American Women Interpreters to Disrupt Traditional Exegetical Models

Reading 2 Peter *through* the context of nineteenth-century African American women's literature demonstrates that the path of historical investigation into early Christian literature is not predetermined and fixed. As the famous theorist of history Marc Bloch states, "The word [*history*] places no *a priori* prohibitions in the path of inquiry, which may turn at will toward either the individual or the social, toward momentary convulsions or the most lasting developments. It comprises no credo; it commits us, according to its original meaning, to nothing other than 'inquiry.'"[43] The meaning and significance of early Christian writings is not locked

---

42. Buell, "Rethinking the Relevance of Race," 451. Scholars such as Paula Fredriksen documented Paul's endeavor to cultivate new religious and social kinships. Tracing the work of people construction, they observe Paul's engagement with diverse literary and pluralistic environments. My work on 2 Peter joins this scholarly endeavor by adding the Petrine epistolary tradition to the conversation about the varieties of early Christianity and the pluralism of the ancient environment reflected in the literature. See Paula Fredriksen, *Paul, the Pagan's Apostle* (New Haven: Yale University Press, 2017), 34–35. Here, Fredriksen notes that ethnicity is not something that can merely be retooled. Rather, she notes that both pagans and Jews were ethnic identities. Consequently, for Paul's audience talking about being an "ex-pagan pagan" was nonsensical because ethnic identity was an essential component of group identity that could not be abandoned.

43. Marc Bloch, *The Historian's Craft* (Manchester, UK: Manchester University Press, 1954), 20; Adele Reinhartz's 2020 Society of Biblical Literature presidential address resourced Bloch as a framing thinker for the work of historical reconstruction in early Christian literature. See Reinhartz, "The Hermeneutics of Chutzpah: A Disquisition on the Value/s of 'Critical Investigation of the Bible,'" *JBL* 140 (2021): 9–10.

in antiquity. Rather, a comparative, phenomenological engagement can unlock its inexhaustibility by focusing on phenomena that gave rise to ancient writings and that reappear in other times and spaces and among other people. Matters related to rhetorical exigency, cultural norms and deviations, literary forms and innovations, and social realities and expectations are sites of comparison.

Within African American and African diaspora (African American/ diaspora) biblical hermeneutics, scholars have variously described or modeled approaches to historical inquiry that move in the opposite direction of traditional historical trends. As early as the 1980s, South African biblical exegete and hermeneutician, Itumeleng J. Mosala, asserted the imperative of valuing contemporary African diaspora cultures and social-political histories before, in turn, drawing on them as ciphers by which to interrogate the meanings of biblical texts. He used the notion and experiences of black struggles to interrogate biblical interpretation and appropriation. To this end, he says, "In particular, I hope that black theologians will take black history and culture seriously enough that they will use it more to interrogate the texts of the Bible. I propose that, in this appropriation of black history and culture for the purposes of appropriating biblical texts, the category of struggle will serve as a critical grid. It is necessary to take sides in the struggles inscribed in black history and culture as a prior step to taking sides in the struggles that produced the Bible and are significant in it."[44] Following Mosala's instruction, this book does fundamentally take a side—namely, the side of a historically minoritized Christian experience forged from the underside of Christian America and expressed through the writings of African American women. In effect, the term *minoritized* in this book conveys "the sense of relegation to the margins or the periphery" by a dominant group in a position to label and sift people groups.[45] To exegete from the location of those rendered minorities, as opposed to the position of those imposing the status, sharpens the exegete's awareness of whose side is mostly canonized and conveyed in 2 Peter and whose version of Christianness is not. More recently, Jennifer Kaaluund used the movement of approximately six million African Americans, known as the Great

---

44. Itumeleng J. Mosala, *Biblical Hermeneutics and Black Theology in South Africa* (Grand Rapids: Eerdmans, 1989), 11–12.

45. Tat-siong Benny Liew and Fernando F. Segovia, eds., *Reading Biblical Texts Together: Pursuing Minoritized Biblical Criticism*, SemeiaSt 98 (Atlanta: SBL Press, 2022), xiii.

Migration (1910–1970) from the southern United States to the Northeast, Midwest, and West of the country, as a site of struggle and experiencing for interpreting Hebrews and 1 Peter's notions of dispersion, foreignness, and belonging.[46] Whereas both Mosala and Kaaluund fundamentally map a linear line of historical inquiry backwards from African American/diaspora historical moments, this monograph transforms the line of inquiry into a cyclical approach. This project, so to speak, goes forward and then backwards only to go forward again.

My approach is not unlike working back to the gospel writers and the historical Jesus by way of recognized twentieth-century exegetical thought leaders, such as Albert Schweitzer and Howard Thurman. Like other critical approaches to biblical texts, the project goes through a particular interpretive door to access the past and understand its literary, social, and rhetorical phenomena. It reassesses the documents of history in a moment of new history. Approaching the exegetical task of 2 Peter in this form follows Hans-Georg Gadamer's characterization of the interpretive process as dynamic ("productive"). The work of interpretation, according to Gadamer, can reproduce meaning intended by the original authors and audiences, but it also goes beyond them. The meaning of a writing, "as it speaks" to the contemporary interpreter, is not identical to its past significance. Meaning is "co-determined" by past and present interpreters.[47] Rather than starting with 2 Peter and tracing its meaning forward to later receiving communities, this book talks backward, both figuratively and literally. Exegesis that resources African American wom-

---

46. Jennifer T. Kaaluund, *Reading Hebrews and 1 Peter with the African American Great Migration: Diaspora, Place and Identity*, LNTS 598 (London: T&T Clark, 2020).

47. "Every age has to understand a transmitted text in its own way, for the text belongs to the whole tradition whose content interests the age and in which it seeks to understand itself. The real meaning of a text, as it speaks to the interpreter, does not depend on the contingencies of the author and his original audience. It certainly is not identical with them, for it is always co-determined also by the historical situation of the interpreter.... Not just occasionally but always, the meaning of a text goes beyond its author. That is why understanding is not merely a reproductive but always a productive activity as well.... It is enough to say that we understand in a different way, if we understand at all" (Hans-Georg Gadamer, *Truth and Method,* trans. Joel Weinsheimer and Donald G. Marshall, 2nd ed. [New York: Crossroad/Continuum, 2004], 296; cf. xxxi, xxviii; quoted in Merold Westphal, "The Philosophical/Theological View," in *Biblical Hermeneutics: Five Views,* ed. Stanley E. Porter and Beth M. Stovell [Downers Grove, IL: InterVarsity Press, 2012], 77).

en's writings, goes *through* history—albeit one strand of history—on its way to hear 2 Peter anew.

Accordingly, this book does not model the path of traditional reception-history studies, though it is informed by them.[48] It does not highlight how nineteenth-century African American women received and interpreted 2 Peter. As source material, their discourses represent an instance in American interpretive history that can texture exegetical analysis of the letter. The path of exegetical inquiry begins by rehearsing some standard topics in critical studies of 2 Peter, analyzing those topics in the context of nineteenth-century African American women's moral discourses and then returning to an exegetical reading of the letter attentive to matters of cultural rhetoric, ethics, and theology with a question about its place in contemporary human relations and rhetoric.[49] Reconsidering critical topics in 2 Peter studies by way of the literary canon of African American women sharpens descriptions about 2 Peter's Christian brand. It also means juggling (1) the use of past tense for discussions about the creation of both kinds of literature as past historical events with (2) the literary present, which approaches literary works as eternally present. Accordingly, the reader will see tense shifts between the past and present in this book. If a historical situation giving rise to either 2 Peter or African American women's writings is addressed, the discussion is set in the past tense, but if what the writing says in its final form is the focus, the book describes it according to the literary present tense.

To this end, a phenomenological approach to early Christian literature leverages the annals of time for two reasons. First, the approach strives to fill gaps in the historical record of biblical studies. African American women from the nineteenth century are conspicuously absent from standard treatments of biblical interpretation from the twentieth and early twenty-first centuries.[50] However, though few in number, these women

---

48. Jeremy Punt, "Inhabiting the World in Front of the Text: the New Testament and Reception Studies," *Neot* 34 (2000): 207–24.

49. For an overview of the variety of configurations in historical studies of biblical texts, see Shively T. J. Smith, "Historical Criticism: Methods," in *The New Cambridge Companion to Biblical Interpretation*, ed. Ian Boxall and Bradley C. Gregory (Cambridge: Cambridge University Press, 2023), 37–54.

50. One reference that reverses the trend and includes nineteenth-century biblical interpreters like Zilpha Elaw and Anna Julia Cooper is Marion Ann Taylor and Agnes Choi, eds., *Handbook of Women Biblical Interpreters: A Historical and Biographical Guide* (Grand Rapids: Baker Academic, 2012). For standard treatments where such

nonetheless engage masterfully in exegetical and existential sense-making of Christian texts in translation, exegesis, and historical reconstruction. For example, barely on the other side of the short-lived Reconstruction effort (ca. 1865–1877) and during the rise of the Redemption campaign's efforts (ca. 1877–1965) to repeal citizenship rights through Jim Crow segregation, Julia A. J. Foote (1823–1900) published her 1879 spiritual autobiography, *A Brand Plucked from the Fire*.[51] In it, she challenges the sexism and patriarchy within her African Methodist Episcopal Zion (AMEZ) church community and provides a reconstruction of early Christian origins informed by her particular social realities.

Standing at odds with the community's prevailing assumptions about the place of women's leadership in church and society, Foote confronted resistance to women's ordination using a sophisticated and eclectic exegetical strategy. She combined methods from literary, historical, and existential approaches to the Bible as she composed a position on the legitimacy of women's ecclesial authority.[52] To capture the full range of her interpretive strategies, Foote is quoted at length:

---

names are absent, see John H. Hayes, ed., *Dictionary of Biblical Interpretation*, 2 vols. (Nashville: Abingdon, 1999); Donald K. McKim, ed. *Historical Handbook of Major Biblical Interpreters* (Downers Grove, IL: InterVarsity, 1998); William Baird, *History of New Testament Research*, 3 vols. (Minneapolis: Fortress, 1992–2013).

51. For discussions about the histories of the Reconstruction and Redemptionist movements in America and the emergence of African American literature in the contested periods of the nineteenth and early twentieth centuries, see Henry Louis Gates Jr., *Stony the Road: Reconstruction, White Supremacy, and the Rise of Jim Crow* (New York: Penguin, 2019); Eric Foner, *Reconstruction: America's Unfinished Revolution, 1863–1877*, New American Nation Series (New York: Harper & Row, 1988); Rayford Whittingham Logan, *The Betrayal of the Negro, from Rutherford B. Hayes to Woodrow Wilson* (New York: Collier, 1965); Dickson D. Bruce, *Black American Writing from the Nadir: The Evolution of a Literary Tradition, 1877–1915* (Baton Rouge: Louisiana State University Press, 1989).

52. I find Michael Gorman's organization of exegetical methods into three tables of dominant approaches a useful pedagogical tool. He supplies a generative heuristic for considering the variety of configurations scholars deploy to analyze texts and histories. While Gorman's table arrangement is, at times, overly simplistic—particularly in the areas of what he calls advocacy and liberationist readings—I see it as a helpful reference for understanding the multiple interpretive questions and strategies for studying early Christian literature. See Michael J. Gorman, *Elements of Biblical Exegesis: A Basic Guide for Students and Ministers*, rev. and exp. ed. (Grand Rapids: Baker Academic, 2010), 233–40.

I could not believe that was short-lived impulse or spasmodic influence that impelled me to preach. I read that on the day of Pentecost was the Scripture fulfilled as found in Joel ii.28,29; and it certainly will not be denied that women as well as men were at the time filled with the Holy Ghost, because it is expressly stated that women were among those who continued in prayer and supplication, waiting for the fulfillment of the promise. Women and men are classed together, and if the power to preach the Gospel is short-lived and spasmodic in the case of women, it must be equally so in that of men; and if women have lost the gift of prophecy, so have men.... But the Bible puts an end to this strife when it says: "There is neither male nor female in Christ Jesus" [Gal. 3:28]. Philip had four daughters that prophesied or preached. Paul called Priscilla, as well as Aquila, his "helper," or as in the Greek, his "fellow-laborer." Rom. xv[i]. 3; 2 Cor. viii.23; Phil. ii.[2]5; 1 Thess. iii.2. The same word, which, in our common translation, is now rendered a "servant of the church," in speaking of Phoebe (Rom xvi.1.), is rendered "minister" when applied to Tychicus. Eph. vi.21.... And in the early ages of Christianity many women were happy and glorious in martyrdom. How nobly, how heroically, too, in later ages, have women suffered persecution and death for the name of the Lord Jesus.[53]

Foote's reconstruction of women's leadership in early Jesus movements exhibits her knowledge of canonical and noncanonical Christian writings, histories, and even koine Greek.[54] She employs literary analysis and theological exegesis, probing the final form of New Testament texts such as Acts 1:12–14 and 2:17–21. In so doing, she is attentive to demographic information about early Christian communities represented in the writings. Moreover, her interpretation discloses a facility with linguistic and

---

53. Quoted in Marcia Riggs, *Can I Get a Witness? Prophetic Religious Voices of African American Women: An Anthology* (Maryknoll, NY: Orbis, 1997), 57–58. For an excellent survey of African American Pauline hermeneutics from this period, see Lisa M. Bowens, *African American Readings of Paul: Reception, Resistance, and Transformation* (Grand Rapids: Eerdmans, 2020).

54. Foote was an itinerant preacher of the AMEZ church tradition and an activist for women's rights. Her theological exegesis reflects her holiness and evangelical traditional roots from the nineteenth century, while also taking a liberationist position that reflects an early instance of womanist and feminist biblical interpretation. The theological strengths and challenges of Foote's reading are not the focus of this book. Rather, it is the fact that she is an example of nineteenth-century African American women writers operating as critical biblical interpreters and historians of early Christian writings.

discourse analysis that investigates the Greek language behind the KJV. She questions the politics of translation legitimating an inequitable power dynamic between women and men in her Christian community.[55]

Without formal training and admittance into the ivory halls of academic biblical studies, women like Foote are, nonetheless, scholars of the Bible. Much of their literary writings qualify as forms of biblical scholarship that intervene in the interpretive trajectories dominating their Christian communities and American society. Readings of Christian literature produced by critical scholarly circles that exclude these African American women (as well as other historically minoritized communities) as interlocutors impoverish the scholastic record in biblical studies. Through such scholarly designs, possibilities in historical reconstruction and interpretation are inevitably missed because entire sets of lived experiences, perspectives, stories, and epistemologies are absent from the proverbial biblical colloquies! In sum, the range of meaning potentials in early Christian discourse has not been realized because not everyone is present at the table of interpretive conversation. Consequently, this book approaches African American women's moral discourse as an untapped interpretive trail for analyzing early Christian history and its literature.

Second, phenomenological exegesis draws upon later contextual histories to identify other models for understanding early Christian texts and contexts. African American women writers are a site for interpretive materials. Resourcing their discourses in service to exegetical endeavors represents a form of Musa Dube's "border crossing practice," which she dubs "intercultural biblical interpretation." Analyzing the moral discourses of African American women from the nineteenth century unearths a particular set of disruptive logics, citational techniques, and treatments of biblical themes. By contrasting features of their cultural rhetoric with 2 Peter, an interpreter participates in the task of inviting "established academic biblical interpretation to be home in strange places (and to strangers)."[56] Such a study forges another path of interpretive enunciation.

---

55. The two Greek words behind Foote's interpretation are *synergos* (Rom 16:3; 2 Cor 8:23; Phil 2:25; 1 Thess 3:2) and *diakonos* (Rom 16:1; Eph 6:21).

56. Dube's model of intercultural interpretive exchange creates new homes for interpretive readings and cultural rhetorical practices heretofore overlooked as resources for examining early Christian literature. One of Dube's generative descriptions of intercultural interpretation upon which this book builds states, "Intercultural Biblical interpretations invite scholars of the Bible to an unsettled practice in bibli-

It can disrupt centuries of exegetical norms in biblical translation and history. This book engages the literary productions of nineteenth-century African American women to reconsider what is most challenging, distinct, troubling, and potentially thrilling about an early Christian writing many scholars continue to overlook and dismiss as inconsequential.

Plan of the Book

Because I am an African American woman using African American women as sources, readers may conclude that the best way to understand this book's contribution is within the rich tradition of African American/ diaspora and womanist biblical interpretation. While the temptation to situate the book's scholasticism in this way is subtle, it is not without consequence. Such a move exchanges the primary objective of the research idea—namely, to understand the culture-making force and rhetorical aim of 2 Peter within the New Testament canon—for the ease created through categorization. Categories assist us in associating discourses rapidly, but it also spotlights the inherent biases in studying biblical literature and history. My white American and European scholarly counterparts do not have to attach their research explicitly to white American (or European) biblical interpretation for scholars to understand (and categorize) it as extending exegetical discourses. Determining the import of this book's research and its appropriate interlocutors solely based upon the racial identity of the scholar and the sources used perpetuates the field's unexamined practices of Othering.

This book is a translation-based, phenomenological exegesis of 2 Peter. It advances critical studies of early Christian texts by focusing on the letter's rhetorical strategy as a culture-making mechanism. It expands what interpreters account for in rhetorical studies of biblical literature by resourcing nineteenth-century African American women's cultural

---

cal interpretation, which is in the uncomfortable space of the borderlands where it will constantly look beyond itself and see itself differently—where it is in a constant encounter and interaction with various other cultures. As a border-crossing practice, intercultural biblical interpretations must inevitably challenge established academic biblical interpretations to be home in strange places (and to strangers)— to make its practices leave the canonized academic ways of biblical interpretation, which as many other scholars have pointed out are not intercultural but Eurocentric" (Dube, "Intercultural Biblical Interpretations," 367).

rhetoric to detail the features and implications of the letter's mode of persuasion. While approaches in African American/diaspora and womanist biblical interpretation guide this study's epistemological genealogy, my research extends critical studies of 2 Peter by also using rhetorical and grammatical analyses and cross-cultural comparisons that are socially and theologically circumspect. This volume's primary disciplinary locations are within 2 Peter and Petrine studies, the history of biblical translation politics, biblical rhetorical analysis, and cultural studies of early Christian literature. Readers should position it at the center of those discussion topics, no matter the interpretive route one takes to arrive.

The goal of this book is twofold. First, it models a unique interpretive interaction with early Christian literature. It does not look past centuries of lived experiences and forms of Christianness as if they were nugatory to the historical inquiry of ancient religious writings. The approach acts on the public proposal I made during the Society of Biblical Literature's virtual #BlackScholarsMatter Symposium in the fall of 2020. In my paper, titled "Preliminary Thoughts: The Hermeneutical Dilemmas of the Allies, Colleagues, and Guild of African American Biblical Scholar-Teachers," I proposed that the guild of biblical scholars follow the guidance of Anna Julia Cooper (1858–1964).[57] A nineteenth-century foremother of the multiform feminist movements of the twentieth century, Cooper describes intellectual communities in her 1886 address, "On Education," as sites where people serve the "gospel of intelligence" committed to inclusive "moral and material uplift" for all.[58] I advocated for the critical study of early Christian literature that dons Cooper's imperative by "confronting

---

57. See Shively T. J. Smith, "Preliminary Thoughts: The Hermeneutical Dilemmas of the Allies, Colleagues, and Guild of African American Biblical Scholar-Teachers," in Byron and Page, *Black Scholars Matter*, 39–45.

58. The 1993 first volume of *Searching the Scriptures*, edited by Elisabeth Schüssler Fiorenza, is dedicated to Anna Julia Cooper. "It must be noted that the first volume of *Searching the Scriptures* (Schüssler Fiorenza 1993) is not dedicated to Stanton but to the memory of Anna Julia Cooper, an African American foremother of feminist biblical studies. The contributors to the volume were not primarily Society of Biblical Literature members but feminist contributors located in different areas of religious studies. The second commentary volume of *Searching the Scriptures* (Schüssler Fiorenza 1994) sought to honor *The Woman's Bible* project of Stanton but did not adopt its title because of the problematic confessional and racist underpinnings of this historic work" (quoted in Taylor, "Celebrating 125 Years of Women," 51; see also Schüssler Fiorenza, *Searching the Scriptures*, vols. 1–2).

the availability and esteem we assign to *diverse and intersectional* primary source material." In so doing, the field gives voice and attention to sources and histories of biblical literature overlooked as starting points for critical exegesis. I do not possess inherent knowledge about Cooper or other nineteenth-century African American women writers because I am an African American woman myself. I had to excavate their texts and contexts critically, as I did for 2 Peter and other early Christian literature engaged in this book. Thus, my approach is one that anyone in the field can take up. As a globally constituted learned society, a normative approach among our membership should entail engaging biblical texts and contexts through the diverse communities colliding with the Bible. Advancing this idea, the book engages the literary productions of nineteenth-century African American women to detail the rhetorical aim of 2 Peter's final form.

Reading 2 Peter through the diverse literary phenomena and cultural rhetoric of nineteenth-century African American women risks misrepresenting the letter. Misrecognition is a persistent danger given that each chapter engages and resources the women's literary canon selectively. But risk is always possible as no exegetical endeavor is without bias, perspective, and investment. Indeed, prejudice and privilege abound in exegetical work as interpreters make decisions about primary sources, translations and cultural equivalence, topics of reconstruction, and preferred configurations of interpretive approaches and methods. Rather than pretending such decisions are not made, this project makes those decisions intentionally. As Gadamer states, "Reason exists for us only in concrete, historical terms.... In fact history does not belong to us; we belong to it."[59] The biblical exegete and historian can never escape herself, even when she most wants to live solely in the worlds of early Christianness. Exegetical readers receive and examine ancient religious texts as historical documents through our own lived historical spaces. Therefore, reading 2 Peter as a writing sitting at the crossroads of multiple histories of religious discourse and cultural rhetoric traces meaning beyond its compositional origins. It can detail the rippling effects of 2 Peter's final rhetorical form on social periods unimagined by its original writers and audiences.

The second goal for the book is to supply a fresh reading of 2 Peter by focusing on its rhetorical aim to nurture a particular culture of Christian-

---

59. Gadamer, *Truth and Method*, 276–78; quoted in Westphal, "Philosophical/ Theological View," 73.

ness. The letter attempts to reform its cultural community from the inside toward a rigid intolerance of theological diversity. To this end, the letter writers deploy a variety of rhetorical strategies, and this book is not an exhaustive examination of them. Rather, each chapter reconsiders a standard topic of discussion in 2 Peter studies through its phenomenological occurrence in the literary moral discourses from a sampling of African American literature. Although engaging in phenomenological comparison, the project does not assert that a genetic or historical progression exists between 2 Peter, composed in the mid-second century, and the moral discourses of African American women composed in the nineteenth century. To avoid any misunderstanding that such an argument might underly my approach, each chapter (except for chapter 2) moves through the rhetorical endeavors of the women first and then shifts to analyze 2 Peter's rhetorical effect.

The monograph probes rhetorical matters of translation (chapter 2), the vocabulary of justice and righteousness (chapters 3 and 4), the literary strategy of pseudonymity (chapters 5 and 6), and the reinterpretation of biblical traditions (chapters 7 and 8). The conclusion (chapter 9) summarizes the implications of the study's phenomenological exegesis of 2 Peter. Questions about the possible relationship between 2 Peter's reception history and canonical influence on the moral discourses of African American women and the contemporary moment are reserved for the final chapter.

Within the field of early Christian literature and history, the literature of nineteenth-century African American women is generally unfamiliar. Therefore, the book quotes relevant excerpts from their writings throughout, providing brief contextual information in addition to commentary to support the phenomenological approach to 2 Peter. Furthermore, among all the writings of the New Testament and early Christian literature from the first two centuries, 2 Peter is likely one of the most overlooked and least read. Therefore, I provide a mediating translation with a brief overview of the translation criteria guiding my approach to 2 Peter. The translation reflects the use of Bryan Wilson's typology of sectarian groups as it accounts for the cultural rhetoric of the letter (chapter 2).[60]

---

60. Bryan R. Wilson, "A Typology of Sects," in *Sociology of Religion: Selected Readings*, ed. Roland Robertson (Baltimore: Penguin Books, 1969), 361–83. The use of Bryan Wilson's typology has proven helpful to Petrine studies with John Elliott's use of it in his sociological exegesis of 1 Peter in 1981. See John H. Elliott, *A Home for*

The writings of African American women from the nineteenth century emerge from existential experiences of cultural inclusion and exclusion and, as such, are a relevant interpretive context for understanding the culture-making force of 2 Peter's rhetoric. Examining 2 Peter through their moral discourses attunes contemporary interpreters to the unique rhetorical voice and cultural conditioning expressed in 2 Peter. The cultural rhetoric of 2 Peter dons the face of the historic Peter and deploys the language of justice to cultivate internal conformity and force the defection of members expressing different Christian views. This book examines how the letter writers selected certain rhetorical ends rather than others, with the moral discourses of African American women as the throughway.

---

the Homeless: A Social-Scientific Criticism of 1 Peter, Its Situation and Strategy, 2nd ed. (Eugene, OR: Wipf & Stock, 2005), 74–76.

2
A Mediating Translation of 2 Peter's Cultural Rhetoric

Translation of 2 Peter

Section 1. Fashioning "the Face" of Peter in the Testament Letter of an Apostle (2 Pet 1:1–21)

Unit 1. 2 Pet 1:1–2: A Salutation in "the Face" of the Historical Peter

> 1:1: Symeōn Peter, an enslaved person and apostle of Jesus Christ, to those having received an allotment of faith, equal in honorable quality as ours in bringing the justice [*dikaiosynē*] of our God and Savior Jesus Christ.[1]
> 1:2: May grace and peace be multiplied to you by knowledge of God and Jesus, our Lord.

Unit 2. 2 Pet 1:3–11: A Cultural Rhetoric of Insider Knowledge

> 1:3: As his divine power has given us everything for life and religious habit [*eusebeian*] through the full knowledge of the One

---

1. Informed by Jerome Neyrey's translation in *2 Peter, Jude*, AB 37C (New York: Doubleday, 1993), 195. For the hybrid form of *Symeōn* Peter, see Joseph A. Fitzmyer, "The Name Simon," *HTR* 56 (1963): 105–12; David R. Nienhuis and Robert W. Wall, *Reading the Epistles of James, Peter, John and Jude as Scripture* (Grand Rapids: Eerdmans, 2013), 130–31. Bauckham supposes the hybrid form of the name reflects a Jewish Christian Petrine circle in Rome, which Horrell refutes. See Bauckham, *Jude, 2 Peter*, 167; David G. Horrell, "The Product of a Petrine Circle? A Reassessment of the Origin and Character of 1 Peter," *JSNT* 86 (2002): 29–60. At minimum, the hybridized name reflects the pluralistic nature of the letter. It presents the discourse as pluralistically aware and conversant, although its ultimate social-theological stance flattens plurality within its membership.

having called us to his own reputation *δοχε* of glorious honor and exceptional civic virtue.*ανετε*

1:4: Through which things he has given to us the socially honorable and great promises that through these you all may become those who fellowship in the divine nature, having escaped the decay of immorality in the world by lust.

1:5: This very thing is the reason why having applied all diligence supply your group faith with exceptional civic virtue, and exceptional civic virtue with knowledge.

1:6: And knowledge with self-control, self-control with endurance, endurance with religious habit [*eusebeian*].

1:7: And religious habit [*eusebeia*] with fraternal-sororal mutuality, and fraternal-sororal mutuality with love.

1:8: For these things being in you all and increasing, keep you all from being unproductive and unfruitful in the knowledge of our Lord Jesus Christ.

1:9: For with whom these things are not present, that person is blind, being shortsighted, having forgotten the cleansing of their past sins.

1:10: Therefore, brothers and sisters, make every effort to ensure your group calling and election firm; for if you all do this, you will never stumble.

1:11: For in this way the entrance into the eternal kingdom of our Lord and Savior Jesus Christ will be provided for you all richly.

Unit 3: 2 Pet 1:12–15: A Testament of the Apostle as an Abbreviated Spiritual Autobiography[2]

1:12: Therefore, I will always intend to remind you all about these things, even though you all know them and have been established in the truth present among your group.

1:13: And I think it just [*dikaios*] as long as I am in this tent, to awaken you all with a reminder.

1:14: Knowing that taking off my tent is soon, as our Lord Jesus Christ made clear to me.

---

2. I adopt the term a *testament of the apostle* from Klauck and Bailey, *Ancient Letters and the New Testament*, 410.

1:15: And I will make every effort to cause you all to always have the memory of these things after my exodus-departure.

Unit 4. 2 Pet 1:16–18: Legacy of the Collective Apostolic Witness of Peter

1:16: For we did not follow cleverly devised myths when we made known to you all the power and coming of our Lord Jesus Christ, but we were eyewitnesses of his majesty. *time* *drta*
1:17: For he received from the God-Father social honor and divine glory when a voice was carried by the magnificent glory to him: "This is my Son, my Beloved, in whom I am well pleased."
1:18: And we heard this voice carried out of heaven when we were with him on the holy mountain.

Unit 5. 2 Pet 1:19–21: The Practice of Prophetic Interpretation Inside the Community

1:19: And we have made firm the prophetic word; to which you all do well to pay attention as to a lamp shining in a dark place until the day dawns and a morning star rises in your hearts.
1:20: Knowing this first: that no prophetic writing is a matter of personal interpretation.
1:21: For not at any time was a prophecy brought by the will of human beings, but people spoke from God who were being carried along by the Holy Spirit.

Section 2. Prophetic Discourses of Paragons and Offenders as Cultural Rhetoric (2 Pet 2:1–22)

Unit 1. 2 Pet 2:1–3: A History of Competing Traditions, Rhetorics, and Teachings

2:1: But there were also false prophets among the people, as also there will be false teachers among your group. They will secretly bring in heresies producing destruction, even denying the Divine Enslaver who purchased them, bringing upon themselves swift *despotes* destruction.
2:2: And many will follow in their unrestrained immorality, and, because of these false teachers, "the way of truth" will be slandered.

2:3: And in their greed they will take advantage of you with fabricated words. The judgment pronounced against them long ago has not fallen idle and their destruction is not asleep.

Unit 2. 2 Pet 2:4–10a: Rehearsing the Paragons of the Way of Truth Tradition

2:4: For if God did not spare angels when they sinned, but God handed them over, casting them into Tartarus in chains of darkness to keep them for judgment.
2:5: And if God did not spare the ancient world but God preserved Noah, the eighth person, a preacher for bringing justice [dikaiosynēs], when God brought a flood upon the world of People Lacking Religious Habit [asebēs].[3]
2:6: And God condemned the cities of Sodom and Gomorrah, having reduced those cities of people and creation to ashes by a catastrophe; having made them an example of things to come for the People Lacking Religious Habit [asebēs].
2:7: And God delivered just [dikaios] Lot, who was made miserable by the conduct of the Lawless Ones in licentiousness.
2:8: By what he saw and heard, the Just [dikaios] One—dwelling among them day by day—was being tormented in his just [dikaios] soul concerning their lawless deeds.
2:9: The Lord knows how to rescue Ones of Religious Habit [eusebeis] from trial and to keep Unjust Ones (adikous) being punished until a day of judgment [hēmeran kriseōs].
2:10a: Especially the Ones Following after Flesh in depraved lust and the Ones Despising Lordship forms of authority.

Unit 3. 2 Pet 2:10b–14: A Model of Cultural Intolerance: Polemics against Others

2:10b: They are bold and self-willed and do not tremble at the act of slandering the Gloriously Honorable Beings.

---

3. The capitalization used in this mediating translation is intentional. Its purpose is to differentiate the social groups that the cultural rhetoric of 2 Peter creates and labels. The letter is not proposing merely conceptions, but it is nurturing particular social relations and interpersonal interactions. The unique capitalization serves to identify the groups and factions the letter's cultural rhetoric creates and the attributes the letter assigns.

2:11: Whereas angels, being greater in strength and power, do not bring against them a slanderous judgment from the Lord.

2:12: These people, however, are like non-speech-oriented animals, having been born by nature for capture and destruction; slandering matters in which they are ignorant in their decay of immorality and, indeed, they will be decayed.

2:13: Suffering injustices [*adikoumenoi*] as payment for their unjust ways [*adikias*]. They consider self-indulgence in the daytime a pleasure. They are spots and blemishes, indulging in their deceits while feasting with you.

2:14: They are always looking for someone with whom to commit adultery. They are always on the lookout for opportunities to sin. They entrap people whose faith is weak. They have hearts trained in greed. Children of a Curse!

Unit 4. 2 Pet 2:15–19: A Model of Cultural Intolerance: Balaam as an Offender of the Way of Truth Tradition

2:15: They went off course, forsaking a straight way, having followed the way of Balaam, the son of Bosor, who loved the wages of injustice [*adikias*].

2:16: But Balaam was censured for his wrongdoing: a speechless donkey having spoken in a man's voice put a stop to the prophet's madness.

2:17: These false teachers are springs without water and mists being driven by storms. Gloomy darkness is kept for them.

2:18: With inflated speech of vanity and with the desires of the flesh in licentiousness, false teachers entice people who barely escaped the people who live in error.

2:19: These false teachers promise them freedom, but they themselves are enslaved to the decay of immorality, for whoever overpowers you, to this one he has become enslaved.

Unit 5. 2 Pet 2:20–22: A Model of Cultural Intolerance: Rehearsing the Wisdom for the Way of Justice

2:20: For if they, having escaped the defilements of the world by a knowledge of our Lord and Savior Jesus Christ, then get tangled up in them again and are overpowered, the last state has become for them worse than the first.

2:21: It would be better for them never to have known the way of justice [*dikaiosynēs*] than, having come to know it, to turn back from the holy commandment that was handed over to them.

2:22: They demonstrate the truth of the proverb: "A dog having returned to its own vomit" and "A sow having been washed only to wallow in the mud."

Section 3. Apostolic Writers, Insider Traditions, and Apocalyptic Revolution (2 Pet 3:1–18)

Unit 1. 2 Pet 3:1–2: Peter as a Writer of Early Christian Literature

3:1: Now this, beloved, is the second letter I am writing to you. In both, as a reminder, I awaken your group's sincere minds.

3:2: To remind you of the words having been previously spoken through the holy prophets and the commandment of the Lord and Savior also spoken through your apostles.

Unit 2. 2 Pet 3:3–13: The Polemics of Cultural Intolerance and Apocalyptic Expectation

3:3: Knowing this first, that mockers will come mocking during the last days, behaving according to their own peculiar passion.

3:4: And saying, "Where is the promise of his coming? For from the time in which the fathers fell into a sleeping death, all things continue from the beginning of creation."

3:5: For this is hidden from them, those who wanting it so—that the heavens existed from long ago, and the earth came into being out of water; and through water, having been formed by the Word of God.

3:6: The water through which the world of that past time perished, having been deluged by water.

3:7: But by the same Word, the heavens and the earth are now stored up in reserve for fire. Why? Because they are being kept for a day of judgment [*hēmeran kriseōs*] and of destruction for the People Lacking Religious Habit [*asebēs*].

3:8: But let this one thing not escape you all, beloved, that one day with the Lord is like a thousand years and a thousand years is like day one.

3:9: The Lord of the promise is not slow as some consider slowness, but he is patient toward you, not wanting any to perish but all to come to repentance.

3:10: But the Day of the Lord will come like a thief, in which the heavens will pass away with a great noise, and the elements will be *stoichein* destroyed, being burned up; and the earth and the deeds done on it will be disclosed.

3:11: So, all these things being destroyed, what kind of people ought you to be? You are to be the kind of people who exist in holy ways of living and in religious habits [*eusebeia*].

3:12: While awaiting and hastening the coming of the Day of God, because of which the heavens being set on fire will be destroyed and the burning elements are melted.

3:13: But, according to God's promise, we await new heavens and a new earth, in which justice [*dikaiosynē*] is at home.

Unit 3. 2 Pet 3:14–16: Paul as a Writer of Early Christian Literature

3:14: Therefore, beloved, while expecting those things, all of you do your best to be found in peace with him, spotless and blameless.

3:15: And you all consider the patience of our Lord as salvation, just as our beloved brother Paul wrote to you according to the wisdom having been given to him.

3:16: As also in all his letters as they speak concerning these things, in which there are some things hard to understand that the Unlearned and Unstable Ones twist as also they do the other Scriptural Writings [*graphē*] to their own destruction.[4]

---

4. This translation deviates from Terrance Callan's division of the letter closing. He identifies 3:14–18 as the closing unit of the entire letter. In contrast, I designate the last "therefore" as the final shift in the discourse and reserve verses 14–16 as the penultimate word, especially since it evokes a new personage who looms large in the history and tradition. The evocation of Paul's identity and writings is too lofty an image in the cultural rhetoric of 2 Peter to conflate with the closing verses of 17–18. See Terrance Callan, *Acknowledging the Divine Benefactor: The Second Letter of Peter* (Eugene, OR: Pickwick, 2014), 188–99.

Unit 4. 2 Pet 3:17–18: Closing Exhortation for a Cultural Rhetoric of Intolerance

3:17: You all, therefore, beloved, knowing beforehand, you all guard yourselves! Unless, having been led away with the error of the Lawless Ones, you all might fall from your own stability.
3:18: But you all grow in the favor and knowledge of our Lord and Savior, Jesus Christ, to him be the divine glory both now and to the Day of the Age. Amen.

A Note about the Translation

Translating 2 Peter and understanding its past and present meaning potentials are two parts of a joint, not separate, task. As one scholar states, "It can be safely assumed that every translation ever done of the biblical text exhibits a definite 'ideology,' whether conscious or unconscious and the factors contributing to translation ideologies or world views include: 'realities of race, class, gender, life-histories, theological persuasions, political alliances, cultural distinctives.'"[5] Rather than deny the existence of these factors or wrongly downplay their significance, the translation above leverages the perspective they provide. Therefore, the book's translation is "up to something"—namely, providing a fresh consideration of 2 Peter that takes seriously *where*, among the polarized masses of Mediterranean ancient peoples, the socially conditioned rhetoric of 2 Peter is aimed. To whom is 2 Peter keyed in a world of limited goods, group-oriented identities and actions, and subsistence-level living, in which less than 3 percent of the population is wealthy and there is no middle class to speak of? What is the response to the world that the letter seeks to cultivate in its hearers? The translation conveys to contemporary readers the social and cultural values, attitudes, and responses that 2 Peter offers, and it seeks to animate the letter's rhetorical discourse. It also prompts contemporary interpreters to measure the significance of 2 Peter's cultural rhetoric for current realities.

The translation preserves the Greek syntax as much as possible—particularly at the level of clauses—and provides a more mediating than

---

5. Steven Voth, "Justice vs. Righteousness: A Contextualized Analysis of 'tsedeq' in the KJV (English) and the RVR (Spanish)," *Journal of Biblical Text Research* 20 (2007): 280.

formal rendering in English. There are adjustments to prepositions, conjunctions, and loaded, overused theological terminology. In addition to translating every *dik*-stem word as some form of "justice" and every *seb*-stem word as "religious habit," the translation renders the second-person plural pronoun "you" into the clunky literal form of "you all." The letter contains no second-person *singular* pronouns, only plural forms.[6] Likewise, there are no verbs in the second-person singular in 2 Peter, only ten instances of second-person plural forms.[7] Such decisions recalibrate readers toward the group and community focus of the document. Second Peter does not speak in, nor conceive of, an individual expression of religious and moral identity and practice. Rather, its social-cultural leaning is entirely community oriented. The challenges and opportunities, the standards and prohibitions to social-religious life that the letter narrates, are for the group. Second Peter describes the community, not the individual, as a beneficiary of a rich and diverse tradition that can withstand the challenges of competing theologies and the apparent delay of God's revolutionary and transformative return.

The letter's language of theology, religion, and the sacred informs how hearers navigate social and cultural proximities, both within their communities and outside them. Chief among these two orientations of 2 Peter—how listeners live within the community or how they manage the world outside the community—reflects the insider experience. Second Peter focuses on a particular group way of being, leaving the actions of the people outside the community in the hands of God. To this end, I sometimes supply additional clauses or phrases to clarify the matters of sociality and peoplehood communicated in the Greek. This is an intentional decision about how to translate the reconstructed Greek of 2 Peter into English. In making this decision, my rendering responds to the translation history of 2 Peter that, at times, conceals the social matters of peoplehood and proximity at work in the rhetoric and grammar of the letter. The history of translations that have overplayed the language of righteousness and social-theological experience of the Western individual is centuries long (see chapters 3 and 4). Despite this long-standing trend, it is anachronistic to the group-oriented personalities of the ancient world. These hearers and readers did not exist at the center or as exemplars of the accepted norms of

---

6. Twenty-one instances: 2 Pet 1:2, 5, 8, 10–13, 15–16, 19; 2:1, 3, 13; 3:1–2, 8–9, 11, 15, 17.

7. Ten instances: 2 Pet 1:4–5, 10, 19; 3:14–15, 17–18.

their world. Rather, the people from whom and to whom the letter speaks existed on the margins of their local environments because of their corporate habitual action and way of life as justice-endowed people of God. Both the opponents and confederates singled out by the letter writers are insiders of a Christian membership, and they navigate the social and cultural fringes of Roman-controlled, mid-second century society. Overall, my translation intentionally resists an English rendering that leaves an overly individualistic and theological impression. The matter of social response and identity formation in 2 Peter is a matter of cultural values and practices as well as social institutions and dynamics—it is a matter of people. The grammar of the testamentary letter of 2 Peter cultivates a corporate body of believers living in a highly pluralistic and conflicting sociocultural environment.

Even though this book puts forth a unique English translation, I recognize that every translation has its own limitations and its own influences. The final translation was produced after engaging the following popular English translations in conversation with critical Greek translations of the New Testament:[8] the Common English Bible (CEB), the New Revised Standard Version (NRSV), the New Revised Standard Version Updated Edition (NRSVue), the Geneva Bible, the Reina-Valera Revisión de 1909 (RVR), La Biblia de las Américas translation (LBLA), and the King James Version (KJV).

Translating 2 Peter's Cultural Rhetoric and Social Theology

My mediating translation of 2 Peter is guided by the impulse to imagine what sort of persons and behaviors the letter persuades its recipients to be and do. The social and cultural systems expressed in the letter endow the activity of its readers—both ancient and modern—with meaning.[9] Second Peter enacts a rhetorical performance. The letter models norms of behavior and attitude its composers sought to map onto the cultural community. Those behaviors lean toward community reforms that approve of a narrow sectarianism. To this end, 2 Peter stigmatizes alternative expressions of

---

8. NA[28]; Barbara Aland, et al., eds., *The Greek New Testament*, 5th rev. ed. (Stuttgart: Deutsche Bibelgesellschaft/United Bible Societies, 2014).

9. Bruce J. Malina, "Understanding New Testament Persons," in *The Social Sciences and New Testament Interpretation*, ed. Richard Rohrbaugh (Grand Rapids: Baker Academic, 1996), 42.

Christianness as, fundamentally, non-Christian rather than mediating conflicting Christian sectarian configurations among its membership.[10]

Underlying my translation is the anthropological work of Bryan Wilson and his typology of seven sectarian group formations: conversionist, revolutionist, introversionist, gnostic manipulationist, thaumaturgic, reformist, and utopian.[11] Each label designates a particular cultural community and social-religious orientation. Although Wilson describes these seven forms as distinct, they are not always mutually exclusive, especially when encountered in literary productions. Features of these seven different social responses blend in religious discourse, producing new sectarian formations and expressions that are both discursive and disruptive, familiar and reinvented into something wholly distinct.[12] Second Peter, for instance, blends three social responses: (1) revolutionist response (2 Pet 3:8–10) intermixed with (2) introversionist and (3) reformist responses (2 Pet 1:3–11, 12–15; 3:1–3, 11–13).[13] This fashions a unique Christian cultural rhetoric that is not easily missed or mistaken for other voices of

---

10. The letter does not use the label of *Christian* (cf. 1 Pet 4:16; Acts 11:26), though it is addressing Christ-believing communities.

11. Recent scholarship rejects, as ahistorical, schemas that divide the varieties of Christianity into dualisms of Christian versus gnostic, protognostic, etc. Current scholarship recognizes astutely the problems with validating theological distinctions that pit some versions of Christian identity against those designated as Other. This book illustrates how 2 Peter may be an early perpetrator in the practice of Othering particular Christian expressions that are different from the norm the letter seeks to impose. See Karen King, *What Is Gnosticism?* (Cambridge: Harvard University Press, 2003), 9–11, 149–90; King, "Translating History: Reframing Gnosticism in Postmodernity," in *Tradition und Translation: Zum Problem der Interkulturellen Übersetzbarkeit religiöser Phänomene; Festschrift für Carsten Colpe zum 65. Geburstag,* ed. Christoph Elsas et al. (Berlin: De Gruyter, 1994), 264–77. As such, some of the language of Wilson's typology is dated. He uses the phrase *gnostic manipulationist* to characterize any religious group Othered by particular theological frames because they use "special knowledge" attained only within the religious movement itself. This book does not analyze 2 Peter through the gnostic manipulationist type Wilson advances for two reasons. First, it is not a dominant social response in 2 Peter. Second, like current scholarly critiques, the label establishes another layer of bifurcation that is ahistorical and mutes the letter's rhetorical endeavor (Robbins, *Tapestry of Early Christian Discourse,* 147–50; Wilson, "Typology of Sects," 361–83).

12. Robbins, *Tapestry of Early Christian Discourse,* 153.

13. Robbins, *Tapestry of Early Christian Discourse,* 147–50.

the tradition (e.g., Paul, the Gospel of Matthew, the Apocalypse of Peter, or even Jude).

Second Peter anticipates change to occur in the community and the world. In the common tongue of contemporary dystopia filmography, "it's inevitable."[14] Second Peter's social and cultural response assumes time will refresh or start anew instigated by the actions of God, not humans. Thus, *revolutionist* elements in 2 Peter do not signify humans agitating for social justice in the world, although members are encouraged to cultivate justice within the community (2 Pet 1:1). Second Peter considers the outside world already on a course that only God can disrupt and change in due time. In the case of believers in the Jesus movement, God has granted them an "escape" from "the decaying immorality in the world" (*phthora*, 2 Pet 1:3–4; cf. 2:12, 19). Though there appears to be a delay, 2 Peter states repeatedly that the day of judgment, in which decay or corruption will be wiped from the earth as the great flood once did, will yet come on God's word (2 Pet 3:4–7) and according to God's timing (2 Pet 3:8–10). Second Peter encourages its readers to anticipate the transformation of the world's natural and material form, which includes its social organizations and cultural practices. Yet, it repeatedly reminds them (*mimnēskomai*, 2 Pet 1:12, 13, 15; 3:1, 2) that they have no control over how and when it occurs. God is the power and force transforming the world while they navigate current realities (2 Pet 2:9–10).

The letter counsels readers to recognize their position as believers of God and Jesus Christ (2 Pet 1:1–2). It encourages radical fidelity that stabilizes Christian identity (2 Pet 3:1–3, 14) when alternative epistemologies about God's movements confront them from *inside* (2 Pet 2:1–3; 3:3–4). Second Peter's revolutionist response to the world is to "stay the course." Strengthening members' sense of insider identity, the letter writers fix the tradition and delineate the community's epistemological source pool. They employ such tactics to withstand rival insider voices, who teach other interpretations of Christian traditions (1:19–21).

Therefore, 2 Peter's discourse is not conversionist argumentation. It does not expect the outside world and its prophets, as well as teachers of alternative Christian formulations living among the membership

---

14. This reference is from *The Matrix* dystopian film trilogy. It is a generative analogy for the letter of 2 Peter because, in some ways, the letter envisions a kind of dystopian reality that is to be undone and revised by divine prerogatives and actions (2 Pet 3:7–13).

(2 Pet 2:1), to change. Even when they have seemingly reversed course and turned toward the truth of the promise (2 Pet 1:12; 2:2), 2 Peter anticipates that people will defect from the community's authentic teaching (2 Pet 2:20–22; 3:5–7). The letter narrates the timing of God as one that provides space for a diminished form of conversion to occur, but the efforts of the believing community and its presence in the world serves no missional purpose. Christian members play no role in instigating a conversion encounter. Rather, conversion remains solely the decision of the individual in relation to God (2 Pet 3:9).

The tension between individualism and group orientation is striking. The letter is group-focused, so individual decision-making is difficult to conceive and, likely, is the reason why the authors think genuine reversals are virtually impossible. Consequently, the view of the outside world through the eyes of 2 Peter is dismal! This letter asserts that the course is unchangeable. Yet within this unwavering destructive course, the letter locates hope for a social order that is functional, humane, lasting, and most importantly, divinely instituted (3:5–7, 10, 13–14). In this way, 2 Peter is primarily revolutionist argumentation. It hopes for change, even if it thinks it highly unlikely at the level of individual agents.

The *introversionist* argumentation of 2 Peter, focusing on the internal identity and workings of the community separate from the broader surrounding society, is telling. The letter distances its envisioned readers from the larger world (2 Pet 1:3–4, 10). The writers do adopt and adapt the cultural resources of the dominant society from which its members hail— especially Hellenistic Judaism and the socioreligious life of Mediterranean polytheisms. They rehearse these traditions in such a way that speaks to and nurtures cultural orientation and continuity among the membership and with the longer kinship chain beyond their chronological moment. Yet, the letter is more concerned with the chronological continuity of Christianness than cross-cultural and translocal connections.

The introversionist religious disclosure of 2 Peter employs the literary device of retelling as a component of its traditioning process. These retellings enculturate the audience into the diverse traditions of the Jesus movement and extend the historical Peter's profile to that of a storyteller. As the authorial face of the letter, Peter recycles traditions from the Synoptics, Paul, the Pseudepigrapha, and even other early Christian writings beyond the New Testament and gives them an interpretive spin that serves the community's formation (for examples, see chs. 4, 8, and 9). The testamental quality of 2 Peter does not merely rehash the voice of other traditions and communities. It fashions old and familiar traditions into new forms, strengthening the in-group identity against alternative formulations. As such, 2 Peter reflects an introversionist social response because it is attentive to developing and fortifying the boundaries of the community.

Second Peter is unique for how it embeds a revolutionist-introversionist response to the world within an energetic prophetic mode that makes it implicitly *reformist*. The letter seeks to remind readers about sources of prophetic knowledge and to inform their understandings about Christian stories and witnesses (1:12; 3:1–2), divine things (2 Pet 3:10–12), holy people (3:2), and their own rank and status within the longer chronological history of the Jesus movement (1:1). Indeed, the letter insists repeatedly it is only through the envisioned reader's proper comprehension of their prophetic place in God's unfolding drama that they can counter and dismiss false teachers and teaching (3:14–18) as well as false prophets and prophecies (1:19–2:1; 3:3–7). The courage and confidence to counter and dismiss wrong teaching represents reformist action set within a diverse theological-cultural setting. The prophetic mode counsels reform from within the community as of primary importance; it is less concerned with reform outside the community.

In summary, conversion happens rarely, and it is not inevitable or even expected in 2 Peter (2:20–21). The letter's discourse features apocalyptic, future-facing expectation molded into testamental letter form. Prophetic reflection (1:19–21) blended with wisdom speech (2:22) fortifies the internal identity of the community (introversionist response; 3:1–2, 15). In turn, 2 Peter's particular rhetoric of Christianness attempts to reform the community's identity and cultural practice into its own separate reality and peoplehood. It crafts an ethic of justice and a homogeneous belief system for inside the community with little diversity of thought and practice tolerated (reformist response), while God takes care of the outside world (revolutionist response).

2 Peter's Sectarian Inhospitality

A striking feature of 2 Peter's blend in sectarian formation and argumentation is how sectarian it becomes. The reforms proposed by 2 Peter include the cultivation of habitual just actions for those within the community who subscribe to a singular teaching. Second Peter's brand of justice, however, does not extend to alternative interpretations of the sources, stories, or the tradition within local communities of Christianness, nor does it extend to the people and society outside the community's borders. The letter writers' response to diversity is a polemical form of domestic harassment. It not only discounts and disregards those in the community with a different understanding of Christian identity and belief, but it also goes as far as to label them ignorant animals (2:12), cursed ones (2:14), enslaved people (2:19), dogs, and pigs (2:22).

Listening to 2 Peter's cultural rhetoric with ears sensitized by nineteenth-century African American women's moral discourse appropriately amplifies the terror, trauma, and dehumanization of its vitriol. Published in 1831, the dictated story of Mary Prince (ca. 1788–?) rehearses details of stigmatization in *The History of Mary Prince, a West Indian Slave, Related by Herself*. She was an enslaved woman from the West Indies who worked as a household servant before she was reassigned to the brutal conditions of the salt mines.

> I am often much vexed, and I feel great sorrow when I hear some people in this country say, that the slaves do not need better usage, and do not want to be free. They believe the foreign people, who deceive them, and say slaves are happy. I say, Not so. How can slaves be happy when they have the halter round their neck and the whip upon their back? and are disgraced and thought no more of than beasts?—and are separated from their mothers, and husbands, and children, and sisters, just as cattle are sold and separated?[15]

Prince dictated her story to an abolitionist and poet ally, Susanna Strickland, and she does not directly address 2 Peter.[16] Yet, her rehearsal of the polemics against African diaspora peoples sounds eerily close to the rhetoric of 2 Peter.[17] It highlights the caution necessary for trusting too easily

---

15. Mary Prince, "Excerpt from *The History of Mary Prince, a West Indian Slave*" (1831), in Robbins and Gates, *Portable Nineteenth-Century African American Women Writers*, 23.

16. Sandra Puchet Paquet, "Prince, Mary," in *The Oxford Companion to African American Literature*, ed. William L. Andrews, Frances Smith Foster, and Trudier Harris (New York: Oxford University Press, 1997), 599.

17. Erving Goffman, "Stigma and Social Identity," in *Understanding Deviance: Connecting Classical and Contemporary Perspectives*, ed. Tammy L. Anderson (New York: Taylor & Frances, 2014), 256–65. Franz Fanon (*Black Skin, White Masks*, trans. Richard Philcox [repr., New York: Grove Press, 2008]) supplies a helpful heuristic for considering the workings of stigmatization concerning ethnic difference that illuminates the rhetorical interventions of African American women writers in the nine-

the accounts of those who cast aspersions on others (*even if the bad actors are authors of the New Testament letter, 2 Peter*).

The letter's cultural rhetoric normalizes social behaviors of stigmatization, inhospitality, and attack that *shrink* diversity, and few exegetical treatments of 2 Peter from the twentieth and early twenty-first centuries question the authors' rhetorical decision. Indeed, a dominant trend in 2 Peter studies is to actually explain away this polemic in one of several ways: either it is a standard form of rhetorical rebuttal found in philosophical debates and Hellenistic Jewish discourses; a distinct Christian formulation directed against the emergence of gnostic thought within Christian circles; or a line of argumentation for combatting Epicurean arguments against providence and judgment.[18] Such reconstructions, however, risk creating a binary of heterodoxy and orthodoxy that is unproductive and ahistorical. Appealing to standard philosophical discourse, for instance, risks veiling legitimate tensions between different expressions of Christian identity and practice. A survey of literature from that century confirms different Christian constructions coexist in ways that are, at times, tolerant and intolerant of alternatives. Within this context, the rhetorical position of 2 Peter reflects a position of intolerance to internal Christian diversity.[19]

The inhospitable and intolerant tone of 2 Peter runs contrary to the growing notoriety of local Christian communities for practicing hospitality, mediation, and pluralism. For example, the Pliny-Trajan correspondences around 111–112 CE attests to popular non-Christian perception about Christian community ethics and behaviors:

---

teenth and twentieth centuries and the rhetorical maneuvers of 2 Peter to impose it in the second century.

18. Regarding the general activity of polemical writing 2 Peter represents, see Luke Timothy Johnson, "The New Testament's Anti-Jewish Slander and the Conventions of Ancient Polemic," *JBL* 108 (1989): 441 n. 66. For argument about 2 Peter's opponents as Gnostics, see Ernst Käsemann, "An Apologia for Primitive Christian Eschatology," in *Essays on New Testament Themes*, SBT 41 (London SCM, 1964), 170–71. For the perspective that 2 Peter responds to Epicurean opponents who dismiss notions of providence, see Jerome H. Neyrey, "The Form and Background of the Polemic in 2 Peter," *JBL* 99 (1980): 420–22.

19. King, *What Is Gnosticism?*, 20–54, 218–37; Denise Kimber Buell, *Making Christians: Clement of Alexandria and the Rhetoric of Legitimacy* (Princeton, NJ: Princeton University Press, 1999), 8–10.

They also declared that the sum total of their guilt or error amounted to no more than this: they had met regularly before dawn on a fixed day to chant verses alternately among themselves in honour of Christ as if to a god, and also to bind themselves by oath, not for any criminal purpose, but to abstain from theft, robbery and adultery, to commit no breach of trust and not to deny a deposit when called upon to restore it. After this ceremony it had been their custom to disperse and reassemble later to take food of an ordinary, harmless kind. (Pliny, *Ep.* 10.96 [Radice LCL])

Similarly, the Letter to Diognetus, an anonymous writing in early Christian apologetics, describes a diaspora Christian manner of life defined by expressions of internal "affection" (Diogn. 1) and fellowship that non-Christian outsiders observe and associate to the community.

For Christians are no different from other people in terms of their country, language, or customs. Nowhere do they inhabit cities of their own, use a strange dialect, or live life out of the ordinary.... They inhabit both Greek and barbarian cities, according to the lot assigned to each. And they show forth the character of their own citizenship in a marvelous and admittedly paradoxical way by following local customs in what they wear and what they eat and in the rest of their lives. They live in their respective countries, but only as resident aliens; they participate in all things as citizens, and they endure all things as foreigners. Every foreign territory is a homeland for them, every homeland foreign territory.... They share their meals but not their sexual partners.... They love everyone and are persecuted by all. (Diog. 5.1–2, 4–5, 7, 11 [Ehrman, LCL])

While Pliny's letter predates 2 Peter and is from a non-Christian observer, the Letter to Diognetus is composed around the time of 2 Peter or later by a Christian insider.[20] Both writings designate hospitality and kinship

---

20. Judith Lieu extends the insider location of Diognetus by demonstrating that while the implied audience is an external non-Christian, "the actual and probably the intended, audience was internal." Lieu argues the author deployed the implied audience as a "literary device" to interrogate and negotiate the meaning of *genos* (and later in the article, also *theosebeia*). Her astute assessment of how Diognetus constructs an identity of its audience in service to a rhetorical agenda to express a particular understanding about the Christian way of life, parallels the arguments of chapters 5 and 6 in this book concerning the constructed nature of authorial "face" Peter and its rhetorical utility. See Judith M. Lieu, "Identity Games in Early Christian Texts: The Letter to Diognetus," in *Identities and Ideologies in Early Jewish and Christian Texts, and in Modern Biblical Interpretation*, ed. Katherine M. Hockey and David G. Horrell

as characteristics of translocal Christian communities. Moreover, both situate persecution and stigmatization as coming from outside those communities.

But the letter of 2 Peter is not cultural rhetoric responding to persecution from outside the community. It is, instead, cultural rhetoric engaged in persecuting and stigmatizing those *inside* the Christian community. Second Peter *forces* the departure of insiders; it does not merely record it as if reporting on voluntary defectors, apostates, and heretics—all of which are yet other terms of stigmatization and defamation. In Wilson's typology, 2 Peter's cultural rhetoric cultivates "a clearly defined community... [that] ... is of a size which permits only a minimal range of diversity of conduct." It works "to rigidify a pattern of behavior and to make coherent its structure of values."[21] Using sociological models, John Gager also recognized the way religious conflict, labeled as "heresy" in early Christian discourses, served "a group-binding function."[22] According to Gager, "the closer the relationship the more intense the conflict" and the more exaggerated the villainy of opponents.[23] Second Peter articulates a response to borders that contemporary readers may find challenging, even off-putting, because it models behaviors and attitudes of intolerance as acceptable practice among Christian members. It takes extreme measures to villainize segments of its membership.

Conclusion

The mediating translation of 2 Peter underscores the polemics the letter performs. The letter puts forward an uncompromising vision of Christian belief and practice, sifting its internal community into two factions: people of justice (1:1) versus people of injustice (2:9) or people of religious habit (*eusebeia*, 1:7) versus people lacking religious habit (*asebēs*, 3:7; more on this in chapters 3 and 4). Along with dividing the community into contending groups, the letter writers engage in vitriolic communication that demeans alternative Christian constructions by calling them names such

---

(London: T&T Clark, 2018), 61; Lieu, "The Forging of Christian Identity and the *Letter to Diognetus*," in *Neither Jew nor Greek? Constructing Early Christianity* (London: T&T Clark, 2002), 171–89.

21. Quoted in Elliott, *Home for the Homeless*, 75.

22. Gager, *Kingdom and Community*, 80.

23. Gager, *Kingdom and Community*, 83, 88.

as "Children of a Curse" (2:14) or even likening them to dogs and pigs (2:22). The letter writers achieve all this while hiding behind the face of Peter and wielding the language of God's justice (1:1, 12–18).

Analyzing the cultural rhetoric of 2 Peter through Wilson's typology of seven sectarian formations demonstrates the letter's rhetorical endeavors of inward-facing reform. The letter writers' reformist efforts mute plurality within Christian community. Although they leverage various traditions from Mediterranean social and literary environments, they do not affirm plurality as a Christian imperative. Moreover, the letter conveys a strong revolutionist tone. God is the prime arbiter of broader social change, while the writers position themselves as the arbiter of change within the Christian community. However, their perspective of just revolution does not expand community but contracts it. Insisting on conformity, the letter writers denominate justice as a chronological thread to Christian traditions and legacies predating the community, but it is not a connecting thread that mediates differences in understanding and practice within the Christian community. In support of this reading, my mediating translation is a reference tool for the analysis of 2 Peter that unfolds in subsequent chapters.

Part 2
The Language of Justice and Righteousness

3

The Rhetoric of Righteousness in the KJV and African American Women's Moral Discourse

Translation matters in the study of 2 Peter.[1] And the translation of the Greek word *dikaiosynē* (and its cognates), which connotes either righteousness or justice, is critical to understanding 2 Peter's past cultural rhetoric for the present moment. The letter is the only writing of the New Testament that opens with *dikaiosynē* in its *first* verse: "Symeōn Peter, an enslaved person and apostle of Jesus Christ, to those having received an allotment of faith, equal in honorable quality as ours in the justice [or righteousness] of our God and Savior Jesus Christ" (2 Pet 1:1). There appears to be a link here between *enslavement to God* and the *justice* [or *righteousness*] *of God.* The language of *dikaiosynē* also extends beyond the opening verse in 2 Peter. In its short three chapters, readers encounter twelve strategic occurrences of *dik*-stem words: (1) four instances of the noun form *dikaiosynē*, translated as either "justice" or "righteousness" (2:5, 21; 3:13); (2) four instances of the adjective form *dikaios*, translated as "just," "righteous," or "right" (2 Pet 1:13; 2:7, 8a and 8b); (3) two occurrences of the negative noun form *adikia*, translated as "unjust," "unrighteous," or "wrong" (2 Pet 2:13, 15); (4) one instance of the negative verb form *adikeō*, translated as "to wrong," "to harm," "to damage," or "to treat unjustly" (2 Pet 2:13); and (5) one instance of the negative adjective form *adikos*, translated as "unjust," "unrighteous," or even "dishonest" (2 Pet 2:9). These terms can either be

---

1. Emerson B. Powery, "'Lost in Translation: Ethnic Conflict in Bibles'—The Gospels, 'Race,' and the Common English Bible: An Introductory and Exploratory Conversation," *Ex Auditu* 31 (2015): 154–68. Powery opens his essay making this assertion broadly, but I appropriate it specifically to the critical study of 2 Peter. For other recent conversation about the politics of translation and matters of social justice, see Voth, "Justice vs. Righteousness," 279–307; Gafney, *Womanist Midrash*, 281–92.

interpreted as addressing (1) matters of *group*-oriented justice and insider *group* actions of justice or (2) matters of *individual* righteousness (piety) and insider *individual* actions of rightness. Either way, *dikaiosynē* is clearly an important concept for the writers of this letter.

The range of meaning potentials accompanying the multiform deployments of the Greek word *dikaiosynē* in 2 Peter reappears in the moral discourses of nineteenth-century African American women. Through their deployment of the words "justice" and "righteousness," African American women compose a cultural rhetoric that produces the same three major social responses to the world as 2 Peter: reformist, conversionist, and revolutionist (see chapter 2). Penned as moral discourse invested in reform, African American women's cultural rhetoric insist that civic, religious, political, and economic institutions can serve good, rather than oppressive ends.[2] They spotlight institutions of enslavement as sites of injustice and manifestations of human unrighteousness, and their cultural rhetoric promotes a mode of suasion advocating economic freedom, political leadership, and cultural plurality. Formulations of Christian identity and practice antagonistic to such imperatives are questioned as legitimate expressions of Christian faith. To this end, they address their cultural communities, the larger society, and even individuals with the expectation that all is changeable. With this belief, they aim their cultural rhetoric at African American and diaspora communities, but also at the entire social order of the American project. These women write their interventions for a larger public to read, consider, and adopt.

In composing their cultural rhetoric, these women respond to a biblical imagination wielded primarily to exclude and diminish their peoplehood and citizenship, an imagination largely shaped by the language of the King James Version (KJV) of the Bible. African American women both critique and use the grammar of the KJV as a rhetorical tool. They intermix language about righteousness and justice with biblical discourses to kindle a variety of social and cultural responses. At times justice and righteousness are separate ideas, operating as different social and theological orientations. Other times, they are two sides of the same coin, signifying Christian formations of community that are both religious and civic, interpersonal and personal. In either situation, the language of justice and righteousness is as central to their message of reform as *dikaiosynē* was for 2 Peter.

---

2. Robbins, *Tapestry of Early Christian Discourse*, 149.

After briefly rehearsing the origins of the KJV translation and its translation choices related to the language of *dikaiosynē*, this chapter surveys a
representative sample of African American women writers. It examines
the use of the phrases "way of righteousness" and "God of justice" in the
moral discourses of four women: Virginia Broughton, Mary Virginia
Cook, Fannie Barrier Williams, and Maria Stewart. Through the language
of righteousness and justice, each writer advocates for social reforms and
seeks the conversion, in both attitudes and behaviors, of white American
Christians regarding race and class and of African American men regarding power inequities (patriarchy) operative within their private households
and religious fellowships. Interacting with the cultural rhetoric of justice
and righteousness in African American women's moral discourses supplies a throughway for encountering the cultural attitudes, behaviors, and
responses 2 Peter communicates.

The Translation Politics of KJV's
"Righteous People" and "Righteous Nation"

Before African American women orators, essayists, educators, activists,
preachers, and poets adopted the language of righteousness and infused it
with their own meaning, it was the language of choice by British translators of the King James Version of the Bible (KJV), first published in 1611.
The translators chose to use "righteousness" as the equivalent term for
the Greek *dik*-root (as well as the *tsedeq* in Hebrew Bible [MT]), rather
than language of justice, which was an option exercised in other Bible
translations circulating in the sixteenth and seventeenth centuries, albeit
inconsistently. For example, the Geneva Bible of 1599 translated the
dik-modifier of Lot in 2 Pet 2:7 (*dikaion Lōt*) as "just Lot," and Spanish
translation traditions, such as the RVR from the Catholic tradition, translated it as "justo Lot."[3] These translations appear to recognize and capture
the relational proximity and dynamics operative in the social world of
the Mediterranean from which and to which the Greek *dik*-terminology
functioned more readily. The people writing, receiving, and referenced
in 2 Peter are Mediterranean communities who have a particular group
orientation distinct from later Western social constructs. Explaining

---

3. Also see the Wycliffe Bible (1382–1395) and the Douay-Rheims Bible (1582),
both of which translate the Greek phrase as "Just Lot."

Mediterranean cultural patterns and dyadic personalities, Bruce Malina states, "Ancient Mediterranean, and nearly all peoples before the sixteenth century CE … lived in collectivistic cultures."[4] Regardless of their religious sensibilities and cultural identities, people from this ancient environment operated with a strong sense of group connection and a less dualistic sense of self and others than later Western English readers.

The use of "righteousness" rather than "justice" in the KJV translation represented a decisive shift from the communal sensibility of ancient Mediterranean conception, and it was an interpretive decision exercised in service to dogmatic theology and monarchical civil religion.[5] Commissioned as a monarchical-endorsed English translation, the KJV was intended to upend popular preference for the Geneva Bible in the Church of England. As Steven Voth rehearses:

> The present situation was that people were not using either the Bishops' Bible (1568) nor the Great Bible (ca. 1535) that had been installed in the churches. The people had turned their attention toward and were buying the editions of the Geneva Bible (1560) that were being produced copiously by the presses of England and the Netherlands.
>
> At the suggestion of Dr. John Reynolds, President of Corpus Christi College, Oxford, and spokesman for the Puritan group, King James I decided to support the production of a new translation and proposed that "this be done by the best learned in both Universities, after them to be reviewed by the Bishops, and the chief learned of the Church; from them to be presented to the Priuie-Councell; and lastly to be ratified by his Royal authority, and so this whole Church to be bound unto it, and none other."

---

4. Although Malina's work has been critiqued as essentializing, it is important that the collectivistic norm of the ancient world guide translation of 2 Peter to account for the cultural implications of its rhetoric more accurately. Malina's descriptions of early Christian communities as forms of group-oriented identities that are distinct from modern Western constructions of identity, can help contemporary interpreters recalibrate their sense of who the rhetoric seeks to serve first, the individual or the collective (Malina, "Understanding New Testament Persons," 46).

5. In American biblical history, particularly from the period of the colonial settlers to the end of the Civil War, the KJV was often referred to as the "Authorized Version" or "King James Bible." See Mark A. Noll, *America's God: From Jonathan Edwards to Abraham Lincoln* (Oxford: Oxford University Press, 2002), 372.

It is evident from this that a very important agenda item in the production of the KJV was to have one and only legitimized version that would unite all the people under one text.[6]

Various social and political exigencies of the time applied pressure to the choices made by the translators. For instance, because of the king's concerns about rousing social opposition to the supremacy of monarchal rule, a persistent tendency among the KJV translators was to moderate notions about the social good and justice for the collective. The Geneva Bible's decision to render terms with the *dik*-stem as "justice" was thus muted. The language of righteousness better served King James I's agenda of stabilizing monarchal civil religion and dogmatic theology. It was an intentional turn toward the individual and the personal as a means of disrupting the occurrence of collective social movements potentially emboldened by a biblical cultural rhetoric of justice.

The decision to swap the dominant translation of *dik*-stem words in the New Testament from "justice" to "righteousness" also shifted the social system from which and to which the Bible catered. As Voth notes, "The meaning and usage of the term 'righteousness' emphasized personal piety, individual holiness, and moral purity. These connotations ... supported the Puritan worldview and theological framework."[7] Rather than nurturing a Christian formation defined by a balanced combination between the orientations of groups and individuals, the KJV's translation preference for "righteousness" served the Puritan commitment to individualistic,

---

6. Voth, "Justice vs. Righteousness," 292. Voth takes the quote from Margaret Thorndike Hills, *A Ready-Reference History of the English Bible* (New York: American Bible Society, 1971), 22. The popularity of the Geneva Bible is further attested to by Harry S. Stout ("Word and Order in Colonial New England," in *The Bible in America: Essays in Cultural History*, ed. Nathan O. Hatch and Mark A. Noll [New York: Oxford University Press, 1982], 21–22): "Despite the fact that the 'Bishop's Bible' was sanctioned by ecclesiastical authority for use in public worship, the Geneva Bible [1560] circumvented official channels and found its way into common dwellings throughout the realm. Within a generation it had outstripped all other versions in circulation and came to stand as the unchallenged emblem of popular piety in the English realm.... The Geneva Bible was, in brief, the first English translation that could legitimately be characterized as a people's Bible.... Aside from the Bible itself, the Genevan commentary was the only literary product all people shared in common and it exerted a far more direct influence on the popular religious imagination than the less widely circulated sermons, devotionals, and spiritual autobiographies."

7. Voth, "Justice vs. Righteousness," 295.

self-sufficient, and introspective persons. It refocused the theological imaginations and conduct of Bible readers and churchgoers from matters of the social, political, and outward-looking to the personal and the private.

Righteousness as a translation choice repositioned the social ethic of the churchgoers of the Church of England and remained a persistent characteristic of Western (Protestant) cultures after the sixteenth century, especially those traditions influenced by Puritan biblicism. "Whether as the 'covenantal society,' 'theocracy,' 'Bibliocracy,' 'new Israel,' or 'Bible Commonwealth,' the Puritan experiment depended on the Bible."[8] Leading biblical historians characterize America as fundamentally "a biblical nation" during the period between the American Revolution (ca. 1765–1791) and the Civil War (1861–1865).[9] Be they located in the North or the South, white or African American, people were well versed in biblical stories, language, and imagery "and they could quote the Authorized Version endlessly."[10] The emphasis on righteousness in the KJV shifted responsibility from group perception to individual consciousness. The first concern became personal salvation, which impacted collective behavior and not vice versa. This was particularly significant for the Puritan settlers, who cast a wide net, spreading the image of America as a "Bible Commonwealth" for its citizens—meaning, European American peoples,

---

8. Stout, "Word and Order in Colonial New England," 19.

9. Mark A. Noll ("The Image of the United States as a Biblical Nation, 1776–1865," in *The Bible in America: Essays in Cultural History*, ed. Nathan O. Hatch and Mark A. Noll [New York: Oxford University Press, 1982], 51) epitomizes the rival interpretive practices of American Bible readers during this period: "In the years between the American Revolution and the Civil War, the Bible offered to many Americans a key for understanding not only private religious reality but also the public life of the country. The Scriptures were so widely used that it is not inaccurate to call the country a biblical nation during this period. The image of the United States as a biblical nation, however, is an ironic one. Those who applied the Bible's teachings to the nation's destiny most directly seemed to have understood its message least. Those, on the other hand, for whom the country itself was least important seemed to have understood it best."

10. Noll, *America's God*, 386. There was vast diversity among antebellum religious sensibilities in which not all people were quoting the Authorized Version of the Bible. Catholics, for example, from both European and African American descent were not using it as a part of their worship life, nor were people of Jewish, Muslim, and other nationalities and languages. The focus on the KJV in this book is informed by the nineteenth century African American women's attested use of the Authorized Version and its teleological influence on the translation history in 2 Peter studies from the twentieth through early twenty-first centuries.

not African Americans and indigenous Americans. But this perception also continues into modernity. As Daniel Bell states: "The fundamental assumption of modernity, the thread that has run through Western civilization since the sixteenth century, is that the social unit of society is not the group, the guild, the tribe, or the city, but the person."[11]

With such a distinction evolving, the Christian Bible became a tool for racializing citizenship. For instance, the language of a "righteous nation" and "righteous people" of God, adopted from the Christian Bible, was particularly popular in the nineteenth century.[12] It was simultaneously a religious and political phrase, and it contradicted the supposed separation of church and state in the American constitution.[13] White American Christian discourses, in both religious and civic arenas, used this language as an instrument to fasten nationalistic typologies of whiteness and providence in place.[14] "Righteous nation" and "righteous people" did not include African American people. In fact, it was heavily employed to counter any notions that "American," "African," and "citizen" belong together through "proslavery" discourses and its attendant forms of racial terrorism and subordination.

The opinion has been announced also of late, that slavery among the Jews was felt to be an evil, and, by degrees, that they abolished it. To

---

11. Daniel Bell, *The Cultural Contradictions of Capitalism* (New York: Basic Books, 1976), 16.

12. In the KJV, the phrase "righteous nation" occurs most explicitly in the Hebrew Bible or Old Testament: Gen 20:4; Deut 4:8; Prov 24:24; Isa 26:2; 41:2. Likewise, the phrase "righteous people": Exod 9:27; Judg 5:11; 2 Sam 4:11; 2 Kgs 10:9; Prov 18:5; 24:24; 29:2; Isa 60:21; Lam 1:18; Ezek 33:12. I use the term *Christian Bible* as opposed to the *Jewish Bible* or *Torah* because within the reception history of the Bible, at this particular moment, the use of "righteousness" that I am referring to has a range of meanings occurring explicitly within American Christian discourse, including politics. American Christian notions of occupation, righteous people, an elect people, and New Israel dominate American political and social discourse, as the examples below will demonstrate.

13. Richard T. Hughes, *Myths America Lives By: White Supremacy and the Stories That Give Us Meaning*, 2nd ed. (Urbana: University of Illinois Press, 2018).

14. See the emerging work of Wongi Gideon Park on whiteness and the Bible for considerations about the politics of biblical translation and interpretation: Wongi Park, *The Politics of Race and Ethnicity in Matthew's Passion Narrative* (Cham, Switzerland: Palgrave, 2019); Park, "The Blessing of Whiteness in the Curse of Ham: Reading Gen 9:18–29 in the Antebellum South," *Religions* 12.11 (2021): 1–18.

ascertain the correctness of this opinion, let the following consideration be weighed: After centuries of cruel *national bondage* practiced upon Abraham's seed in Egypt, they were brought in godly contrition to pour out "the effectual fervent prayer" of a **righteous people**, to the Almighty for mercy, and were answered by a covenant God, who sent Moses to deliver them from their bondage—but let it be remembered, that when this deliverance from bondage to the nation of Egypt was vouchsafed to them, they were extensive domestic slave owners. God had not by his providential dealings, nor in any other way, shown them the sin of domestic slavery—for they held on to their slaves, and brought them out as their property into the wilderness. And it is worthy of further remark, that the Lord, *before they left Egypt*, recognized these slaves as property, which they had bought with their money, and that he secured to these slaves privileges above hired servants, *simply because they were slaves.*—Exod. xii: 44, 45.[15]

This quotation, taken from a sourcebook of American proslavery rhetoric from the 1700s–1800s, expresses an opinion grounded in what it calls "The Scriptural View of Slavery." It uses language of righteousness as a way of defining peoplehood and society as righteous when it affirms the institution of enslavement as not only a civilized institution but one orchestrated and instituted by God.

Similarly, language about the "righteous nation" was often presented to enslaved African Americans by white Christian missionaries using excerpts from the KJV to evangelize them. For example, one sourcebook documents the instructions provided to missionaries in an essay called "The Manner in which the Gospel should be communicated to the Negroes, so as to meet the character, condition, and circumstances of the people." This source reads:

I would commend the work also to every *Lover of his Country*. The moral and religious improvement of *two million eight hundred thousand persons*, must be identified with our individual peace and happiness, and

---

15. Thornton Stringfellow, "The Bible Argument: Or, Slavery in the Light of Divine Revelation," in *Cotton Is King and Pro-Slavery Arguments: Comprising the Writings of Hammond, Harper, Christy, Stringfellow, Hodge, Bledsoe, and Cartwright on This Important Subject*, ed. E. N. Elliott (Augusta, GA: Pritchard, Abbott & Loomis, 1860), 517. The italics included are in the original source, but the bold emphasis is mine.

with our national prosperity and honor. "**Righteousness** exalteth a **nation**, but sin is a reproach to any people."[16]

This protreptic resource distinguishes between those enslaved in America righteously and those who are righteous in their ownership of America and its resources, be it natural, land, or human chattel. The passage makes moral and religious instruction a matter of righteous individualism first and corporate identity second. In both cases, however, righteousness is reserved as a virtue of white America, not African Americans, be they enslaved or free. Furthermore, the language of righteousness presupposes the legitimacy of enslavement. It does not question the institution of captivity although it is concerned about the condition of the captive's introspective self. Righteousness, in this case, is branded as a spiritual and personal matter distinct from civic justice and inclusion for African Americans. The phrase "Lover of His Country" is a patriotic designation for white America, not the enslaved African American. In this discourse, the conception of righteousness supplies no critique regarding social morality, and justice appears irrelevant to discussions about the improvement and elevation of African Americans to full citizenship and freedom.

Reviewing the history of American enslavement and violence against disenfranchised persons, the Equal Justice Institute's (EJI) report, *Lynching in America*, also records the prominent use of the "righteous nation" in its investigations of America's historic legacy of racial difference and violence. Detailing the history of the rise of the Ku Klux Klan and white backlash in the form of vigilante terror of African American citizens, the report records righteousness as popular parlance for a particular American conception of dominance and civic access.

> Varied white groups took up the cause of restoring labor discipline in the absence of slavery. Vigilantes whipped and lynched Black freedmen who argued with employers, left the plantations where they were contracted to work, or displayed any economic success of their own. White terror groups also focused intense energy on imposing "their own vision of a **righteous society**," which usually meant targeting Black men.[17]

---

16. Charles Colcock Jones, *The Religious Instruction of the Negroes in the United States* (N.p.: 1842), 192–93; Kindle loc. 4059, 192–93, bold emphasis added.

17. Equal Justice Initiative, *Lynching in America: Confronting the Legacy of Racial Terror*, 3rd ed. (Equal Justice Initiative, 2017), 15, bold emphasis added. See also Shively T. J. Smith, "Witnessing Jesus Hang: Reading Mary Magdalene's View of Crucifixion

According to this description, "righteous," among other theological and biblical terminology (like "slavery," "slave," etc.), was the language of choice among a particular Bible-*speaking* segment of the American population. Deploying Bible vernacular infused with notions of personal piety and rightness before God, dominant white American culture normalized a sensibility that racial enslavement was an institution devised by God, particularly for people of African descent.[18] From this perspective, a righteous society engendered second-class citizenship devoid of legal protection, political voice, and social access for the designated Other of white America.

But the KJV grammar functioned also as the language of choice for nineteenth-century African American women biblical interpreters. The KJV Bible was widely available to them as the source from which many learned to read and write in various missionary schools and at their own kitchen tables. For example, Anna Julia Cooper describes helping her mother learn to read, "My mother was a slave and the finest woman I have ever known. Tho untutored she could read her Bible and write a little. It is one of my happiest childhood memories explaining for her the subtle differences between q's and g's or between b's and i's."[19] Following her intimate recollection about her mother's endeavor to improve how she reads and writes using the Bible as the textbook, Cooper comments on her father:

---

through Ida B. Wells's Chronicles of Lynching," in *Stony the Road We Trod: African American Biblical Interpretation*, ed. Cain Hope Felder, 30th anniv. exp. ed. (Minneapolis: Fortress, 2021), 303–5, nn. 20–21, 25–26.

18. The social and linguistic roles of race in New Testament studies and early Christian history continue to be explored and nuanced in relationship to contemporary social constructions of race. For an introduction to those conversations, see Laura Nasrallah and Elisabeth Schüssler Fiorenza, eds., *Prejudice and Christian Beginnings: Investigating Race, Gender, and Ethnicity in Early Christian Studies* (Minneapolis: Fortress, 2009); Gay L. Byron, *Symbolic Blackness and Ethnic Difference in Early Christian Literature* (New York: Routledge, 2002); Buell, *Why This New Race*; Katherine M. Hockey and David Horrell, *Ethnicity, Race, Religion: Identities and Ideologies in Early Jewish and Christian Texts, and in Modern Biblical Interpretation* (New York: Bloomsbury Academic, 2018); David G. Horrell, "'Race,' 'Nation,' 'People': Ethnic Identity-Construction in 1 Peter 2.9," *NTS* 58 (2012): 123–43; Anthony J. Blasi, Paul-André Turcotte, and Jean Duhaime, *Handbook of Early Christianity: Social Science Approaches* (Walnut Creek, CA: AltaMira, 2002).

19. Anna J. Cooper, *The Voice of Anna Julia Cooper*, ed. Charles Lemert and Esme Bhan, Legacies of Social Thought Series (Lanham, MD: Rowman & Littlefield Publishers, 1998), 331.

"Presumably my father was her master, if so I owe him not a sou[l] and she was always too modest and shamefaced ever to mention him."[20] Cooper's recollection about her parents captures the tension between the function of biblical language with those ranked as "the enslaved" versus "the enslaving" classes in America. The KJV in the hands of Cooper's mother supplied an avenue for access and human actualization whereas the Bible in the hands of Cooper's father supplied him little in terms of moral critique against the enslavement of his fellow human beings or even the rape of those under his authority. The Bible with its language and theological imperatives of righteousness did not yield the same patterns of human relations when viewed through the phenomenon of Cooper's parentage.[21]

The Bible was "the talking book" for these women like Cooper and her mother and many African Americans of the period. The language of the Bible talked to them while also equipping them with language and rhetorical forms to talk back to the Bible, their communities, and society. It gave them the language of freedom and possibility, but it also gave them the language of those interested in the enslavement and colonization of human beings and the earth. Allan Callahan depicts this tension, explaining how the Bible was an artifact that was received by the larger African American community and then used as a source that both talks and poisons.

> African Americans were learning en masse to read the Bible as a book both opened and closed. As the Word of God, it spoke to them with words that lent a new language to their dreams and their nightmares. As a written text, it greeted them with silence. But as they struggled to make

---

20. Cooper, *Voice of Anna Julia Cooper*, 331.

21. In his presidential address, Vincent Wimbush used Fredrick Douglass's 1845 edition of his autobiography, *Narrative of the Life of Frederick Douglass, an American Slave, Written by Himself*, to identify and describe three types of interpreters and consciousness "who are differently positioned—the enslaving, the enslaved, and the runagate." Recognizing these "sites" of interpretive "insight" are not mutually exclusive, Wimbush acknowledged "they can be and in history have been complexly intertwined, yet there is justification for their isolation for the sake of analysis." See Vincent Wimbush, "Interpreters—Enslaving/Enslaved/Runagate," *JBL* 130 (2011): 9, 11. Anna Julia Cooper's autobiographical details about her parents, like Douglass, attests to the three types of interpreters at work in the nineteenth century. This chapter extends Wimbush's analysis by attending to the translation history of 2 Peter as another site where one can trace the interpretive positionality of "the enslaving, the enslaved, and the runagate."

the book talk to them, African Americans would make the Talking Book their own.

Once the Bible began to speak to them, African Americans heard it saying some things that were hard for them to hear. It spoke with a voice that sometimes echoed their oppressors. The words of life could deal death, and its text could become noxious. The Talking Book was also a poison book. Toxic texts in the Old Testament seemed to condemn Africans and their descendants to slavery because they were Africans. Toxic texts in the New Testament seemed to condemn Africans and their descendants to slavery because they were slaves.[22]

The dilemma of translating *dik*-stem words of 2 Peter is another site for considering how the Bible was simultaneously the talking and poison book for African Americans and, perhaps, even the writers of 2 Peter.

With this history of the politics of the KJV translation and dominant trends in nineteenth-century American interpretation practices at the forefront, I am reticent to deploy "righteousness" as the preferred translation for *dik*-stem Greek terms to understand 2 Peter in its ancient rhetorical moment *then*. To maintain righteousness as the translation of choice is to disregard the multiple colonial histories of KJV translation as though it is inconsequential. Moreover, maintaining such a stream of translation risks distorting the culture-making endeavor of 2 Peter by subsuming it under contemporary translation decisions and racially, ideologically charged deployments of its discourse.

The Language of Righteousness and Justice in African American Women's Moral Discourses

Another conundrum is comprehending the meaning potential of righteousness in African American women's moral discourse from the nineteenth century, which preserves a rich selection of African American women's use of both justice and righteousness language. For these women and their cultural communities, the boundaries between their lived sociopolitical situations and their religious experiences blur. Within African American communities, Christian churches are more than religious institutions. They are sites for social, political, economic, and educational

---

22. Allen Dwight Callahan, *The Talking Book: African Americans and the Bible* (New Haven: Yale University Press, 2008), 20, 25–26.

activities. African American Christian institutions nurture communities of culture and interpretation and supply sanctuary for the creation and maintenance of a contested people seeking civic inclusion and committed to civic duty. Located within Christian denominations such as Baptist, Methodist, or holiness fellowships, these women variously employ the language of both justice and righteousness to address matters of equality and inclusion within their local and regional communities and white dominant society. In their writings, God is both ethical and righteous. And God expects the virtues of justice and righteousness to be replicated within creation, starting with the liberation, care, protection, and inclusion of the disenfranchised, terrorized, and oppressed African American citizens. Because of the intersectional blend of their identities as women, American, and African, these interpreters wield the language of righteousness and justice from the margins of *both* their cultural communities and larger society. They employ this vocabulary, therefore, to expand cultural practices and theological imaginations for authorizing African American citizenship and women's leadership. A few representative examples below showcase the ubiquitous usage of both terms in African American women's moral discourse. They inform reconsiderations of 2 Peter's translation and cultural rhetoric of justice that follows in chapter 4.

The Path of Righteousness

African American women's moral discourses often employ the phrase the "path of righteousness" or "way of righteousness." The same construction appears in biblical Greek in 2 Pet 2:21 as *tēn hodon tēs dikaiosynēs*. My translation departs from standard Bible translation treatments (KJV, NKJV, NRSV, NIV, NRSVue, CEB) by rendering the Greek as "the way of justice."[23] But African American women's moral discourse appears to

---

23. Indeed, the entire translation history of the phrase in dominant mainline translations treat the term as "way of righteousness" even when they treat the opening verse occurrence of the *dik*-stem word as "justice," as is the case of the CEB. In similar form, some scholarly translations provided in exegetical commentaries also behave like the CEB. Even when they render the *dik*-stem word of 1:1 as "justice" they treat the term of 2:21 as "righteousness." Thus, they slip back into normative Eurocentric ideologies of the theological significance and effect of the language of *dikaiosynē* and its cognates. See Neyrey, *2 Peter, Jude*, 217; Lewis R. Donelson, *1 and 2 Peter and Jude: A Commentary*, NTL (Louisville: Westminster John Knox, 2010), 256, 257. "The noun *dikaiosynē* was translated 'justice' in 1:1. However, the more general English term

follow the linguistic cues of the KJV rendering of 2 Pet 2:21. In the KJV, the phrase the "way of righteousness" occurs five times: Prov 8:20; 12:28; 16:31; Matt 21:32; 2 Pet 2:21. No evidence exists among the extant literature that 2 Peter was impactful. However, African American women resource Proverbs and Matthew to craft moral discourses about fair treatment, charity, and neighborliness and were thus likely influenced by the KJV's "way of righteousness" language found there.

For example, a prodigious opinion editorialist, Jennie Carter draws explicitly from Prov 16 in an essay for the *Elevator* titled "Letter from Nevada County" in 1867. She quotes an emended form of verse 32 in the conclusion, which addresses the quality of self-rule contrasted to city rule. Her use of this verse is significant for this discussion about the phrase "way of righteousness" because it immediately follows one of its occurrences in the KJV (Prov 16:31).

> Children, do you wish pleasant memories when you grow old? Do nothing in anger; treat your playmates with gentleness; be obliging, sharing with them always. They will soon imitate your example, and you find yourselves growing better day by day. A great man said, thousands of years ago, "He that ruleth his own spirit is greater than he that taketh a city."[24]

Carter cites Proverbs and the wisdom tradition associated with Solomon as an authoritative source about godly and humane treatment of others. While she quotes the chapter partially, her citational use signals a familiarity with the entire discourse. She deploys Prov 15:31–32 establishing appropriate contextual markers from the biblical past and her contemporary moment.

Likewise, Jarena Lee and Maria Stewart cite the Gospel of Matthew— the other biblical text in which the KJV phrase "way of righteousness" occurs—multiple times. For example, Lee's spiritual autobiography, explicitly references Matt 3 and 16, while stories, and images recur throughout her biography. Similarly, Stewart cites the gospel explicitly in some of

---

'righteousness' seems to fit better." It is intriguing that Donelson shifts so abruptly to righteousness here, abandoning the conceptual meaning of justice he initiated with 2 Peter with little explanation.

24. Jennie Carter, *A Black Journalist of the Early West*, ed. Eric Gardner, Margaret Walker Alexander Series in African American Studies (Jackson: University Press of Mississippi, 2007), Kindle loc. 446–48.

her speeches, and she uses Matthean phrases freely without citation.[25] All three women are skilled biblical interpreters who regularly selected biblical books and chapters in which the phrase "way of righteousness" occurred. However, they do not select 2 Peter nor reference the occurrence of the phrase in 2:21 in those same writings. The 2 Peter occurrence does not rise above a biblical echo that affirms it is a recurring theme of Christian discourse.

Nonetheless, the point here is not to examine the reception history of 2 Peter in African American women's moral discourses but to parse what reference to righteousness as "a way" or "a path" means in African American women's writings.[26] These women employ the phrase as a discursive strategy for legitimating cultural communities formally operating as marginalized minorities in a dominant society. The phrase functions as both an affirmation and behavioral tactic. The women interpreters deploy it to counter dehumanizing stereotypes, to oppose distortions about their capabilities, and to contest social techniques that reclass citizenship populations. For example, Virginia Broughton refers to the "path of righteousness" in her 1894 essay called "Woman's Work":

---

25. For example, Maria Stewart explicitly provides a citational reference to Matt 15:14 in her essay, "Religion and the Pure Principles of Morality, the Sure Foundation on Which We Must Build," in *America's First Black Woman Political Writer*, ed. Marilyn Richardson (Bloomington: University of Indiana Press, 1987), 28–42. She quotes without citation her version of Matt 24:36 in her "Address Delivered before the Afric-American Female Intelligence Society of Boston," April 28, 1832, Iowa State University Archives of Women's Political Communication: https://tinyurl.com/SBL4533a/: "It will be a great day of joy and rejoicing to the humble followers of Christ, but a day of terror and dismay to hypocrites and unbelievers. Of that day and hour knoweth no man; no, not even the angels in heaven, but the Father only."

26. For the sake of chapter length, all the instances of the phraseology cannot be rehearsed. But another nineteenth-century African American woman deploying the phrase explicitly as "way of righteousness" in her spiritual autobiography is Zilpha Elaw, an itinerant preacher and contemporary of Jarena Lee. She says, "May I ever be preserved to 'trust in the Lord with all my heart, and not lean to my own understanding.' Lord! ever teach me the way wherein I should go. 'Oh, may thy Spirit guide my feet, In ways of righteousness; Make every path of duty plain.'" See Zilpha Elaw, *Memoirs of the Life, Religious Experience, Ministerial Travels, and Labours of Mrs. Elaw*, ed. Kimberly D. Blockett, Regenerations (Morgantown: West Virginia University Press, 2021), 53.

God help us to examine this subject in the light of his Word! Do it for the sake of the children, who need the united wisdom of men and women to guard their wayward feet in the **path of righteousness**; do it for the sake of our homes, where we want love, order, peace and purity; but know we cannot have them unless husband and wife work and plan together. Let us do it for the sake of our country, where good and **just** laws are so much needed for the protection and encouragement of both man and woman; and above all for the sake of the Lord Jesus, who has prayed the Father that we might be one even as he and his Father were one; that the World might believe he was sent of the Father.[27]

From the 1880s to the first decade of the twentieth century, Broughton advocated for biblical interpretation that defended women's rights in her black Baptist traditions and the larger society. Broughton was both an educator and Christian missionary activist in her local communities and across the Tennessee and Kentucky regions. Her autobiography, *Women's Work, as Gleaned from the Women of the Bible* (1904), sifted through biblical precedents to establish gender equality in African American church communities and beyond. Broughton's "feminist interpretation of the Bible shaped her understanding of women's roles in her own day."[28] Those understandings compelled her to form women's biblical societies (which she called "bible bands") for the study and interpretation of the Scriptures. Broughton was a formidable actor within her African American Baptist traditions in the South, advocating for equal educational opportunities for women through biblical literacy and for egalitarian leadership roles between men and women of the denomination. She was a foremother of womanist and feminist biblical interpretation and scholarship.

The quotation above conveys what Broughton designates as fundamental characteristics of the path of righteousness—namely, love, order, peace, and purity within the household, which ripples out to the larger society. In this essay, Broughton responds to formerly enslaved southern African American communities as they struggle to establish stable households and communities under the violent resurgence of white nationalist Redemption efforts, less than twenty years after Reconstruction. She departs from the

27. Virginia W. Broughton, "Woman's Work" (1894), in Robbins and Gates, *Portable Nineteenth-Century African American Women Writers*, 412, bold emphasis added.

28. Evelyn Brooks Higginbotham, "Baptist Church," in *Black Women in America: An Historical Encyclopedia*, ed. Darlene Clark Hine, Elsa Barkley Brown, and Rosalyn Terborg-Penn, vol. 1 (Bloomington: Indiana University Press, 1993), 86.

KJV's usage of deploying righteousness to emphasize individual pietism. Instead, she pens the phrase as a device for reforming nuclear family practices and the larger American society. She pitches the imagery of a righteous path to address matters of household management and shared parental oversight. Having activated the image of a pathway, she advances a vision of "good and just laws" for "protection and encouragement of both man and woman," which the larger society has not yet achieved. Righteousness, in Broughton's usage, concretizes justice as a social commitment to protect, encourage, and include people across gender, racial, and cultural differences. Linked as complementary concepts, the language of path and righteousness convey Broughton's sensibilities that Christian belief and experience are corporate and accountable to civic life.

Like Broughton, Mary Virginia Cook (1862–1945) spoke as a denominational woman of the African American Baptist tradition. She deploys the phrase the "path of righteousness" in her 1887 essay, "Women's Place in the Work of the Denomination." Linking righteousness and peace with love, she contrasts the current arrangement of male-only power holders within the community. According to Cook, the more authentic organization for the denomination should involve a joint sharing of power and acknowledgement between men and women.

> Dear women, the cry comes to us from afar to bring the light of love, and to lead into the **paths of peace and righteousness**. From your ranks, as mother, wife, daughter, sister, friend, little as you have hitherto thought of it, are to come the women of all professions, from the humble Christian to the expounder of His word; from the obedient citizen to the ruler of the land. This may be objectionable to many, but no profession should be recognized that fails to recognize Christ, and all the Christians have a legal right where He is, for "with Him there is neither Jew nor Greek, there is neither bond nor free, there is neither male nor female, for ye are all one in Christ Jesus."[29]

Cook's essay is an insider text, written from her African American Baptist experiences to persuade both women and men members toward a new cultural standard characterized by legal rights for all. She addresses the imperatives of women's work and coleadership within her Baptist denom-

---

29. Mary V. Cook, "Women's Place in the Work of the Denomination" (1887), in Robbins and Gates, *Portable Nineteenth-Century African American*, 479, bold emphasis added.

ination, deploying the path of righteousness as a discursive strategy to critique inequitable social arrangements that privilege male leadership over women.

Born in Bowling Green, Kentucky, Cook was a lifelong activist for the rights of black women, particularly in their African American church communities. Like Broughton, Cook advocates for educational equality between gendered classes within her community and racialized populations in the broader society.[30] She defends women's historical importance through a Christian lens, rehearsing the stories and roles of women from the Bible as contributors to the development of Israelite and Christian faith traditions.

> If, indeed, the King of all the Universe chooses a woman to kill a man who had opposed Israel for twenty years, it is all right, and who dare question God's right, if he raise up a woman who shall become a judge, and a leader of his people?... Should woman be silent in this busy, restless world of missions and vast church enterprises? No! A long, loud No! Give place for her, brethren.[31]

In contending with male leadership about their censorship of women's voices and roles, Cook appeals to biblical women as authoritative precedents. She uses biblical authority as an authorizing source for elucidating the path of righteousness as a corporate experience of group equality. She does not advocate a form of Christian universalism that dissolves the differences between women and men or the intellectual inheritances of those locations as found in the Scriptures and lived experience. Rather, she uses the "path of righteousness" rhetorically. It is a mechanism for disrupting ideologies of power installed in African American communities that reinscribe dominant white American hierarchies, which victimizes the entire community.[32] Cook uses language of righteousness coupled with theological virtues of peace and love to flatten caste structures that valued and

---

30. Hollis Robbins and Henry Louis Gates Jr., "Mary V. Cook (1863–1945)," in Robbins and Gates, *Portable Nineteenth-Century African American*, 463.

31. Cook, "Women's Place in the Work of the Denomination," 479. Bold and italics added.

32. Anthony B. Pinn, *Understanding and Transforming the Black Church* (Eugene, OR: Cascade, 2010); Anne H. Pinn and Anthony B. Pinn, *Fortress Introduction to Black Church History* (Minneapolis: Fortress, 2002); Marcia Riggs, *Plenty Good Room: Women versus Male Power in the Black Church* (Cleveland: Pilgrim, 2003).

empowered certain particularities over others. The current arrangement of her Christian denomination relies on women Others and their presence, work, and contributions. For her, the path of righteousness is a just path of equality across difference. She deploys the path of righteousness as a rhetorical metaphor to illustrate the journey of expanding the community's cultural practice toward a more inclusive and equitable power arrangement, as opposed to a more constricted one.

The God of Justice and Judgment

The phrase "the God of justice" appears in the multiform moral discourses of African American women, especially "race women" like Stewart. Race women, among African American writers and activists of the nineteenth and twentieth centuries, addressed racialized discourses that obscured and diminished their experiences. Figures like Stewart, Cooper, and even the towering twentieth-century pioneer, Mary McLeod Bethune, demanded America fulfill its principles of freedom and equality while they actively worked to uplift African Americans socially, economically, educationally, and spiritually.[33]

Influenced by the blended prophetic and apocalyptic style of David Walker's black nationalist rhetorical mode exemplified in his 1829 pamphlet, *Walker's Appeal ... to the Colored Citizens of the World*, Stewart operated on the public lecture circuit wielding a similar rhetorical style.[34]

---

33. Joyce A. Hanson, "The Making of a Race Woman," in *Mary Mcleod Bethune and Black Women's Political Activism* (Columbia: University of Missouri Press, 2003), 11–55; Brittney Cooper, "A'n't I a Lady? Race Women, Michelle Obama, and the Ever-Expanding Democratic Imagination," *MELUS* 35.4 (2010): 39–57.

34. David Walker (ca. 1785–1830), an early African American abolitionist, was a contemporary of Frederick Douglass and Sarah Louisa Forten. Known by some scholars as "the father of black nationalist theory," Walker advocated for the violent overthrow of the American institution of enslavement and championed the establishment of racial equality. He was a public and vocal supporter of black civil rights and self-help organizations such the Massachusetts General Colored Association, and he operated as an agent for the first African American newspaper, *Freedom's Journal* (1827–1829). Walker is most known for his scathing critique of enslavement and the colonization of African nations. His antislavery pamphlet exhorted enslaved persons to revolt against their enslavers and to embrace America as much their home as Africa and in the contemporary moment, even more so. Walker asserts African Americans helped build the country by saying, "America is more our country than it is the whites—we have

She confronts matters of race, womanhood, freedom, citizenship, God, and faith. Woven tightly together, she pens these themes through literary forms from the Bible, particularly the traditions of the prophets. Her addresses showcase innovative deployments of the KJV in which she endeavors to persuade her hearers toward a different end. Rather than shaping biblical language to mute the Christian imperative of social action and political accountability, as the KJV translation was commissioned to achieve, Stewart seeks to define Christian identity by sociopolitical action.

When she uses the language of the justice of God, Stewart departs from the KJV preference for the God of judgment. For example, she deploys the phrase in an address to an all-male audience at the African Masonic Hall in Boston on February 27, 1833:

> African rights and liberty is a subject that ought to fire the breast of every free man of color in these United States, and excite in his bosom a lively, deep, decided and heart-felt interest.... Or has it been for the fear of offending the whites? If it has, O ye fearful ones, throw off your fearfulness, and come forth in the name of the Lord, and in the strength of the **God of Justice**, and make yourselves useful and active members in society; for they admire a noble and patriotic spirit in others; and should they not admire it in us?[35]

Stewart positions the God of justice on the side of advocacy and allyship with the African American community, as opposed to the God who judges them. Moreover, the justice of God is defined by civic inclusion and activity, as opposed to sectarianism and inaction. Stewart describes the justice of God as making a demand on African American communities to con-

---

enriched it with our blood and tears.... Will they drive us from our property and homes, which we have earned with our blood?" See James Clyde Sellman, "Walker, David," in *Africana: The Encyclopedia of the African and African American Experience*, ed. Kwame Anthony Appiah and Henry Louis Gates Jr. (New York: Basic Civitas Books, 1999), 1955. Stewart's cultural rhetoric mirrored Walker's literary style and content by assuming a prophetic tone that opposed the colonization movement that sought to resettle free African Americans in Africa. Like Walker, she encouraged her African American audiences to embrace their right and place as full and contributing citizens to the American project despite white American resistance.

35. Maria W. Stewart, "An Address Delivered at the African Masonic Hall" (1833), in Robbins and Gates, *Portable Nineteenth-Century African American*, 30–31, bold emphasis added.

tend for their citizenship and social recognition of their human rights to be a free people in the land of their birth.[36]

In addition to characterizing God as justice, Stewart interprets God as a judge of righteousness. She conjoins "God's cause" and basic human rights of liberation and access. For example, in an address made to the all-female membership of the "Afric-American" Female Intelligence Society of Boston on April 28, 1832, themes of God's judgment, justice, and cause of freedom are constituting strands of the gospel that Stewart puts forward.

> And I make bold to say that many who profess the name of Christ at the present day, live so widely different from what becometh the **Gospel** of our Lord Jesus Christ, that they cannot and they dare not reason to the world upon **righteousness** and **judgment** to come. Be not offended because I tell you the truth; for I believe that God has fired my soul with a holy zeal for his cause.... A few remarks upon moral subjects, and I close. I am a strong advocate for the cause of God, and for the cause of **freedom**.[37]

Here, Stewart locates divine judgment outside the victimized Christian communities of African Americans. The chief subjects of God's judgment in Stewart's discourses are often the active and complicit enslaving classes of America, especially Christian-identifying slaveholding constituencies.

According to Stewart, God exercises judgment also against African American Christian communities who do not strive for full inclusion through the model of exemplary religious and civic morals. She describes God's judgment laid upon those within the community in her address to the all-male Masonic Hall audience (also quoted above):

> You have a right to rejoice, and to let your hearts cheer you in the days of your youth; yet remember that for all these things God will bring you into **judgment**. Then, O ye sons of Africa, turn your mind from these perishable objects, and contend for the cause of God and the rights of man. Form yourselves into temperance societies. There are temperate men among you; then why will you any longer neglect to strive, by

---

36. For another example of Stewart's position on what the Christian vision of the justice of God looks like regarding sociopolitical activism, see her "Address Delivered before the Afric-American Female Intelligence Society of Boston."

37. Stewart, "Address Delivered to the Afric-American Female Intelligence Society of Boston," bold emphasis added.

your example, to suppress vice in all its abhorrent forms? You have been told repeatedly of the glorious results arising from temperance, and can you bear to see the whites arising in honor and respectability without endeavoring to grasp after that honor and respectability also?[38]

Stewart advocates for her male audience to embrace the practice of temperance and the politics of respectability based on securing God's righteous judgment. But this is not merely an introspective endeavor; it is also a public civic endeavor. She strategizes that by keeping matters of God's justice and judgment in the forefront rhetorically, she can encourage a manner of life that challenges the prejudicial perspectives of their white Christian neighbors. Consequently, even when Stewart locates God's judgment internal to African American cultural experience, she persists in her attentiveness to the intercultural dynamics and power inequities between African Americans and dominant white America.

Stewart did not create the phrases "God of judgment" and "God of justice." Her masterful use of the two conceptions appears to foreshadow the history of these two phrases in American translation postdating Stewart herself. In the KJV, the phrase "the God of judgment" occurs explicitly in Isa 30:18 and Mal 2:17.[39] But English translations emerging in the latter part of the twentieth century, such as the New Revised Standard Version (NRSV, 1989), and its 2021 revision, the New Revised Standard Version Updated Edition (NRSVue, 2021), render both phrases as "justice" instead of "judgment."[40]

---

38. Maria Stewart, "An Address: African Rights and Liberty," February 27, 1833, African Masonic Hall, Boston, bold emphasis added. Accessed online through Iowa State University Archives of Women's Political Communication: https://tinyurl.com/SBL4533b.

39. Beyond this specific phrase, other variations of that construction occur in the English translation of the KJV over 160 times: Exod 12:12; Deut 1:17; 4:1; 12:1; 17:8; 32:4; 1 Kgs 2:3; 3:11, 28; 10:9; 11:33; 2 Chr 24:24; Ezra 7:26; Neh 10:29; Ps 76:9; Eccl 11:9; Isa 5:16; 30:18; Jer 1:16; 5:4–5; Ezek 5:7–8; 28:22; 45:9; Amos 5:15; Mal 2:17; Luke 11:42; Rom 1:32; 2:2–3, 5; 11:33; 1 Cor 7:40; 2 Thess 1:5; 1 Pet 4:17; 2 Pet 2:4; Rev 14:7; 16:7; 20:4.

40. The CEB, published in 2011, also renders the phrase "God of justice." Isa 30:18: "Nonetheless, the LORD is waiting to be merciful to you, and will rise up to show you compassion. The LORD is a **God of justice**; happy are all who wait for him." Mal 2:17: "You have made the LORD tired with your words. You say, 'How have we made him tired?' When you say: 'Anyone doing evil is good in the LORD's eyes,' or 'He delights in those doing evil,' or 'Where is the **God of justice**?'"

Isa 30:18, NRSVue. Therefore the LORD waits to be gracious to you; therefore he will rise up to show mercy to you. For the LORD is a **God of justice**; blessed are all those who wait for him.
Isa 30:18, KJV. And therefore will the LORD wait, that he may be gracious unto you, and therefore will he be exalted, that he may have mercy upon you: for the LORD *is* a **God of judgment**: blessed *are* all they that wait for him.

Mal 2:17, NRSVue. You have wearied the LORD with your words. Yet you say, "How have we wearied him?" By saying, "All who do evil are good in the sight of the LORD, and he delights in them." Or by asking, "Where is the **God of justice?**"
Mal 2:17, KJV. Ye have wearied the LORD with your words. Yet ye say, Wherein have we wearied *him*? When ye say, Every one that doeth evil *is* good in the sight of the LORD, and he delighteth in them; or, Where *is* the **God of judgment?**

Stewart's translation politics and interpretive emphasis in the 1830's— approximately two hundred years before the NRSVue was ratified—position her as a primogenitor of contemporary translation preferences. She focuses on historical matters of relationality, proximity, and social constructions as opposed to the triumphalism and individuality of English Puritan ideology and American colonial theologies. Stewart's translation play is dialectical. It vacillates between conceptions of righteousness and justice, disrupting trends in biblical translations that make it a matter of either/or: either righteousness or justice. Stewart's interaction, therefore, can attune interpreters to both the introspective and cultural group implications of translating *dikaiosynē* as "justice" or "righteousness" in 2 Peter. That decision is not automatic or a given. Translation decisions influence the overall interpretation of 2 Peter's persuasive action toward cultivating internal community identity and behavior.

Justice as Interpersonal and Intragroup

African American women characterize justice as an interpersonal and intragroup experience. According to their moral discourses, justice is an attitude and practice that cuts across the diversities of American race logic within Christianity, transgressing the boundaries of separation, segregation, and difference as a value of God. One example is Fannie Barrier Williams's plea to her white American Christian sisters in 1833. She assigns the Christian imperative of justice as the duty of white Christian women to subscribe to and practice humane treatment of their African American Christian sisters.

> Women who are tender enough in heart to be active in humane societies, to be foremost in all charitable activities, who are loving enough to unite Christian womanhood everywhere against the sin of intemperance, ought to be instantly concerned in the plea of colored women for **justice and humane treatment**. Women of the dominant race can not afford to be responsible for the wrongs we suffer, since those who do **injustice** can not escape a certain penalty.
>
> But there is no wish to overstate the obstacles to colored women or to picture their status as hopeless. There is no disposition to take our place in this Congress as faultfinders or suppliants for mercy. As women of a common country, with common interests, and a destiny that will certainly bring us closer to each other, we come to this altar with our contribution of hopefulness as well as with our complaints....
>
> The colored women, as well as all women, will realize that the inalienable right to life, liberty, and the pursuit of happiness is a maxim that will become more blessed in its significance when the hand of woman shall take it from its sepulture in books and make it the gospel of every-day life and the unerring guide in the relations of all men, women, and children.[41]

Williams's address defines justice and humane treatment as a Christian requisite. Without explicitly using the word "righteousness," she assigns, as a righteous endeavor, concern about the prejudices against Christian African American women. She deploys the nineteenth-century ideology that Christianity is a nonraced identity as a rhetorical strategy for not only critiquing the silence of her white Christian sisters but shaming their complicity. Moreover, Williams suggests God's judgment remains for those who do not act on behalf of what is morally expedient—namely, actualizing life, liberty, and happiness as the Christian gospel manifest in America.

Buell argues that the nineteenth-century notion of Christian identity operative among minoritized populations, like African American women, diminished race as a marker of Christian identity. According to Buell, women like Williams and Stewart contended that "racial or ethnic divisions among Christians (and indeed among all humans) are incompatible

---

41. Williams, "Intellectual Progress of the Colored Woman," 404–5, bold emphasis added.

with Christianity." Buell notes correctly that women like Williams and Stewart highlight a fundamental incompatibility between the egalitarianism of Christianity, as they conceive of it, and the racialized prejudice of white American Christianity and its behaviors.[42] What she misses, however, is that many of them were not advocating for a total erasure of their ethnic identities and locations, but rather an affirmation of its fully human nature and legitimacy. All the women referenced in this chapter (Williams, Stewart, Cooper, Carter, Broughton, Cook, etc.) valued the cultural resources of their African American background. Dissolving racial identities under the Christian banner did not require erasure of the African diaspora traditions and lineages, but a ratification of it as just as American as their European America Christian neighbors. They rejected Christian cultural formations that promoted and expected forms of ethnic assimilation into a white Christian majority so completely as to extinguish their identity. They imagined an authentic moral Christian society created the conditions for "a multiethnic, multiclassed American society."[43]

---

42. "On the positive side, at least since the early nineteenth century, the notion of Christian origins as racially inclusive and egalitarian has supported opposition to Christian and non-Christian practices that sanction differential treatment on the basis of 'race.' Especially in North America, certain biblical passages have been crucial in formulating the transcendence of racial difference as an original Christian ideal, especially within the African American biblical interpretation, to combat white Christian racism. 'God is no respecter of persons: But in every nation one who fears [God], and works righteousness, is accepted with [God]' (Acts 10:34–35); 'For [God] has made of one blood all the nations of the world to dwell on the face of the earth' (Acts 17:26); and 'There is neither Jew nor Greek, neither slave nor free, male and female: for you are all one in Christ Jesus' (Gal. 3:28) are three of the most well-known New Testament passages cited to challenge racist forms of Christianity. The interpretation of these New Testament passages as indicative of explicitly non-racialized Christian origins depends on a historical model of Christian history that moves from 'pure' origins to less pure realizations of Christianity over time. When Christian practices and structures contribute to racist and ethnocentric oppression, this outcome has often been interpreted as a failure to realize the universalistic and egalitarian ideals inherent in earliest Christianity. This argument presupposes a sharp distinction between universalism and ethnic/racial particularity. While important for antiracist interventions, especially the North American civil rights efforts, defining Christianness in contrast to race has not solved the problems of modern racism. This construction of universalism also paradoxically perpetuates anti-Judaism in the name of antiracism" (Buell, *Why This New Race*, 11).

43. Darryl M. Trimiew, "The Social Gospel Movement and the Question of Race," in *The Social Gospel Today*, ed. Christopher H. Evans (Louisville: Westminster John Knox, 2001), 28.

Conclusion

Language of both justice and righteousness frequently occurs throughout many nineteenth-century writings of African American women. These two terms carry the connotative baggage of Western Christianity and its global colonial histories. Within the women's literary archive, however, righteousness language was often deployed in more socially focused discussions on the patterns and strivings of collective life for their Christian African American communities. Even when they followed the KJV translation's use of righteousness to describe their personal religious experience, these women often conceived those experiences reverberating throughout their communities and society. Individual religious experience, mainly as they expressed in their personal call stories and denominational literature, extended beyond the personal to the collective lived experiences of their people.

In summary, African American women essayists critique Christian cultures that assign segregation and separation as features of God's righteous judgments or justice. They penned discourses on righteousness and justice to counter social formations of caste, prejudice, differentiation, and expulsion and designated them as outside the moral field of God and authentic Christian practice and community. African American women were not oblivious nor averse to notions of Christian pluralism, although their antagonists—namely, dominant forms of white American Christianity—were. Their Christian cultural rhetoric did not advocate the dissolution of ethnic identity within the cross-racial Christian community but the protected coexistence and equal treatment of ethnic pluralism as the most authentic reflection of God's justice manifest in society. Their cultural rhetoric champions internal reform within their Christian communities as well as the broader society in which they find themselves. As modes of suasion, their cultural rhetorics seek to nurture and fortify a diverse people through prophetic Christian messages of tolerance, plurality, and kinship.

4
The Rhetoric of Justice in 2 Peter

Popular English translations and exegetical commentaries from the twentieth century and beyond frequently translate the twelve occurrences of
dik-stem words in 2 Peter as "righteousness."[1] As the previous chapter

---

1. A brief review of standard exegetical commentary treatments of the term in
2 Pet 1:1 illustrates the translation preference for "righteousness" as opposed to justice:
Jörg Frey, *The Letter of Jude and the Second Letter of Peter: A Theological Commentary*,
trans. Kathleen Ess (Waco, TX: Baylor University Press, 2018), 247; Andrew M. Mbuvi,
Jude and 2 Peter, New Covenant Commentary Series (Eugene, OR: Cascade, 2015), 68;
Bo Reicke, *The Epistles of James, Peter, and Jude*, AB (Garden City, NY: Doubleday,
1964), 150; Earl Richard, *Reading 1 Peter, Jude, and 2 Peter: A Literary and Theological
Commentary* (Macon, GA: Smyth & Helwys, 2000), 321; Nienhuis and Wall, *Reading the Epistles of James, Peter, John, and Jude as Scripture*, 131; Peter H. Davids, *The
Letters of 2 Peter and Jude*, The Pillar New Testament Commentary (Grand Rapids:
Eerdmans, 2006), 159; Ruth Anne Reese, *2 Peter and Jude*, Two Horizons New Testament Commentary (Grand Rapids: Eerdmans, 2007), Kindle loc. 1865–66. Representative of this larger trend, one commentary states the significance of righteousness as
a theme in 2 Peter in these terms: "Righteousness is an important theme for the letter,
appearing seven times (1:1, 13; 2:5, 7, 8, 21; and 3:13) as a binding theme. As the theme
unfolds, it becomes apparent that Peter primarily uses the term with an ethical dimension." See Richard B. Vinson, Richard F. Wilson, and Watson E. Mills, *1 and 2 Peter,
Jude*, Smyth & Helwys Bible Commentary (Macon, GA: Smyth & Helwys, 2010), 291.
Some scholars have begun to depart from this tradition, preferring the translation
of "justice" though they rarely acknowledge and trace the history of translation that
makes this decision a significant turn in the politics of meaning-making in critical
studies of 2 Peter. One of the closest discussions about this matter, states, "Translations are divided between rendering *dikaiosynē* as 'justice' or 'righteousness.' The
somewhat more traditional translation of 'righteousness' suggest that the gift of faith
is part of the redemptive righteousness of Christ. However, all other occurrences of
dikaiosynē or *dikaios* in 2 Peter (1:13; 2:5, 7, 8, 21; 3:13) have an ethical or moral sense.
The translation 'justice' conveys somewhat better the ethical dimensions of *dikaiosynē*
and fits nicely with the imagery of receiving a faith that is 'of equal honor' to that of

demonstrated, such translations activate the vocabulary of individual piety as the standard starting point for understanding the meaning and significance of 2 Peter. In doing so, these translations conceal the social investment and culture-making endeavor of the letter's rhetoric and incorrectly affirm the institution of enslavement as a social arrangement of God. African American women's use of the language of righteousness and justice, on the other hand, helpfully highlights the social aspect of these terms. Unlike the KJV, these women deployed both terms to cultivate a communal Christian identity that cut across racialized cultural divisions of black and white. They played dialectically with notions about the righteousness and justice of God to oppose the pressures of a racist, classicist, and sexist society—inside and outside African American communities. They used the terms to privilege equity and access and, in turn, cast a different American Christian vision about the workings of justice than the dominant, white American Christian discourse.

Examining 2 Peter alongside the discourses of these African American women helpfully highlights the social element of the letter and opens up the potential to examine its positions toward enslavement. However, unlike the moral discourses of the nineteenth century women, 2 Peter depicts justice as a social dynamic that occurs *only* within the Christian community. It is an insider Christian experience that is most noticeable at the local level. Second Peter is neither individualistic (as KJV-based translations would suggest) nor universally egalitarian (as the rhetoric of African American women would like). Second Peter's cultural rhetoric is rooted in social concern and group action, but its scope is limited.

Second Peter's Esteem-Building Enterprise

Like the nineteenth century women interpreters discussed in the previous chapter, the authors of 2 Peter are situated in a strongly pluralistic society. Most of their recipients are located within the multicultural and syncretistic urban centers of the Greco-Roman world and overwhelm-

---

the apostles" (Donelson, *1 and 2 Peter and Jude*, 213–14). Other exegetical commentaries preferring "justice" include Neyrey, *2 Peter, Jude*, 143; Ben Witherington III, *A Socio-rhetorical Commentary on 1–2 Peter*, vol. 2 of *Letters and Homilies for Hellenized Christians* (Downers Grove, IL: IVP Academic, 2007), 293; Callan, *Acknowledging the Divine Benefactor*, 40; Bauckham, *Jude, 2 Peter*, 165; Daniel J. Harrington, *Jude and 2 Peter*, SP (Collegeville, MN: Liturgical Press, 2003), 239.

ingly live on the margins of their larger religious-social world.[2] As such, their understanding of *how* they are perceived and received by others in their extended groups matter in a way that is unconventional to Western notions of modern or postmodern people. Similar to their nineteenth century counterparts, Broughton and Stewart, the authors of 2 Peter focus specifically on the circumstances and self-understanding of their believing community, who appears to feel that they are devalued by society and their broader Christian networks. In response, the letter writers make a concerted effort to assert that the intended audience collectively has an honorable quality. In this case, their honor is equal to that of the letter's implied author, the historical Peter, as well as the broader circle of apostles and prophets referenced in the discourse (2 Pet 1:1; 3:2). In making this argument, the authors concentrate their epistolary mode of persuasion, much like Cook did writing "Women's Place in the Work of the Denomination," toward the deliberative task of esteem building. The letter reminds readers that they are members of a corporate kinship with equal share (1:4) and purpose (1:10–11). The rhetorical aim is to heighten their sense of authority, ownership, and place (1:3–8; 3:17–18) within the chronological stream of early Christian history. The authors, therefore, are involved in a group-oriented "traditioning" process.[3] By encouraging readers to adopt

---

2. Social scientists in critical biblical studies and social anthropologists of the ancient Mediterranean world offer various statistics about the percentage of the population made up by the marginal and disenfranchised classes (the advanced agrarian society's "peasant class," as they often label it) at the time the writings of the New Testament, with proposals as high as 90 percent. See Dietmar Neufeld and Richard E. DeMaris, *Understanding the Social World of the New Testament* (New York: Routledge, 2010), 197; Jerome H. Neyrey and Eric C. Stewart, *The Social World of the New Testament: Insights and Models* (Grand Rapids: Baker Academic, 2008), 151; Warren Carter, *The Roman Empire and the New Testament: An Essential Guide* (Nashville: Abingdon, 2009); Adam Winn, ed., *An Introduction to Empire in the New Testament*, RBS 84 (Atlanta: SBL Press, 2016). A minority of scholars estimate as low as 60 percent. What is clear is that most of the ancient Mediterranean world of 2 Peter consisted of people living outside the comforts of resources, power, and economic and food security. These were corporate groups functioning outside of the certainty of leisure and individual wealth, power, and access. Reading 2 Peter with this social reality in mind requires emphasizing the social unit on the margins, not just individual actors.

3. Malina, "Understanding New Testament Persons," 48. Positing such tactics as a distinguishing feature of group-oriented selves, Malina describes ancient Mediterranean people as "codependent on a range of others who dominate their ever-changing in-groups.... They need other people to continue to know who they really are." Malina

a particular viewpoint about authority while discouraging alternative understandings of Christianness, the letter's cultural rhetoric exemplifies a process of identity adoption. The authors of 2 Peter instruct readers about who they are and who they are not to be, what they are to do and what they are not to do (2 Pet 2:13–14; 3:11–13) as agents of God's justice.

The authors of 2 Peter, however, are more extreme than their nineteenth century counterparts. The women discussed in the previous chapter, like Stewart and her address to the African Masonic Hall, encourage those who hold different opinions to change their behavior and remain part of their community. The ancient letter writers, on the other hand, exclude those who disagree with them. They designate adversaries to their version of Christian belief as apostates, individuals who should be completely cut off from the community for abandoning their beliefs. According to the letter's depiction, these apostates voluntarily returned to their former non-Christian identities and practices after failing to consistently conform to the Christian "way of truth" (2:2). Thus, declare the authors, "It would be better for them never to have known the way of justice [*dikaiosynēs*] than, having come to know it, to turn back from the holy commandment that was handed over to them" (2:21).[4] Traditional scholarship often follows the letter's description, viewing the defectors (be they current or future actors) as voluntarily deserting the Christian community. However, these rival teachers may not have *voluntarily* left the community. Rather, 2 Peter's cultural rhetoric seems to have *forced* defection due to its rigid, intransigent stance on Christian identity, practice, and community.

Second Peter's Cultural Rhetoric of Justice

Second Peter's rigidity is seen especially in its employment of *dikaiosynē* and related terms. Reading these terms sensitized by the moral discourses of African American women helps attune interpreters to this rigidity. As discussed in the previous chapter, nineteenth century African American women, following the KJV, adopted the connotation of "righteousness" as focused on individual piety, but that individuality was never divorced from the social and civic predicaments of their Christian African American

---

also describes the dyadic identity by saying ancient Mediterranean people were "very concerned to adopt the viewpoints of the groups (their in-groups) whose fate they shared" (45).

4. Informed by the CEB translation.

communities. Thus, they often deployed righteousness interchangeably with language for "justice" to promote socially focused behavior.

A similar complementary use of the language of righteousness and justice can be found in a literary source for 2 Peter, the Apocalypse of Peter.[5] For example, the Apocalypse describes an angel escorting victims of homicide to the site of their offenders' hellish judgment. The victims state, "Righteousness and justice is the judgment of God. For, we heard but we did not believe that we would come to this eternal place of judgment" (Apoc. Pet. 7.11).[6] The quotation sets notions of righteousness and justice in complementary relation and establishes it as a group experience of reflection.

The Apocalypse of Peter, like 2 Peter, also juxtaposes righteous people to unrighteous people. Referring to unrighteous people as "sinners," Apoc. Pet. 3:2 says, "And how the righteous and sinners will be separated and how the upright in heart will act and how the wicked will be rooted out from eternity to eternity."[7] In the Apocalypse of Peter, righteousness is not only individual, but also collective. The Apocalypse of Peter 2:12–13 conveys this group dynamic, saying, "Enoch and Elijah will be sent in order to instruct them that this is the deceiver who will come into the world and perform signs and wonders to deceive.... Therefore, all who die by his hand will be martyrs and will be counted in the company of the good and righteous martyrs who pleased God with their life."[8] In this text, righteousness is a shared attribute that produces a collective of "righteous ones" who are martyrs. Implicitly juxtaposed to the righteous martyrs are those swayed by the influence of the "deceiver," a theme that recurs in 2 Peter. Unrighteous or unjust actors in the letter are cast as a collective involved in deeds and words of deception (*plastois logois*, 2 Pet 2:3).

---

5. The Apocalypse of Peter is preserved in two main text types, an Ethiopic text (discovered in 1910) and the Akhmīm text (discovered in 1886/87). The Ethiopic text is recognized as representing "a more original reading." See Eric J. Beck, *Justice and Mercy in the Apocalypse of Peter: A New Translation and Analysis of the Purpose of the Text*, WUNT 427 (Tübingen: Mohr Siebeck, 2019), 7, 169.

6. The versification and translation of the Apocalypse of Peter is taken from the Ethiopic text in Beck, *Justice and Mercy in the Apocalypse of Peter*, 69. Beck observes that the passage in which this quote is located is in chapter 25 of the Akhmīm version (Beck, *Justice and Mercy in the Apocalypse of Peter*, 78).

7. Beck, *Justice and Mercy in the Apocalypse of Peter*, 67.

8. Beck, *Justice and Mercy in the Apocalypse of Peter*, 67.

Translating the *dik*-stem words of 2 Peter as "justice" rather than "righteousness" recalibrates readers to the social dimension of 2 Peter's cultural rhetoric that it inherits from its use of the Apocalypse of Peter and that is reflected in the moral writings of nineteenth-century African American women. Using the translation of justice in 2 Peter highlights the letter's predilection for targeting community members who subscribed to a different understanding of the tradition. The brief tour of the twelve instances of justice language in 2 Peter that follows maps the range of sensibilities about justice articulated in the early Christian writing of 2 Peter and provides an entry into the way the letter's rhetoric focuses on the creation of a particular community culture.

A Tour of 2 Peter's Cultural Rhetoric of Justice

The four noun forms of *dikaiosynē* in 2 Peter use the concept of justice to establish group identity for both the local and dispersed believing communities spanning across the first 120 years of the Jesus movement. Each instance places justice as a value *within* the community, not outside it.

> 2 Pet 1:1. Symeōn Peter, an enslaved person and apostle of Jesus Christ, to those having received an allotment of faith, equal in honorable quality as ours in the bringing of **justice** [*dikaiosynē*] **of our God** and Savior Jesus Christ.

> 2 Pet 2:5. And if God did not spare the ancient world but God preserved, Noah, the eighth person, a preacher for **bringing justice** [*dikaiosynēs*], when God brought a flood upon the world of People Lacking Religious Habit [*asebōn*].

> 2 Pet 2:21. It would be better for them never to have known the way of **justice** [*dikaiosynēs*] than, having come to know it, to turn back from the holy commandment that was handed over to them.[9]

> 2 Pet 3:13. But, according to God's promise, we await new heavens and a new earth, in which **justice** [*dikaiosynē*] is at home.

God's heavenly kingdom is a place of "justice," and the earthly community is the "way" that leads to it. Those who "bring justice" now do so primarily

---

9. Informed by the CEB translation.

for the benefit of the Christian community who awaits the coming of God's kingdom. Thus, from 2 Peter's use of the *dik*-stem noun form, justice is inward facing. It creates and re-creates a believing community focused on the care and maintenance of itself, and it designates those activities as the acts of God's justice among them.

The adjective form of the *dik*-stem, which assigns the attribute of justice to people and things in 2 Peter, is also inward facing. It describes the quality of the believing communities' interactions with one another.

> 2 Pet 1:13. And I think it **just** [*dikaion*] as long as I am in this tent, to awaken you all with a reminder.

> 2 Pet 2:7. And God delivered **Just** [*dikaion*] Lot, who was made miserable by the conduct of the lawless ones in licentiousness.

> 2 Pet 2:8. By what he saw and heard, the **Just** [*dikaios*] One—dwelling among them day by day—was being tormented in his **just** [*dikaian*] soul concerning their lawless deeds.

Christian membership operates with its own internal compass. The behavior of community members distinguishes them from the larger world located outside the community, and the attitudes they espouse render Christians recognizable to each other among their local memberships. According to 2 Peter, justice is the defining feature that makes the community recognizable as a faithful fellowship.

The letter writers shrink the culture of shared recognition by appropriating criteria that sifts the membership into opposing factions. To this end, the writers deploy the negative form of justice to identify who or what amounts to injustice.

> 2 Pet 2:9. The Lord knows how to rescue Ones of Religious Habit [*eusebeis*] from trial and to keep **Unjust** Ones [*adikous*] being punished until a day of judgment.

> 2 Pet 2:13. Suffering **injustice** [*adikoumenoi*] as payment for their **unjust ways** [*adikias*]. They consider self-indulgence in the daytime a pleasure. They are spots and blemishes, indulging in their deceits while feasting with you.

> 2 Pet 2:15. They went off course, forsaking a straight way, having followed the way of Balaam, the son of Bosor, who loved the wages of **injustice** [*adikias*].

The four occurrences of *dik*-stem negative forms denote those who are not oriented toward God's justice within the believing communities. Their religious habits are the antithesis to the God-oriented actions the letter seeks to cultivate among its membership.

Two observations are worth noting about the occurrences of *dik*-words in the letter of 2 Peter. First, the experience of justice in 2 Peter is keyed toward the group and not the individual. Its mode of persuasion is characterized by a social-theological concern for group-oriented selves, and its rhetoric is directed toward people accustomed to adopting the viewpoints of the in-group whose fate they shared. Like other Mediterranean people of the time, the authors and the recipients expect to receive honor or shame *from* the community and *for* the community based on their behaviors.[10] Therefore, even when a *dik*-word is explicitly assigned as an attribute for an individual, as in "Just Lot" (2 Pet 2:7, 8) or Noah, "a preacher for bringing justice" (2 Pet 2:5), the adjective is used to cultivate a collective attribute of justice. The individual and by extension their community is either honorable or shameful, just or unjust. Consequently, English translations should eschew anachronistic projections that miss how 2 Peter originates from and speaks to corporate persons. The letter maintains and creates the social unit; it mirrors and responds to the corporate entity, not pietistic commitments or a self-sufficient individual. The use of the language of "righteousness" masks the original significance of the Greek *dik*-stem in such a way that an important dimension of the voice and concern of 2 Peter is misrepresented. Using the language of "justice" recovers this important corporate dimension.

The second observation about the twelve occurrences of *dik*-stem words details the experience of group-oriented justice as an insider phenomenon of the believing community. The letter writers assign justice as an insider experience. Rather than talk about righteousness as personal characteristics within individual believers and unbelievers, the letter defines justice as habitual actions that repeatedly affect Christian communities living in highly diverse social, cultural, and theological environments. Thus, justice interacts with the letter's notions of habitual action, expressed through the vocabulary of *eusebeia* or *asebēs* (2 Pet 1:3, 6–7; 2:5–6, 9; 3:7, 11).[11]

---

10. Malina, "Understanding New Testament Persons," 48.

11. Tord Fornberg (*An Early Church in a Pluralistic Society: A Study of 2 Peter.* ConBNT 9 [Lund: Gleerup, 1977], 2–3) points to this vocabulary as evidence of the

The language of *eusebeia* in 2 Peter articulates the distinction between insiders-outsiders and patriots-apostates, creating the conditions for a forced departure of the letter's targeted Other. Four instances of the noun form *eusebeia* and one instance of the adjective form (*eusebēs*) occur in 2 Peter.

2 Pet 1:3. As his divine power has given us everything for life and **religious habit** [*eusebeian*] through the knowledge of the One having called us to his own reputation of glorious honor and exceptional civic virtue.

2 Pet 1:6. And knowledge with self-control, self-control with endurance, endurance with **religious habit** [*eusebeian*].

2 Pet 1:7. And the **religious habit** [*eusebeia*] with fraternal-sororal mutuality, and fraternal-sororal mutuality with love.

2 Pet 2:9. The Lord knows how to rescue **Ones of Religious Habit** [*eusebeis*] from trial and to keep Unjust Ones [*adikous*] being punished until a day of judgment.

2 Pet 3:11. So, all these things being destroyed, what kind of people ought you to be? You are to be the kind of people who exist in holy ways of living and in **religious habits** [*eusebeiais*].

The decision to translate *eusebeia* and its cognates as "religious habit and sensibility," rather than the more standard preference of "godliness," is based on the same reason as the decision to activate the English language of justice as opposed to righteousness.[12] It is an attempt to use translation

---

Hellenism of 2 Peter: "There is widespread agreement that 2 Peter is strongly influenced by Hellenism: in this thesis Hellenism refers to the more or less homogeneous culture which had predominated in the countries round the eastern shores of the Mediterranean ever since the time of Alexander the Great. This agreement is usually justified by the use of certain expressions in 2 Pet 1:3–4, 16, which are seldom encountered elsewhere in Jewish or Christian writings. The 'Hellenistic' vocabulary often prompts the assumption that 2 Peter is Hellenistic in content as well. Yet it is a moot point whether a description of 2 Peter as 'Hellenistic' is relevant. The Jews of both Palestine and the Diaspora had been influenced by the surrounding cultures since Alexander's time."

12. A brief review of standard exegetical commentary treatments of the term *eusebeia* in 2 Pet 1:3 illustrates the translation preference for "godliness," "piety," or

to retrieve and interpret the social and cultural sensibility of the letter. In each instance of *eusebeia*, religious habit is not simply a static quality but a collective action and way of being.

Like the *dik*-stem words, 2 Peter deploys the negative form of *seb*-stem words. Two instances of the negative adjective form of religious habit (*asebēs*) and one instance of the negative verb form (*asebeō*) occur.

> 2 Pet 2:5. And if God did not spare the ancient world but God preserved, Noah, the eighth person, a preacher for bringing justice [*dikaiosynēs*], when God brought a flood upon the world of **People Lacking Religious Habit** [*asebōn*].

> 2 Pet 2:6. And God condemned the cities of Sodom and Gomorrah, having reduced those cities of people and creation to ashes by a catastrophe; having made them an example of things to come for the **People Lacking Religious Habit** [*asebesin*].

> 2 Pet 3:7. But by the same word, the heavens and the earth are now stored up in reserve for fire. Why? Because they are being kept for a day of judgment and of destruction of the **People Lacking Religious Habit** [*asebōn*].

The letter illustrates the appearance and ramifications of nonreligious habit among believers and nonbelievers. The communities of believers can practice a kind of religious habit that creates justice within their ranks or not. Both forms of religious habit impact the relational dynamics among members.

In terms of translation, therefore, the letter of 2 Peter calls for habitual religious action that embodies and nurtures justice, rather than an individ-

---

"godly life"—all of which continue to emphasize individual faith orientations and conceal the corporate focus of the term: Daniel J. Harrington, "Jude and 2 Peter," in *1 Peter, Jude and 2 Peter*, ed. Daniel J. Harrington, SP 15 (Collegeville: Liturgical Press, 2008), 243; Donelson, *1 and 2 Peter and Jude*, 217; Jonathan Knight, *2 Peter and Jude*, New Testament Guides (Sheffield: Sheffield Academic, 1995), 59; Neyrey, *2 Peter, Jude*, 150; Davids, *Letters of 2 Peter and Jude*, 166. Although they continue the convention of translating *eusebeia* as "piety" in their translation, Duane F. Watson, Terrance D. Callan, Mikeal Parsons, and Charles Talbert situate their translation as occurring within the social and cultural values" of honor versus shame and benefaction. See Duane F. Watson, Terrance D. Callan, Mikeal Parsons, and Charles Talbert, *First and Second Peter*, Paideia (Grand Rapids: Baker Academic 2012), 156, 160. Frey translates *eusebeia* as "a pious life" (*Letter of Jude and the Second Letter of Peter*, 247–48.

ually focused pietism of godliness that nurtures individual righteousness. Translation matters—particularly in conveying the religious habits of justice (*dikaios-eusebeia*) expressed in 2 Peter. No one translation can capture all potential meanings of a text written in a different language, from a different time, within a different context than later interpreters. But when interpreters attune themselves to the culture-making force of the language in 2 Peter, the more culturally equivalent term here is justice as opposed to righteousness.

Second Peter juxtaposes justice against injustice, or religious habit against lacking religious habit, as a rhetorical mechanism for sifting its community into two factions. Whether or not the letter is recording a historical reality that exist prior to its composition, the rhetoric of 2 Peter, at the very least, inscribes these divisions. Moreover, it takes a second violent step. It targets one Christian expression within the community by labeling it the way of injustice and religiously inferior. Essentially, the authors assign group shame to alternative expressions without any signs of Christian mediation or hospitality. Consequently, the cultural rhetoric of 2 Peter is accomplishing more than merely historical description. It is a social intervention that targets, labels, and ultimately displaces a particular segment of its own membership.

The writers reclassify Christians into adversaries and partisans by labeling an alternative position a heresy or faction (*haireseis*, 2:1). The matter here, however, is less about who the targets of 2 Peter's rhetoric were and more about what 2 Peter's rhetoric achieves through the literary face of the historic Peter. Using twelve *dik*-words, the letter writers model an endeavor in cultural rhetoric that is not only intolerant but violently so.

Justice as a Cultural Rhetoric of Uniformity

The imperatives of God's justice enacted on the group in 2 Peter is diametrically different from the interactions of justice and community conveyed in the writings of nineteenth century African American women. Women such as Fannie Barrier Williams, Virginia Broughton, and Mary Cook deployed justice vocabulary as a disruptive logic (see chapter 3 for examples). They merged justice, righteousness, and community together to challenge racialized differentiation under the banner of Christianity. The writers of 2 Peter, in contrast, use justice vocabulary to enforce distance between forms of Christianness. Rather than using justice as a disruptive strategy that knits together diversity, 2 Peter uses justice as a discursive strategy that unwinds intragroup plurality in favor of cultural uniformity in experience, thought, and practice.

The seemingly general and global scale of 2 Peter's opening salutation does not actually embrace plurality.[13] Rather, the letter champions a universalistic form of Christianness by imposing uniformity. Second Peter describes the current iteration of Christianness as if it is the sole chronological heir to the prophets (1:19–21; 3:2), Jesus (1:16–18), the apostles (1:1; 3:2), and Paul (3:15–16). Indeed, if one were to read 2 Peter without an awareness of the varieties of Christian communities, locations, and experiences scattered across the Greco-Roman world, the letter would supply no clues that such a diverse and dispersed Christian canvas existed other than the internal rivalry it chronicles in 2:1–3:5, 16, which it classifies as fundamentally non-Christian. Second Peter's cultural rhetoric situates Christian experience within a chronological stream of actors and history without explicitly acknowledging current geographical and diverse local identities.

Consequently, the letter's cultural and social position is significantly different from the cultural rhetoric of 1 Peter and Jude, which were both literary sources for 2 Peter. First Peter cultivates an identity of mutuality and kinship across cultural, social, and geographical pluralities. For example, 1 Pet 3:8–9 says, "Finally, all of you be of one mind, sympathetic, lovers of your fellow believers, compassionate, and modest in your opinion of yourselves. Don't pay back evil for evil or insult for insult. Instead, give blessing in return. You were called to do this so that you might inherit a blessing." The letter does not, however, insist that believers are uniform.

In its first and final chapters, for instance, 1 Peter characterizes its communities as a translocal kinship in which each local formulation of Christianness inevitably carries its own cultural markers and identities. For example, 1 Peter's encyclical form lists a diverse set of regional coordinates in Asia Minor as the letter's target recipients (1:1). These

---

13. Ben Witherington labels 2 Peter "the very first document and the very first encyclical ever written to the entire extant church." As the quote reveals, Witherington esteems the universalistic character of 2 Peter without interrogating the kind of universalism it advances. He also does not critique the amoral pattern of behavior the letter models, which risks reinscribing such moralist attitudes and patterns as acceptable in contemporary contexts (Witherington, *Socio-rhetorical Commentary on 1–2 Peter*, 283).

five locations (Pontus, Galatia, Cappadocia, Asia, and Bithynia) possess regional indigenous dialects and traditions and distinct cultural,
social, and historical markers as they relate to the unfolding of Roman
imperialism in their local areas.[14] Those land and regional stories of the
people who lived there for generations is not erased under the banner of
"Christian" (1 Pet 4:16). The letter works overtime to assert an identity
of fellowship and collectivity across these different regional coordinates
and histories while expanding it to include Christian communities situated beyond the borders of Asia Minor who the letter designates as
"fellow believers" who "are enduring the same suffering throughout the
world" (1 Pet 5:9; cf. 5:13). In 1 Peter, the diverse translocal formulations of Christianness share with each other both the sufferings of Christ
(1 Pet 4:13) and the glorious apocalyptic revelation of Christ (1 Pet 5:1).
Even the letter of Jude, with its strong sectarian focus similar to 2 Peter,
nonetheless leaves room for mercy and mediation to occur between
diverse articulations within the community. Jude does target a particular expression of Christianness it rejects, but it concludes by trying to
nurture some pathways for mercy and reconciliation by saying, "Have
mercy on those who doubt. Save some by snatching them from the fire.
Fearing God, have mercy on some, hating even the clothing contami-
nated by their sinful urges" (CEB, Jude 22–23). The recipients of the
letter, designated as "holy people" (v. 3), are told to "have mercy" and
"save others" who are members of Jude's specific community subscrib-
ing to a different understanding of the faith. The "holy people" in Jude
refers to multiple forms of Christianness that may yet be narrowly medi-
ated and negotiated in the letter.

Second Peter contains an understanding of collective sharing. Still, it
does not carry the same notion of plurality as attested in 1 Peter, nor does
it provide the opportunity for mediation as gestured towards (however
slight) in Jude. Regional identities of Christianness go unacknowledged,
and the letter does not register a global collective of translocal communities. Indeed, when it speaks of "sharing," the letter limits the attribute to
its particular community. According to 2 Pet 1:4, God "has given to us
the socially honorable and great promises that through these you all may

---

14. Brigitte Kahl, *Galatians Re-imagined: Reading with the Eyes of the Vanquished*
(Minneapolis: Fortress, 2010), 5, 31–76. For specific histories of Asia Minor areas
("Anatolia"), see Stephen Mitchell, *Anatolia: Land, Men, and Gods in Asia Minor*, 2
vols. (Oxford: Clarendon, 1993).

become those who fellowship [or "share," *koinōnoi*] in the divine nature, having escaped the decay of immorality in the world by lust." Although the letter writers deploy a *koin*-stem word (*koinōnos*), they assign it as a characteristic of one segment of the membership ("us"). They do not attach it to the entire diverse fellowship.

Another example of 2 Peter imposing uniformity resides in its sifting and weighing the diversity of interpretations surrounding Paul's writings. In 2 Pet 3:15–16, the authors refer to Paul's apostolic teaching. While acknowledging the authority of Paul's legacy, the authors also acknowledge divergent interpretations of Paul's writings.

> And you all consider the patience of our Lord as salvation, just as our beloved brother Paul wrote to you according to the wisdom having been given to him. As also in all his letters as they speak concerning these things, in which there are some things hard to understand that the Unlearned and Unstable Ones twist as also they do the other Scriptural Writings [*graphē*] to their own destruction.

The description of Paul's letters as containing "some things hard to understand" does not convey the authors' reservations about the authority and significance of Paul but a disregard for rival interpretations, which they call the interpretations of "the Unlearned and Unstable Ones." The name-calling devalues the identity of the rival interpreters and casts them as unworthy of the letter's community.

The idea that Paul's writings produce a diversity of interpretations is not uncommon in the tradition. Origen's commentary on the Epistle of Romans opens by declaring the difficulty of Paul's expressions, which lend themselves to various contentious interpretations. Like 2 Peter, Origen asserts there are both legitimate and heretical uses of Paul's writings that can reinforce or undermine Scripture (*graphē*):

> It seems to me that there are two reasons why the letter that was written to the Romans is considered to be harder to understand than the Apostle Paul's other letters. First, because he makes use of expressions which sometimes are confused and insufficiently explicit. Second, because he stirs up very many questions in the letter and the heretics, especially propping themselves up on these, are accustomed to add that the cause of each person's actions is not to be attributed to one's own purpose but to different kinds of natures. And, from a handful of words from this letter they attempt to subvert the meaning of the whole of Scripture,

which teaches that God has given man freedom of will. (Origen, *Comm. Rom.* preface 1 [Scheck])

The diverse Christian articulations related to Paul, as presented in Origen's statement and 2 Peter, center around Paul's letters, not his legend. Paul is an authority figure; he is just misunderstood as a writer, a point with which Paul himself would likely agree.[15]

Unlike Gal 2:1–10, which sees Paul and Peter as representing different emergent formulations of Christian identity and practice, the letter of 2 Peter does not set Paul and Peter at odds.[16] Rather, Paul is described a "beloved brother" who possesses "wisdom" from God (3:15). The letter depicts their positions as aligned. In this, 2 Peter is similar to Acts 15, which stages a moment where various formulations of the emerging Jesus movement negotiate coexistence. Acts narrates a setting in which Judeans (15:1), Pharisees (15:5), and a variety of regional identities such as Phoenicia and Samaria (15:3) believers are in conversation with marquee figures such as Peter (15:7), Paul (15:2–3), and James (15:3). These diverse orientations convene to discuss how to respond to the question of gentile inclusion in the messianic Jewish community (Acts 15:22–29). The Jerusalem Council, in other words, is a site of exchange across diverse Christian understandings. In this episode, Acts flattens the rivalry between Peter and Paul. Peter supports Paul and authorizes his gentile mission (Acts 15:7–12). Within the larger storyline of the book of Acts, there is little difference in content, message, and form between what Peter and Paul proclaim publicly.[17] As George A. Kennedy remarks, the speeches in Acts "show the apostles, Peter and Paul in particular, performing their duty of preaching the gospel, both to Jews and to gentiles" and indicate that they share "the same message before different audiences."[18] The book of Acts and 2 Peter both portray an amicable relationship between Peter and Paul, with each directing the same message to a different audience.

---

15. See Rom 3:8; 6:1; 1 Cor 6:12; 10:23; Phil 3; 2 Thess 2:2.

16. Fornberg, *Early Church in a Pluralistic Society*, 30–31.

17. For an example, compare Peter's Pentecost speech with its evocation of David in 2:14–36 to Paul's speech in Acts 13:15–41. For discussions about the speech forms in Acts, see Marion L. Soards, *The Speeches in Acts: Their Content, Context, and Concerns* (Louisville: Westminster John Knox, 1994); Janusz Kucicki, *The Function of the Speeches in the Acts of the Apostles*, BibInt 158 (Leiden: Brill), 2018.

18. George A. Kennedy, *New Testament Interpretation through Rhetorical Criticism*, Studies in Religion (Chapel Hill: University of North Carolina, 1984), 115.

While Acts uses Peter and Paul to emphasize the peaceful coexistence of multiple forms of Christianness, 2 Peter uses the pairing to collapse the plurality. In the letter, there is no hierarchy between Peter and Paul. They are both depicted as progenitors of early Christian writings who embrace their status as "enslaved persons" of Jesus Christ (2 Pet 1:1; 3:15; cf. Rom 1:1; Gal 1:10). They carry the same literary weight and influence. They bear the same wisdom to the letter's Christian community. But whereas strong Pauline traditions like 1 Cor 1:11–12 preserve the witness that diverse Christian beliefs and practices coexisted and collided, the legacy of Peter cast in 2 Peter is one that quells such variety.[19]

Justice as a Cultural Rhetoric of Enslavement

Reading the letter of 2 Peter through the moral discourses of African American women foregrounds the link between the justice of God and the social institution of enslavement. Sensitized by the stories and challenges of American enslavement recorded by women writers (some of whom were enslaved persons themselves) slows the rush to distance the positive metaphorical usages of enslavement in the New Testament from the physical experience of enslavement in the Roman world. From this vantage point, the metaphorical usage of enslavement in 2 Peter is more than an ancient institutional relic with diminished historical relevance for the present. It is an important element of the letter's cultural rhetoric.

The opening verse of 2 Peter is jarring to contemporary readers attentive to matters of justice and liberation. The Peter persona is labeled an enslaved person of God in the same breath as the letter recipients are affirmed to be sharers in the justice of God. Readers are left to wonder about the quality of justice if the devotees who commend this God so highly are enslaved people. Moreover, the language of enslavement is not limited to verse 1. Language of enslavement and affirmations of that experience also occurs in 2 Pet 2:19: "These false teachers promise them freedom, but they themselves are enslaved [*douloi*] to the decay of immorality, for whoever overpowers you, to this one he has become enslaved [*dedoulōtai*]." In addition to the explicit language of enslaved persons, the book uses language denoting the stakeholder in institutions of enslavement, the "enslaver" (*despotēs*; 2:1), and the alternative social

---

19. Karen L. King, "Which Early Christianity?," in *The Oxford Handbook of Early Christian Studies*, ed. Susan Ashbrook Harvey and David G. Hunter (New York: Oxford University Press, 2010), 66–67.

condition—namely, liberation and freedom (*eleutheria*, 2:19 above). Enslavement is presupposed, while ownership by a particular personified force is not. The weight of justice in 2 Peter is not on the dismantling of institutional enslavement but upon whom one commits to being owned.

The complexity of enslavement rhetoric in early Christian writings and the moral dilemma of its lived experience is fully displayed in 2 Peter's small sampling of occurrences. The letter implies that the state of enslavement, as either a positive or adverse condition, is determined by whom one is enslaved to. The letter opens by designating the historic Peter an "enslaved person ... of Jesus Christ" (1:1). This is an authorizing status. It links the role of enslavement to the function of a Christian apostle, in turn depicting enslavement as an empowered position. In contrast, the letter writers portray their adversaries as enslaved. But instead of Jesus as the adversaries' enslaver, the letter writers personify "decaying immorality" as the overlord (2:19). The writers portray their adversaries' condition of enslavement in delegitimating terms. Both cases indicate that enslavement is a required condition for one in a position of authority. Following the letter's logic, enslavement is ethical or unethical, righteous or unrighteous, depending on the power to which enslaved persons subject themselves. But, in both cases, the institution of enslavement remains intact.

In the cultural reasoning of the ancient Mediterranean, enslavement was not in itself amoral. It was simply part of the social system. When a city was conquered, its citizens were enslaved. When an individual could not support his family, his children were sold to pay off the family debt.[20] Even if people were not formerly enslaved, one of the most ubiquitous institutions of the ancient world was the patron-client hierarchy in which even free persons relied upon the patronage of those with greater power and resources. The interconnectedness of the ancient world made such systems less a matter of morality and more a matter of survival. Second Peter, however, misrepresents the workings of enslavement. It depicts enslaved people as empowered agents who are free to determine the terms of enslavement. It neglects to account for how enslavement is an imposed arrangement forced by those with power upon those who lacked power, needed services, or had limited available resources.[21] As such, 2 Peter's use of enslavement

---

20. Richard A. Horsley, "The Slave Systems of Classical Antiquity and Their Reluctant Recognition by Modern Scholars," *Semeia* 83–84 (1998): 35, 36, 40.

21. I am indebted to my colleague Luis Menéndez-Antuña for allowing me to read an unpublished paper on enslavement that helped to nuance this concern. See

as a didactic metaphor recasts cultural realities and reconfigures power dynamics. It takes one of the most pervasive realities of the Mediterranean world, enslavement, and reshapes it into a voluntary condition that it can then use to clarify the boundaries of Christian conformity.

Second Peter also manipulates other presuppositions about the social hierarchy of the ancient world, fiddling with its configuration but not challenging it. In 1:1–2, for instance, the letter reshapes the typical social contract of the patron-client system. The patron-client contract is an asymmetrical relationship in which "the partners are not social equals and make no pretense to equality." Instead, in the patron-client relationship, partners hold "significantly different social statuses" and exchange different types of goods, services, favors, and gifts.[22] In conventional New Testament adoptions of the patron and client system, the apostles are the patrons, and the letter recipients are the clients (e.g., 1 Cor 1:12–15; 4:1–2).

Second Peter, however, reframes the power dynamics between the apostles and believers as a contract among colleagues. The collegial contract "is a type of reciprocity among equals. It is symmetrical reciprocity between persons of the same social status."[23] The opening verses of 2 Peter evokes the language of reciprocity by deploying the word *isotimon* (translated as "equal in honorable quality"). The lexeme *isotimos* does not appear in any other writing of the New Testament or the LXX.[24] The novelty of the term reflects its function in the letter. Peter shares the status of an apostle

---

now published Luis Menéndez-Antuña, "Of Social Death and Solitary Confinement: The Political Life of a Gerasene (Luke 8:26–39)," *JBL* 138 (2019): 643–64. For book-length studies on the cultural rhetoric of enslavement in early Christian discourse that inform this brief analysis of 2 Peter, see Marianne Bjelland Kartzow, *The Slave Metaphor and Gendered Enslavement in Early Christian Discourse: Double Trouble Embodied* (New York: Routledge, 2018); J. Albert Harrill, *The Manumission of Slaves in Early Christianity* (Tübingen: Mohr Siebeck, 1995); Mary Ann Beavis, *The First Christian Slave: Onesimus in Context* (Eugene, OR: Wipf & Stock, 2021); Chris L. De Wet, *The Unbound God: Slavery and the Formation of Early Christian Thought*, Routledge Studies in the Early Christian World (New York: Routledge, 2018); De Wet, *Preaching Bondage: John Chrysostom and the Discourse of Slavery in Early Christianity* (Oakland: University of California Press, 2015).

22. Robbins, *Exploring the Texture of Texts*, 79.

23. Robbins, *Exploring the Texture of Texts*, 79.

24. The term *isotimos* appears outside the canonical tradition, occurring in the writings of Josephus and Philo: Josephus, *A.J.* 8.8.2; 12.3.1; *B.J.* 4.5.2; 4.7.1; Philo, *Leg.* 2.18; *Sacr.* 1.8, 91, 95, 131; *Deus* 1.13, 57; *Sobr.* 1.4, 54; *Conf.* 1.170; *Her.* 1.159, 177; *Abr.* 1.62; *Ios.* 1.232; *Mos.* 1.324; *Decal.* 1.37; *Spec.* 1.170, 181, 228–229, 238; 2.157;

with others; their status is "as ours" (that is, the same as Peter; 1:1). That shared position is reinforced later in the letter by a narrative rehearsal of the group-witness experience at the transfiguration (2 Pet 1:16–18) and the designation of the apostles as like the prophets of Israel (2 Pet 3:2).

The language of *isotimon* is not merely an affirmation of shared apostolic authority and influence. It undermines the disproportionate power dynamic between apostles and believers. The letter flattens the hierarchy of client-patron relations in which the direction of influence and authority flows downward from the apostles to their followers. The letter writers esteem the larger Christian constituency by diminishing—though not abandoning entirely—the notion of a special class of people embedded within the larger Christian community. In 2 Peter, the apostolic tradition is ratified, and the letter recipients are elevated to the status of colleagues, partners, and kinspeople on par with the apostolic tradition they espouse.

Once again, the letter writers exercise a rhetorical strategy that camouflages their actual culture-making endeavor. They put forward a façade that they are flattening apostolic authority, subsuming it under social forms of reciprocity and using the language of *isotimon*. Yet, they produce the opposite rhetorical effect. By downplaying apostolic authority, the letter writers amplify their own authority and embolden their membership to use that authority against their opponents. Despite the letter's attempt to elevate the recipients' place in the social hierarchy of the corporate identity of Christianity, the recipients are still dependent on the authority of the apostles for their power.

All of this, moreover, does not erase the fact that the letter leaves institutional enslavement and power hierarchies intact. The difficulty of 2 Peter for modern readers remains: the letter attaches human identity and agency to a spiritual caste system. The writers not only presume the institution of enslavement is an empirical social reality but also validate it as a moral one. Second Peter's cultural rhetoric supplants a human caste system with an enslavement to Jesus Christ (1:1) and God, the divine Enslaver (2:1). A power hierarchy remains. The letter's constructed hierarchy divides humanity into those who lord and those who are lorded over. The only question the letter raises implicitly through its use of enslavement imagery is who the lording power is, not whether lordship should be exercised.

3.202; *Virt.* 1.154, 185, 223; *Praem.* 1:112; *Prob.* 1:130, 148; *Legat.* 1.98, 341. Among the Greek apologists, it appears in Athenagoras's *Leg.* 22.

Conclusion

This chapter contrasts 2 Peter's usage of *dik*-stem words with the literary archives of nineteenth-century African American women analyzed in the previous chapter. The moral discourses supply a mechanism for interrogating the rhetorical force of righteousness and justice language in 2 Peter. Located firmly within American formulations of Christian community, the women employ justice and righteousness to address matters of human equality and treatment. They use the terms to promote cultural practices that authorized inclusion and leadership within and outside their respective communities.

In contrast, 2 Peter commands the language of justice in the form of *dik*-stem Greek words from the center of its Christian community. Instead of characterizing the justice of God as pluralistic and mediating, the letter models a polemical and conformist approach. Justice is antagonistic to difference in 2 Peter. The letter writers make their understanding of justice plain by piling one derogatory description on another for their rivals (2 Pet 2:13b–14). The justice of God within the Christian community, according to 2 Peter, identifies and targets other understandings of Christianity. The cultural rhetoric of 2 Peter minoritizes Christian Others and labels those tactics as the work of God.

Positioned as an influential voice, the writers of 2 Peter set the norms of social behavior from the center of power and privilege. They police the boundaries of belief and practice, profiling and marginalizing alternative formulations that do not fit their Christian construction. Justice in 2 Peter polices in the name of God, profiles in the name of God, marginalizes in the name of God, and even enslaves in the name of God. It is not difficult to understand why African American women made little use of 2 Peter as a biblical resource. They penned their moral discourses of Christian justice from the margins of denominational and American cultures that subordinated, disregarded, and even enslaved them. How just, or even righteous, could the Christian letter of 2 Peter be for African American women who articulated that the justice of God is one that promotes inclusion, humane treatment, and shared community?

Part 3
The Face of Another

5

Pseudonymity as African American
Women's Strategy for Social Response

Second Peter and the moral discourses of nineteenth-century African American women both address matters of cultural identity and belonging. Despite their historical distance and literary differences, they also both deploy the rhetorical strategy of pseudonymity as a persuasive technique to establish credibility, expand the literary tradition, and provide witness to their different conceptions of of justice and injustice.

Literary Pseudonymity

Pseudonymity, as opposed to anonymity, is the most appropriate label for this conversation. Anonymity literally means writings that have "no name" (from Greek *a-*, "no" or "without," and *onoma*, "name"), and typically connotes writings whose authors are unknown, like the homily of Hebrews.[1] In contrast, in pseudonymous writings, *be they ancient or modern*, the writers deliberately identify themselves "by a name other than their own" (from Greek *pseud-*, "false," and *onoma*, "name"). Pseudonyms mask the real identities of authors by either inventing a name with minimal previous notoriety or borrowing a name from a recognized figure within that particular community.[2] Both 2 Peter and the writings of Sarah Louisa Forten (1814–1883)

---

1. See Origen's reflections on Hebrews in his Homilies of Hebrews cited in Eusebius, *Hist. eccl.* 6.25.11–14. Although Origen frequently attributes Hebrews to Paul, he did pen the famous statement, "Who wrote the epistle [Hebrews]? Only God knows."

2. Dennis Duling, *The New Testament: History, Literature, and Social Context*, 4th ed. (Belmont, CA: Wadsworth, 2003), 257; Klaus Koch, "Pseudonymous Writing," *IDBSup* 712; David G. Meade, *Pseudonymity and Canon: An Investigation into the Relationship of Authorship and Authority in Jewish and Earliest Christian Tradition* (Grand Rapids: Eerdmans, 1987), 1–2.

and Ida Bell Wells-Barnett (1862–1931)—exemplars from the nineteenth-century African American literary canon—have names attached to them.[3] Second Peter uses a hybrid Semitic-Hellenistic name borrowed from the persona of the Galilean fisherman turned apostolic leader of the eclectic Jewish movement, the historic Symeon Peter (1:1; also see 3:1). Wells invents a name and literary persona called "Iola" (referred to here as Wells-Iola), and Forten publishes under two pseudonyms, one borrowed from biblical tradition (referred to here as Forten-Ada) and one borrowed from a character in a popular novel (referred to here as Forten-Magawisca).

Be it a name borrowed from another (as is the case of 2 Peter and Forten) or invented to create a new public literary face (as is the case of Wells), the names assigned to respective writings perform identity. By choosing different names for their writings, the authors enact identities (personas) that serve their respective social positions inside and outside their communities. In contemporary literary and rhetorical theories, personas are the artificial creation of authors. They are voices and faces purposefully chosen by authors for cultural suasion. They represent the authors but stand invariably distinct from them, hiding their true identity. Indeed, the very word persona comes from Latin, where it means an "actor's mask." Authors use the rhetoric of a persona as a literary performance. They are neither fully disclosed nor entirely hidden while masked behind their created faces.[4]

What modern rhetorical studies refer to as textual personae, classical Greek handbooks on rhetoric refer to as the ethos of the writing. In Aristotle's classical formulation, ethos is the self-portrayal of the writer as a reliable character. It is a mechanism for building the audience's confidence in the speaker (Rhet. 1.2.1356a413). Similarly, Cicero considers ethos a vital and dynamic ingredient in persuasive speech alongside logos ("logic") and pathos ("emotions"), which he refers to as the three officiae ("officials"; De or. 2.115).

Among Greek and Roman textbooks on rhetoric and prose composition, prosopopoeia ("putting on the face of another") is another concept that describes the literary strategy of character building. Prosopopoeia is

---

3. Ida Bell Wells-Barnett is conventionally referred to in short form as Ida B. Wells, following her standard journalist title. The rest of the chapter will follow that convention.

4. Robert C. Elliott, The Literary Persona (Chicago: University of Chicago Press, 1982), 19–32.

different from merely establishing the ethos of the rhetor. It distinguishes between the rhetor's personal ethos and the ethos of the rhetorical persona that the speaker assumes in her composition. For example, the mid-first to early-second-century rhetorical textbook attributed to Aelius Theon describes the rhetorical practice of *prosopopoeia* as follows:

> Personification [*prosopopoeia*] is the introduction of a person to whom words are attributed that are suitable to the speaker and have an indisputable application to the subject discussed.... Under this genus of exercise fall the species of consolations, exhortation, and letter writing.
>
> First of all, then, one should have in mind what the personality of the speaker is like and to whom the speech is addressed: the speaker's age, the occasion, the place, the social status of the speaker; also the general subject which the projected speeches are going to discuss. Then one is ready to try to say appropriate words. (Aelius Theon, *Exercises* 10.115)[5]

Rhetorical teachers such as Theon designate persona-creation as a rhetorical strategy especially well-suited for creating the author's alter ego in letter writing. The persona created in a composition, however, is not necessarily the same as the author's character. Later handbooks, for instance, delineate *prosopopoeia*'s general designation into three different rhetorical personas. A composition can either convey the character of a known living person ("*ethopoeia*," *ēthopoiia*), a deceased person ("apparition making," *eidōlopoiia*), or an invented person ("*prosopopoeia*," *prosōpopiia*).[6] Each of these can have a different personality than the author herself and can be used to convey a different message: that the author has authority based on personal accomplishments, that the author stands in continuity with and expands upon tradition, or that the author attends to a perspectival gap she fills with an unknown voice. In other words, attribution is a rhetorical activity that performs a practical function. It is a feature authors deploy to persuade readers toward a particular social understanding, action, and response.

Writing under the Name of Another as an African American Woman

Compared to their counterparts—be it white American women and men or African American men—the group of African American women

---

5. Translation from Kennedy, *Progymnasmata*, 47–48.
6. See Aphthonius the Sophist, *Preliminary Exercises* 11 in Kennedy, *Progymnasmata*, 115.

participating in the larger literary production of the nineteenth century (circa 1746–1892) was small.[7] The rhetorical tactics of pseudonymity elevated their visibly marginal status, transforming their works into a site of authorized cultural knowledge and social discourse. In doing so, their cadre forged a pathway of influence that proved literary representation, rhetorical skill, and "by extension humanity, knew no color."[8]

Writing under the name of another was a discursive tactic for women such as Sarah Louisa Forten Purvis (1814–1884) and Ida B. Wells (1862–1931). As the daughter of a leading free black family of the north, Forten joined the philanthropy and social activism of her parents, James (1766–1842) and Charlotte Vandine Forten (1837–1914). She was a regular contributor to the newly established abolitionist newspapers *The Liberator* (1831–1865) and *The Emancipator* (1833–1850), where she wrote under the names "Ada" and "Magawisca."[9] Such newspapers endeavored to showcase "the rising genius of our colored brethren."[10] After refining her skills in African American women's literary societies in the North, like Philadelphia's Female Literary Association (established 1831), Forten wrote for a general readership of women and men, white and African American, and any international readers of the American abolitionist movement.[11] In contrast, Wells was the daughter of formerly enslaved parents from the South, who wrote under the name of "Iola." Wells invented the name to explore and develop her literary skill and social voice while working as a teacher to support herself and her impoverished family. Unlike Forten, the target audience Wells wrote for under the name Iola was primarily African American readers—men and women.

Both Forten and Wells used pseudonyms to present their social and political views forcefully and to mute some of the effects of their intersectionality as literate and outspoken women, Americans, and people of

---

7. Foster, *Written by Herself*, 16.

8. Gay Gibson Cima, "Black and Unmarked: Phillis Wheatley, Mercy Otis Warren, and the Limits of Strategic Anonymity," *Theatre Journal* 52.4 (2000): 495.

9. Scott A. Miltenberger, "Forten, James," in *Encyclopedia of African American History, 1619–1895: From the Colonial Period to the Age of Frederick Douglass* (New York: Oxford University Press, 2006).

10. Quoted in Mary Kelley, "'Talents Committed to Your Care': Reading and Writing Radical Abolitionism in Antebellum America," *New England Quarterly* 88.1 (2015): 71.

11. Marie Lindhorst, "Politics in a Box: Sarah Mapps Douglass and the Female Literary Association, 1831–1833," *Pennsylvania History* 60 (1998): 263–78.

African descent.[12] Whereas Forten spoke from the position of a northern, wealthy, and free African American family, Wells spoke from the experience of a southern, poor, formerly enslaved African American family. Both social positions faced challenges of reception within African American and white American reading communities. The normative social and literary venues in which they sought to contribute as public writers were unaccustomed to their embodied voices, perspectives, and skills.

Sarah Louisa Forten Purvis

The early nineteenth-century American women's literary period in general was "an era of pseudonymous authorship" in which "the identities of abolitionist poets were often veiled" both for white American and African American women, though they did so for different reasons.[13] Inventing or borrowing names to mask one's identity moderated the literary enterprise, enabling the disclosure, acknowledgment, and inclusion of both African American and white American women who might otherwise be ignored. There were, of course, exceptions. For example, Jarena Lee (1783–1855), an African American woman itinerant preacher from the African Methodist Episcopal Church, refused to write under another name. Despite the lack of formal education, she published two autobiographies in her name during her lifetime. Opting for full disclosure, Lee used literary conventions to tell her stories of activism, faith, and ministry, but she did not use the literary strategy of pseudonymity. For Lee, her name and personal story went hand in hand:

> In 1836 I travelled 556 miles, and preached 11 sermons; and felt under much exercise to print a book, and I had some friends to encourage me...; and every circumstance was so favorable that I finally succeeded, and when they were brought home, I sat down in the house and wondered how I should dispose of them; to sell them appears too much like merchandize.[14]

---

12. Patricia Hill Collins and Sirma Bilge, *Intersectionality*, Key Concepts (Malden, MA: Polity Press, 2016); Cima, "Black and Unmarked," 484.

13. Todd S. Gernes, "Poetic Justice: Sarah Forten, Eliza Earle, and the Paradox of Intellectual Property," *New England Quarterly* 71.2 (1998): 230 n. 3.

14. Jarena Lee, *Religious Experience and Journal of Mrs. Jarena Lee: Giving an Account of Her Call to Preach the Gospel; Revised and Corrected from the Original Manuscript Written by Herself* (repr., Philadelphia, 1849), 296.

As one scholar notes:

> In writing "for the satisfaction of such as may follow after me," Jarena Lee was testifying to her belief that her life and her experiences had meaning not only to her family and friends but to the public at large and especially to coming generations. Hers was a consciously political act, directly defying conventions of female self-effacement and modesty which made many women writers apologize for publishing, avoid the persona narrative form, or assume pseudonyms.[15]

According to this description, writers like Lee viewed pseudonymity as a diminished literary endeavor. It hid the names and identities of women, especially white American women, who sought to uphold normative American standards of virtuous womanhood as humble, genteel, submissive, and silent. In contrast, society denied African American women such femininity markers, so there was no need to deploy a rhetorical strategy designed to maintain their appearance.

African American women masked their identity behind the rhetorical strategy of pseudonymity for other reasons—namely, as another form of *visibility* akin to Lee's decision of personal disclosure. For example, one of the pseudonyms Forten employed was a popular nom de plume among both African American and white American women in literary communities of the early nineteenth century, "Ada." The name means "bright one" and derives from one of the first females named after Eve in the Jewish Scriptures and Christian Bible, Adah, who was one of two wives of Lamech (Gen 4:19).[16] For many white women, the pseudonym was a way to maintain their social respectability while writing potentially controversial content. For instance, Eliza Earle Hacker (1807–1846), a contemporary of Forten's and a white American Quaker woman, often used Ada pseudony-

---

15. Foster, *Written by Herself*, 74.

16. As one scholar describes it, "The nom de plume is derived from the first female name in the Old Testament. Genesis. 4:19 states that 'Lamech took unto him two wives: the name of the one was Adah, and the name of the other, Zillah.' 'Adah' is a Hebrew word for 'ornament,' 'but since Lamech's other wife was named Zillah (meaning in shadow), Adah may signify brightness.'... 'Ada' also has classical, dynastic resonances, for an ousted Carian satrap of that name successfully petitioned Alexander the Great to reinstate her authority and the status of her ancestors in 334 B.C." (Gernes, "Poetic Justice," 230 n. 3).

mously.[17] Earle donned an Ada persona to conceal her privileged status as a respected and conforming white American woman who sought to engage other respected white American women readers while advancing otherwise unpopular social movements. In a poem titled "Petitioning Congress," published in the *Massachusetts Spy* on February 1, 1837, Earle concealed her identity under the pen name of Ada while championing women's rights publicly:

> Yet MORAL COURAGE had been freely given,
> By Him whose wisdom never has erred,
> And shall we trample on his gift of Heaven,
> For high and holy purposes conferred?
>
> Ours be the "Duty," not the "Rights of woman,"
> Knowing the strength of nature's dearest ties,
> May we yet "prove that ours are feelings human,"
> Holy affections, kindly sympathies.[18]

Safely hidden behind her Ada persona, Earle invited her sister readers to consider the correlations between abolitionism, social change, and Christian belief. One scholar describes Earle's appropriation of Ada, saying, "Apart from obvious codes of public behavior for some in 1830s America, anonymity must have held different meanings for Earle...: genteel amateurism, concern for personal safety, communitarian spirit, Quaker demureness."[19] Earle's Ada persona was a literary strategy of concealment for someone who wanted to assert public voice and influence, but from a place that maintained her security, access, and status when she was not hidden behind her veil.

Forten, in contrast, donned an Ada persona to raise her visibility and to step out from behind the security of her status. Her persona enabled her to write for a more general audience that was both male and female, white and African American, within literary publications recognized for their antislavery advocacy and position. For example, under her pseudonym

---

17. "In 1837, at the age of thirty, Eliza began publishing in the *Spy* using the pen name 'Ada.' Eliza and her siblings were engaged in a variety of social causes, including the Indians' plight, antislavery, African American enfranchisement, legal reform, the treatment of prisoners, and the care of the mentally ill" (Gernes, "Poetic Justice," 249).

18. Gernes, "Poetic Justice," 251.

19. Gernes, "Poetic Justice," 264.

Ada, Forten wrote a poem called "Appeal to Woman," which was reprinted in the *Liberator* on February 1, 1834. Forten-Ada's poem champions a unified and equitable interracial Christian sisterhood. It invited white American women to rethink their perceptions and treatment of African American women. In this poem, Forten's "Ada" attribution only hides her name but not her social markers as an educated writer and African American woman. The poem is transcribed at length to capture the message conveyed through the persona of the African American Christian, "Ada":

> Oh, woman, woman, in thy brightest hour
> Of conscious worth, of pride, of conscious power,
> Oh, nobly dare to act a Christian's part,
> That well befits a lovely woman's heart!
> Dare to be good, as thou canst dare be great;
> Despise the taunts of envy, scorn and hate;
> **Our "skins may differ," but from thee we claim**
> **A sister's privilege, in a sister's name.**
>
> **We are thy sisters,—God has truly said,**
> That of one hand, the nations he has made.
> Oh, Christian woman, in a Christian land,
> Canst thou unblushing read this great command?
> Suffer the wrongs which wring our inmost heart
> To draw one throb of pity on thy part;
> Our "skins may differ," but from thee we claim
> **A sister's privilege, in a sister's name.**
>
> Oh, woman!—though upon thy fairer brow
> The hues of roses and of lilies glow—
> These soon must wither in their kindred earth,
> From whence **the fair and dark have equal birth.**[20]

Through her poetic moral rhetoric, Forten-Ada claims kinship and equality as a Christian imperative. She asserts that differences in skin color do not diminish the sisterhood established by God's hands and words. An implicit assumption of Forten's appeal is a particularly nineteenth-century conceptualization that race is a biological, inheritable, and immutable

---

20. Quoted in full in Gernes, "Poetic Justice," 239; partially quoted in Kelly, "Talents Committed to Your Care," 64, bold emphasis added.

identity that authentic Christianity should be unbothered by, because, in its original form, Christianness was a universalistic religion. It belonged to no single people or nation. Forten deploys Christianness as a "racially inclusive ideal" that transgresses cultural differences.[21] Forten's pseudonymity was not an act of concealment but a social disclosure and cross-cultural address. Through her understanding of Christian kinship, Forten-Ada championed something entirely different for both cultural locations—a cultural hybrid that includes and involves all equitably and equally.[22]

The phenomenon of literary pseudonymity in Forten's writings generated public acknowledgment. It attached her social perspectives and theological beliefs to her intersectional identities. Even when her real name was unknown, her biography was known. For instance, before Forten's poem "Appeal to Woman" was reprinted in the *Liberator*, a local Massachusetts circular called *The Lowell Observer* published it. While the newspaper did not disclose her full name, it acknowledged Forten's multiple cultural and social identities: "The following lines were written by a young and intelligent lady of color, who, with the other members of the family to which she belongs, has by her perseverance and study, &c., forced the respect even of those who would wish to crush the people of color to the earth. May her appeal not be in vain!"[23] The newspaper's brief description showcases Forten's identity by alluding to her family's collective abolitionist endeavor, which her pen name, by itself, does not communicate. Her literary networks acknowledged her identity and published her writings. They also broadcast Forten-Ada's social status and platform proudly.

For nineteenth-century African American women writers such as Forten, membership in literary societies preceded the rhetorical strategy of public pseudonymity. African American women's literary societies began to appear in the early to mid-nineteenth century in northern cities

---

21. Buell, "Rethinking the Relevance of Race," 452.

22. Richard A. Rogers offers a useful working description for cultural hybridization that leads to a form of transculturation: "Transculturation involves cultural elements created through appropriations from and by multiple cultures such that identification of a single originating culture is problematic. Transculturation involves ongoing, circular appropriations of elements between multiple cultures, including elements that are themselves transcultural." See Richard A. Rogers, "From Cultural Exchange to Transculturation: A Review and Reconceptualization of Cultural Appropriation," *Communication Theory* 16 (2006): 474–503, esp. 491.

23. Gernes, "Poetic Justice," 239 n. 20.

like Philadelphia, Boston, New York, and Washington, DC. Those societies focused on "developing literacy skills in a supportive environment and
promoting 'racial uplift' by improving the education of black children."[24]
They played a vital role in forming women's literary and political leadership. Nurturing safe and affirming reading communities, African
American women participated to "develop leadership abilities, practice
framing constitutions and bylaws, and hone their writing skills."[25] These
societies had a basic structure, though each one had its own variations
and protocols.[26] For example, the Female Literary Association, in which
Forten-Ada refined her literary craft and pseudonymous voice, met each
Tuesday night at a member's home "for the purpose of 'mental improvement in moral and literary pursuits.'"[27] Describing Forten's participation,
one scholar noted that "many of the women, including Sarah Forten,
wrote original essays, poems, and stories. Submitted without names, the
writings were placed in a box and later criticized."[28] Anonymity was a

---

24. Gernes, "Poetic Justice," 232.

25. As one scholar notes, "Some of the most able officers of the women's antislav-
ery conventions … served their apprenticeship in Philadelphia's female literary soci-
eties" (Julie Winch, "'You Have Talents—Only Cultivate Them': Philadelphia's Black
Female Literary Societies and the Abolitionist Crusade," in *The Abolitionist Sisterhood:
Women's Political Culture in Antebellum America*, ed. Jean Fagan Yellin and John C.
Van Hornes [Ithaca, NY: Cornell University Press, 1994], 103).

26. African American women's literary societies promoted antislavery, abolition,
and the education and assimilation of African Americans as full citizens. Some of the
most prominent collectives included (1) the Edgeworth Society, formed by admir-
ers of the Irish novelist Maria Edgeworth (Philadelphia); (2) the Minerva Literary
Association (Philadelphia); (3) the Female Literary Association (Philadelphia 1831);
(4) the Bethel Literary and Historical Association (Washington, DC), and (5) the
Afric-Intelligence Society (Boston). The Female Literary Association of Philadelphia
included members like the Forten Sisters and Grimké, whereas the DC Bethel Literary
Society included nineteenth-century activist and educator Anna Julia Cooper, and the
Afric-Intelligence Society of Boston invited the lectureships from Maria W. Stewart.
See Gernes, "Poetic Justice," 232.

27. Gernes, "Poetic Justice," 232.

28. Gernes summarizes the ethnographic description supplied by a white American woman observer of one of the meetings: "Soon after all were quietly seated, a
short address, prepared for the occasion, was read by the authoress [Sarah Douglass],
a copy of which is herewith sent: it speaks its own praise, therefore comment from me
is unnecessary. The fifty-fourth beautiful and encouraging chapter of Isaiah was then
read. After sitting a short time under a solemn and impressive silence that ensued the
reading of the chapter, one of the company vocally petitioned our heavenly Father for

pedagogical strategy within the societies. The personal identity of the original composer was a second-order matter to the literary contents, rhetorical strategy, and relevance of the address to the plight of African Americans in society. Women, like Forten, forged their literary capacities through collaborative authorship and interpersonal connection. Their organizational cultures of anonymity operated as sites for literary experimentation, freedom of exploratory expression, and the development of social and religious convictions.

After honing their craft through the anonymous pedagogies of the literary societies, skilled writers could use pseudonymity to take their work into the broader literary world. This pseudonymity was not a device for conveying individuality. Even though women writers claimed a name and persona through their pseudonyms, their fundamental formation remained intact—pseudonymity was a rhetorical tool fashioned *from the collective* in service *to the collective*. The editorial introduction to Forten-Ada's poem "The Grave of the Slave," published in the *Liberator* on January 22, 1831, evinces the collective quality of African American women's pseudonymous writings: "To the anonymous writer of the following effusion we offer our thanks, and request a continuance of favors." Associational networks supported the women's learning, development, and publication, even when those same associates and cultural communities did not know the identities behind the pen names. Authorship was a collaborative enterprise to be celebrated and promoted by all rather than a solo project.[29]

---

a continuance of his favor, &c. The remainder of the evening was occupied principally by their severally reading and relating affecting slave tales, calculated to bring forcibly into view the deplorable situation of our fellow-creatures at the south—both the oppressor and oppressed. This interesting interview was closed with singing an appropriate hymn." Cited in Gernes, "Poetic Justice," 232–33 from original source: *Liberator*, July 21, 1832, in Carter, et al., *Black Abolitionist Papers*, 1:204. See also Dorothy Sterling, ed., *We Are Your Sisters: Black Women in the Nineteenth Century* (New York: Norton, 1984), 110–11.

29. Mary Kelly notes that "authorship was not always or necessarily a solitary project but was also a sociable enterprise in which individuals collaborated in the making of literature. Looking at writing from this vantage draws us into associational networks founded by a range of participants, African American women among them, and encourages us to go beyond our concentration on print and consider the equally important oral and scribal forms in which ideas circulated" (Kelly, "Talents Committed to Your Care," 39).

In the tradition of African American women's literary societies, Forten's use of pseudonyms may have started as a form of literary conceal-ment, but it quickly transformed into a *transparent* literary fiction."[30] It served the purpose of public disclosure, recognition, and endorsement. For example, several of Forten's essays published under the name Ada in the *Liberator* included the following editorial introduction, "By a young lady of color," or "The following simple, but beautiful lines, by a young lady of color, will meet a response in many hearts."[31] When Forten's essay "Appeal to Woman" was reprinted in *The Liberator*, the editors revealed her identity in response to the proud behest of her father: "Our correspon-dent 'Ada' and 'Magawisca,' we are proud to learn, is a young colored lady of Philadelphia."[32]

Forten's father, James Forten, wrote a letter a few months before the publication of "Appeal to Woman" to abolitionist William Lloyd Garrison (1805–1879), editor of *The Liberator*. In this letter, Father Forten attrib-uted the writings bearing the signature of Ada to his daughter by saying, "As you are not acquainted with the author of 'Ada' and of 'A,'... I have discovered by accident that these pieces were written by one of my Daugh-ters––."[33] Such public endorsement, from both her family's patriarch and a publisher, amplified Forten's authority. It authenticated her social voice, perspectives, and advocacy. With her signature pseudonyms, Forten not only participated in the unfolding literary tradition that later interpretive communities now label the abolitionist writings of the nineteenth cen-tury, but she also extended that tradition. Pseudonymity, in this case, did not simply recall a historical and literary tradition of a person. Instead, *pseudonymity created a tradition*. It enabled the author—in this case, Sarah Forten—to leave a more significant literary and social imprint of critique, disruption, and correction than she might otherwise have been able to. Through her pseudonymity, she was able to focus attention off of herself

---

30. Meade, *Pseudonymity and Canon*, 4, emphasis added.

31. Sarah Louise Forten, "A Mother's Grief," the *Liberator*, July 7, 1832, https://blackfreedom.proquest.com/a-mothers-grief/; Forten, "Hours of Childhood," the *Lib-erator*, December 15, 1833, https://blackfreedom.proquest.com/hours-of-childhood/; Forten, "To the Hibernia," in *Liberator*, May, 1833, https://blackfreedom.proquest.com/to-the-hibernia/.

32. Quoted in Gernes, "Poetic Justice," 234–35.

33. Quoted in Gernes, "Poetic Justice," 234 n. 11. Also see James Forten Sr. to William Lloyd Garrison, February 23, 1831, in Carter, *Black Abolitionist Papers*, 1:35.

and onto shifting America from an enslaving nation to one genuinely committed to its highest ideals of liberty. As Forten said, writing under her pseudonym Ada, "But will not justice soon arise, / And plead the cause of the depised? / For oh! my country, must it be, / That they still find a foe in thee?"[34]

Forten's pseudonymity was also a mechanism for bearing witness to the African American experience, particularly enslavement and prejudice. Known for her poetic writings, Forten often combined the narrative and existential testimonies of enslaved African Americans with lyrical poetry. For instance, stylized as testimonies of enslaved people in poetic form, her 1831 poem "The Slave" opens as a collective first-person witness: "Our sires who once in freedom's cause, / Their boasted freedom sought and won, / For deeds of glory gained applause, / When patriot feelings led them on."[35] Whether Forten herself or her family personally experienced enslavement was not the issue. Through the voice of Ada, she was able to express the collective experience of enslavement by African Americans and the struggles associated with it.

Forten often combined the stylistic writing of essays and treatises with the more personal letter form as a way to mediate between two cultural communities. For instance, in her letter essay entitled "The Abuse of Liberty" in the *Liberator* on March 26, 1831, Forten adopted her second pen name from a popular literary character, Magawisca:

> I know no evil under the wide-spread canopy of Heaven, so great as the abuse of man's liberty; and no where has this vice a more extensive sway, than in this boasted land of Philanthropy, that offers to every white man the right to enjoy life, liberty, and happiness. I say every white man, because those who cannot shew a fair exterior, (no matter what be the noble qualities of their mind) are to be robbed of the rights by which they were endowed by an all-wise and merciful Creator, who, in his great wisdom, cast a sable hue over some of the "lords of creation."[36]

Forten borrowed the name Magawisca from the 1827 historical romance novel by Catharine Maria Sedgwick, *Hope Leslie; or Early Times in Massachusetts.*

---

34. Sarah Louisa Forten, "The Slave," in the *Liberator*, 1831, https://blacktreedom. proquest.com/the-slave/.

35. Forten, "Slave."

36. Sarah Forten Purvis, "The Abuse of Liberty" (1831), in Robbins and Gates, *Portable Nineteenth-Century African American Women Writers*, 253.

The book conveys early overtones of cross-cultural feminist ideas of equity, exchange, and relationship between Indigenous Americans and colonial settlers and their violent collisions. In turn, the book assumes a rare position for early nineteenth century popular literary fiction by espousing an Indigenous American female heroine who moves between two racialized cultural worlds. Primarily set in 1643 as "a story that echoes the history of Pocahontas," the fictional Magawisca was a daughter of the Pequot chieftain Mononotto.[37] Facing racially charged attacks and Puritan colonial imprisonment, Magawisca expresses revolutionary defiance near the end of the book. She addresses her Christian jailers, saying, "I demand of thee death or liberty."[38] Throughout the book, Magawisca is a mediating and liberationist actor, moving between the racial-religious groups of her Indigenous people and Christian settlers, warning both about the dangers of discord and distrust. Four years after the novel's successful publication, Forten adopted the character's name as a statement about her own mediating role between white American and African American communities and about her defiant task to speak against the misuse of liberty and its corrupted, one-sided form in American society.

Forten viewed herself as joining God's preference for justice and equality by wading in the pool of revolution. Behind the relative safety of her Magawisca pseudonym, she was free to exhort her readers to participate in God's actions rather than stand aside while God remakes creation:

> Awake from your lethargy; exert every nerve; cast off the yoke from the oppressed; let the bondmen go free; and cry unto your offended God to send freedom with its strong battlements to impede the progress of

---

37. Sedgwick describes her character saying, "The Indian stranger was tall for her years, which did not exceed fifteen. Her form was slender, flexible, and graceful; and there was a freedom and loftiness in her movement which, though tempered with modesty, expressed a consciousness of high birth. Her face, although marked by the peculiarities of her race, was beautiful even to the European eye. Her features were regular, and her teeth white as pearls; but there must be something beyond symmetry of feature to fix the attention, and it was an expression of dignity, thoughtfulness, and a deep dejection that made the eye linger on Magawisca's face, as if it were perusing there the legible record of her birth and wrongs." See Catharine M. Sedgwick, *Hope Leslie; or Early Times in Massachusetts* (New York: White, Gallaher, & White, 1827), vi, 40–41; Ashley Reed, *Heaven's Interpreters: Women Writers and Religious Agency in Nineteenth-Century America* (Ithaca: Cornell University Press, 2020), 25–52.

38. Quoted in Jeffrey Insko, "Anachronistic Imaginings: 'Hope Leslie's Challenge to Historicism," *American Literary History* 16.2 (2004): 179.

this raging flood;—I say, cry unto Him for aid; for can you think He, thee Great Spirit, who created all men free and equal—He, who made the sun to shine on the black man as well as on the white, will always allow you to rest tranquil on your downy couches? No,—He is just, and his anger will not always slumber. He will wipe the tear from Ethiopia's eye; He will shake the tree of liberty, and its blossoms shall spread over the earth.[39]

In this address, Forten prompts her readers, particularly her white American male readers, to join God's revolutionary activity of justice and equality for all human beings. The name Magawisca was assigned not merely out of the need to wield power, authority, and influence. It was penned as a dynamic literary action to prompt cross-cultural religious responses.

When she took on the nom de plume of Ada, Forten did not erase the markers of her African American identity. Similarly, when Forten took on the face of Magawisca, she preserved her own heritage, casting the indigenous literary character into the body and literary voice of an African American woman. It was a rhetorical endeavor of owning her identity and a mechanism for being seen, not unseen. This hybridization also implicitly signaled a relationship between indigenous and African Americans. It aligned her cultural community (African Americans) with indigenous Americans, who negotiated similar experiences of racism, genocide, displacement, and disenfranchisement. [40]

---

39. Purvis, "Abuse of Liberty," 254.

40. Forten's appropriation of a name taken from an indigenous American character in a novel raises questions about the complicated interactions between various nonindigenous racial and ethnic groups with indigenous Americans in the nineteenth century. For example, Sylvester Johnson (*The Myth of Ham in Nineteenth-Century American Christianity: Race, Heathens, and the People of God* [New York: Palgrave, 2004], 48) discusses the experiences of victimization and othering shared between African Americans and indigenous peoples during the colonial period by saying, "The 'other' as Native American or as Negro was frequently victimized by historical forces of identity conquest and physical domination." Forten's appropriation of an indigenous voice and face as a pseudonym raises questions about Others in relation to African American and white American Christians. It highlights that she recognizes a resonance, even authority, in assuming the literary face of an indigenous American woman. However, more research on that relationship is necessary beyond this book's scope to analyze where such appropriation also goes awry and potentially distorts and/or betrays both communities.

Ida B. Wells

Like Forten, Ida B. Wells also participated in a literary association, specifically one in Memphis, Tennessee, which she described as "a lyceum composed mainly of teachers of the public schools." Wells said they met weekly on Fridays at a local church, where they collaborated on literary exercises that "consisted of recitations, essays, and debates interspersed with music." She described those literary events as "a breath of life to me, for this program was like the Friday afternoon oratoricals in school. The exercises always closed with the reading of the *Evening Star*—a spicy journal prepared and read by the editor."[41] As a participant in this literary association, Wells eventually became the editor of the Memphis *Evening Star*; from this platform, she invented her Iola persona:

> All of this, although gratifying, surprised me very much, for I had had no training except what the work on the *Evening Star* had given me, and no literary gifts and graces. But I had observed and thought much about conditions as I had seen them in the country schools and churches. I had an instinctive feeling that the people who had little or no school training should have something coming into their homes weekly which dealt with their problems in a simple, helpful way. So in weekly letters to the *Living Way*, I wrote in a plain, common-sense way on the things which concerned our people. Knowing that their education was limited, I never used a word of two syllables where one would serve the purpose. I signed these articles "Iola."[42]

Pseudonymity in Forten's writings operated as a device for witnessing *about* the African American experience; Wells, writing under the name Iola, engaged pseudonymity for witnessing *to* the African American experience. Wells wanted to speak directly to the lives of the community she was most concerned about. More importantly, she wanted to engage her African American readership in social matters they were experiencing that were unnamed and unaddressed by other newspaper outlets, churches, or even service organizations. Her pen name enabled her to speak into an unfilled space.

---

41. Ida B. Wells, *Crusade for Justice: The Autobiography of Ida B. Wells*, 2nd ed., Negro American Biographies and Autobiographies (Chicago: University of Chicago Press, 2020), 42–43.

42. Wells, *Crusade for Justice*, 43–44.

While pseudonymity gave some nineteenth-century African American women a platform for their progressive voices and perspectives, it also provided cover for others experimenting with their social voices and developing their public literary style. As one of few African American women with the literary skills and opportunities to embark on the courageous endeavor of journalism in the late nineteenth century, Wells took on the pen name Iola to shield herself from uninvited backlash and censure as she explored how to write:

> Although I had made a reputation in school for thoroughness and discipline in the primary grades, I was never promoted above the fourth grade in all my years as a teacher. The confinement and monotony of the primary work began to grow distasteful. The correspondence I had built up in newspaper work gave me an outlet through which to express the real "me" and I enjoyed my work to the utmost.[43]

"Iola" was the product of Well's rhetorical strategy of "person-making."[44] The name was previously unknown by Wells's African American communities; thus, it carried no built-in authority, platform, or standing. Wells was able to not only take on the persona, but she was able to infuse it with rhetorical aim and audience. As a blank slate, the Iola persona gave Wells room to experiment with her literary voice and increase her influence. Iola was both detached from Wells's personal story and informed by it. The Iola pseudonym did not render Wells invisible; instead, it was the reverse. Over time, her larger readership came to know who she was as both simultaneously Iola and Wells.[45]

Writing on the topic of race in America, Wells-Iola was an investigative reporter for the African American community. Black newspapers

---

43. Wells, *Crusade for Justice*, 51.

44. Some of the ancient Greek rhetorical handbooks theorists connote the character-making endeavor of rhetoric *ethopoeia*. See the discussion of *ethopoeia* by Aphthonius the Sophist, *Preliminary Exercise*, in Kennedy, *Progymnasmata*, 115.

45. Wells's Iola identity may have been commended by a renowned literary writer and contemporary, Frances Ellen Watkins Harper, who wrote a book published in 1892 titled *Iola Leroy*. Scholars continue to debate whether it was Harper's homage to Wells, which appears plausible. For literary attestation of the friendship shared between Wells and Harper, see Wells, *Crusade for Justice*, 78; John Ernest, "From Mysteries to Histories: Cultural Pedagogy in Frances E. W. Harper's Iola Leroy," *American Literature* 64.3 (1992): 509.

recognized her writings as one with a versatile and compelling voice. One of her journalistic contemporaries, Lucy Wilmot Smith (1861–1889), reported that Wells was dubbed the "Princess of the Press" by her predominantly male editorial colleagues. Smith further reports,

> No writer, the male fraternity not excepted, has been more extensively quoted none struck harder blows at the wrongs and weaknesses of the race. Her readers are equally divided between the sexes. She reaches the men by dealing with the political aspect of the race question, and the women she meets around the fireside.... By the way it is her ambition to edit a paper. She believes there is no agency so potent as the press in reaching and elevating a people. Her contributions are distributed among the leading race journals.[46]

Wells's alternate attribution functioned as an extension of her identity. She fabricated Iola to provide practical advice on race and citizenship, which informed African American communities' knowledge of current events impacting them. Mainstream white American newspapers did not provide such information and perspectives.[47] The writings of Wells-Iola, therefore, offered a vital service to the literary tradition of the nineteenth-century black press. She both participated in and extended that tradition by deploying Iola as an insider voice and discursive literary tactic for addressing her community.

Pseudonymity was neither a strategy of deception nor a mechanism for invisibility. Wells's rhetorical strategy of deploying transparent literary fiction in the persona of Iola correlates with descriptions of *ethopoeia* and *prosopopoeia* supplied in ancient Greek textbooks:

> *Ethopoeia* [*êthopoiia*] is imitation of the character of a proposed speaker.... *Ethopoeia* has a known person as speaker and only invents the characterization, which is why it is called "character-making."... In the case of *prosopopoeia*, everything is invented, both character and

---

46. Wells, *Crusade for Justice*, 54.

47. Otis Sandford, Hardin Chair of Excellence in Economic and Managerial Journalism at the University of Memphis and leading scholar of journalist history, described the contribution of Wells and the larger black press by saying, "The white press, the newspapers of the day ... ignored Black people unless they were committing crimes or being lynched." The quote is recorded at an online resource titled, "Exposing the 'Thread-Bare Lie': How Ida B. Wells Used Investigative Journalism to Uncover the Truth about Lynching," *Chicago Stories*, WTTW, https://tinyurl.com/SBL4533c.

speaker ... which is why this is called "person-making." (Aphthonius, *Preliminary Exercises* 11)[48]

Like the rhetorical expectations of *ethopoeia* and *prosopopoeia*, Wells used the rhetorical strategy of pseudonymity to find her voice and build a trustworthy rapport within her cultural community. Through this compositional strategy, she infused her Iola-persona with credibility, relevance, and affirmation of the lived experiences of her audience. Moreover, she nurtured intragroup conversations and reflections on the social currents of African Americans and their broader locations and interactions with their white American neighbors.

The Rhetoric of Titling African American Women's Discourses

Another integral feature of nineteenth-century African American women's literature was the phenomenon of titling. Titles did more than provide an enticing tagline. They often identified writers' social locations and identities, such as when the *Liberator* introduced Forten's testimony poems by identifying her as "a young lady of color."[49] This was particularly the case in African American spiritual autobiographies. For example, Jarena Lee published her spiritual autobiography in 1839 under the title, *The Life and Religious Experience of Jarena Lee, a Colored Lady: Giving an Account of the Call to Preach the Gospel.* Similarly, a contemporary of Lee, Mary Prince (ca. 1788–after 1833), published her autobiography in 1831 under the title *The History of Mary Prince, a West Indian Slave.* Publishing her story almost thirty years later in 1860, Elizabeth Keckley (c. 1818–1907) titled her story *Behind the Scenes, or, Thirty Years a Slave, and Four Years in the White House.* Others titled their works by identifying their cultural communities, which in turn identified their embodiments and social location, such as Maria Stewart's (1803–1879) *Productions of Mrs. Maria W. Stewart Presented to the First African Baptist Church and Society, of the City of Boston* in 1835. Like pseudonyms, the titles of African American women's writings help shape reader expectations about their authors' identities.

Titles were a rhetorical mechanism for asserting presence and legitimacy in a literary tradition that sought to Other, silence, and even overlook these women and their larger communities. As one scholar summarizes:

---

48. See Kennedy, *Progymnasmata*, 115–16.
49. Forten, "Mother's Grief."

From the earliest examples of *Briton Hammon, Negro Man* (1760) to *Olaudah Equiano, or Gustavus Vassa, the African* (1789) to *Solomon Bayley, Formerly a Slave* (1825), *A Colored Female of Philadelphia* (1832), and *Jarena Lee, a Colored Lady* (1836), the names of African American authors were regularly identified by race. Obviously, such insertions manifest the assumption of a crucial difference. And, the very significance of that difference becomes apparent when one considers the rarity of white writers who identify themselves by race and of male writers who include the fact of their sex. The writings of blacks, and women, were the unusual, the Other, and were so identified even when their form and content were visually indistinguishable from those of white men.[50]

At the outset, how these women described their work was how the writers identified themselves. A persistent feature in African American religious writings of the nineteenth century was "to acknowledge a difference important enough to mention specifically" while implying "an equality of experiences and the legitimacy of erecting an African American life as an example."[51] Like the pseudonyms they employed, their book titles functioned as rhetorical strategies that accorded visibility to the women writers who penned literary productions to capture the struggles and genius of their African American communities—many of whom identified as "Christian" in some form.

Conclusion

Pseudonymity was a rhetorical strategy for erecting African American lives as authoritative conveyors of theological truth and social justice. Writing under the name of another—be it borrowed or invented, character-making or person-making—enabled African American women to speak from and toward configurations of Christianness, citizenship, and community. It was a mechanism for creating authority and rendering legitimacy to its authors, as opposed to a mechanism for leveraging a preestablished authority that the authors hid behind.

Pseudonymity approached from African American women's literary tradition is not a matter of deception but voice. It was an attempt to be counted as participating in the social experiment instead of being

---

50. Foster, *Written by Herself*, 66.
51. Foster, *Written by Herself*, 66.

discarded. Nineteenth-century African American women invented and adopted alternate literary personas to experiment with their public literary voices and to develop their craft. These women used pseudonyms to participate as full members of established literary traditions, even as they attempted to rework their structures. They created forms of cultural adaptation, exchange, and transculturation in order to increase their cultural communities' visibility and speak to the injustices they experienced. It was a true paradox. Pseudonyms, within nineteenth-century African American writings, were not attempts at concealment and deception but rather transparency and truth-telling.

6
Pseudonymity as 2 Peter's Strategy for Othering

Interpreting 2 Peter through the phenomenon of the transparent literary fiction practiced by nineteenth-century African American women provides a fresh examination of the letter's pseudonymous status. When viewed through the circumstances surrounding pseudonyms in the writings of Wells and Forten (see chapter 5), the matter of 2 Peter's pseudonymous character becomes less important than its rhetorical suasion and cultural practicality. The question becomes: what does assuming the name of another allow the authors of 2 Peter to *do* culturally and socially? The $pl.$? women's use of pseudonymity produced a different outcome than we will see in 2 Peter, but the answer to this question is almost the same. Like their nineteenth century counterparts, the authors of 2 Peter use pseudonymity to establish credibility, expand the literary tradition, and provide witness to injustice.

The Evidence for the Pseudonymity of 2 Peter

The letter of 2 Peter provides the necessary details to establish the historic Peter as the face of its discourse. Its salutation invokes the authoritative legacy—both in story and influence—of its implied author, the historical Peter: "Symeōn Peter, an enslaved person and apostle of Jesus Christ …" (2 Pet1:1), and the opening verses acknowledge that the letter has an intended audience ("you"), though specifics regarding their location, demographics, and identities are unnamed. Later, the letter positions itself as "the second letter I [Peter] write to you" (3:1), a statement that helps prompt the letter's designation as 2 Peter.

Despite this façade, 2 Peter is not written by the apostle Peter, who was likely executed under Emperor Nero around 60–63 CE, almost a century before the probable composition date of the letter around 140–160 CE.[1] A number of features betray the letter's pseudonymous character. First is the controversy in 2 Pet 3:15–16, which concerns Paul's letters. In this passage, the writers mention that "our beloved brother Paul wrote" to the community and spoke "in all his letters" about the same issues 2 Peter addresses. The tenses here signal that time has elapsed. Paul's letters have circulated beyond their original destinations to a broader audience. Not only did Paul's letters go further geographically, but they also transcended their original timestamp. One need only read 1 Clement's reference to Paul's original letter(s) to the Corinthians almost fifty years after Paul's ministry to observe how his popularity and authority are assumed in contemporary conversation: "Take up the epistle of the blessed Paul the apostle. What did he first write to you at the beginning of the gospel?" (1 Clem. 47.1–3 [trans. Holmes] // 1 Cor 1:11–12). Similarly, the letter of 2 Peter does not advocate for the apostolic authority and significance of Paul's writings as a future goal but names it as a present reality, which is more consonant with the message of 1 Clement in the latter part of the first century (i.e., after the deaths of both Peter and Paul) than references within Paul's letters and Acts earlier in the century. Furthermore, 2 Pet 3:15–16 refers to Paul's letters as "scripture," a development establishing the authority and concept of a canon that dates well after the apostles' death.[2]

Second, the authors infuse into 2 Peter the generic character of a testament (1:12–15) and a "mini apocalypse" (3:3–13), both of which "were wholly dominated by a pseudo-epigraphic authorship."[3] As Richard Bauckham argues, "In Jewish usage the testament was a fictional literary genre.... In most cases they were entirely free invention. It is highly probable that they were normally accepted as such."[4] Second Peter adopts the

---

1. For the dominant tradition about Peter's crucifixion under Nero, see Acts Pet. 30–41; Eusebius, *Hist. eccl.* 2.25.5–8; 3.1.2–3; Tertullian, *Scorp.* 15; cf. 1 Clem. 5.4; Apoc. Pet. 2.10–13. The translation and versification of the Apocalypse of Peter referenced follows the schema provided by Beck, *Justice and Mercy in the Apocalypse of Peter,* 67. For an alternative tradition that suggests Peter survived Nero's *Christos*-targeted persecution movement in Rome, see Tertullian, *Praescr.* 32; Epistle of Clement to James 2.

2. Meade, *Pseudonymity and Canon,* 180.

3. Fornberg, *Early Church in a Pluralistic Society,* 16.

4. Bauckham, *Jude, 2 Peter,* 134, emphasis original. Bauckham's assertion about the known pseudonymous quality of testament literature has been recently tested and challenged in scholarship. See E. Randolph Richards and Kevin J. Boyle, "Did

literary form and rhetorical invention of a testament and similarly functions as "transparent fiction." This should not be seen as some form of
deceptive fiction and identity concealment. Rather, like the pseudonyms
of nineteenth-century African American women writers, the transparent
fictive authorship of 2 Peter can be understood as a mechanism for preserving sources and traditions from the past deemed applicable for later
situations. As one scholar says, "Second Peter ... bears neither the form
nor the character of a pseudepigrapha, and since it includes some genuine Petrine material, it is understandably attributed to its first and most
famous contributor."[5] Pseudonymity in 2 Peter was not an attempt to pass
false source material to unsuspecting readers. Instead, 2 Peter's pseudonymity repackages recognizable Petrine source material and updates the
relevance of the stories and experiences archived in its pages for the current readership.

Third, 2 Peter demonstrates an unquestionably post-Petrine *Sitz im
Leben*. One of the central problems of 2 Peter is the delay of the Coming
(*parousia*, 1:16; 3:4, 12). As one hypothetical critic asks, "Where is the
promise of his coming? For ever since the fathers fell asleep, all things
have continued as they were from the beginning of creation" (3:4). Such
statements would have been impossible if Peter were alive (cf. Mark 9:1).
Pseudonymity is further substantiated by the fact that this concern is not
characteristic of earlier traditions, as captured in 1 Pet 4:7 with its earnest
expectation of Christ's imminent return. Instead, 2 Peter reflects upon
the problem of Christ's delay in coming (3:4) and the vacancy left with
the passing of apostolic leadership (3:2). A similar concern is acknowledged in writings like those found in the Clement tradition. For example,
2 Clem. 11.2 records, "For the prophetic word says: 'Wretched are the
double-minded, those who doubt in their heart and say, "We heard all
these things even in the days of our fathers, and though we have waited
day after day we have seen none of them"'" ([trans. Holmes]; see also
1 Clem. 23.3). Although the authors of 2 Peter reach back to the legacy of
Peter to address the matter of God's coming, the crisis of fulfillment is a
later, post-Peter phenomenon.

A fourth feature betraying the pseudonymous character of 2 Peter is
the use of the second-person plural reference for the early apostles. Second

---

Ancients Know the Testaments Were Pseudepigraphic? Implications for 2 Peter," *BBR*
30 (2020): 403–23.

5. Witherington, *Socio-rhetorical Commentary on 1–2 Peter*, 271.

Peter 3:1b–2 says, "I awaken your group's sincere minds. To remind you of the words having been previously spoken through the holy prophets and the commandment of the Lord and Savior also spoken through *your apostles*." Here, the letter writers do not refer to the apostles using a first-person plural referent ("us") or in terms like the shared apostolic witness rehearsed earlier in 2 Pet 1:18, which uses "we": "And *we* heard this voice carried out of heaven when *we* were with him on the holy mountain." Ownership of the apostolic witness slips in 3:2, and the artificial creation of the Peter mask lapses. It is an unintended disclosure of the identity behind the literary persona put forward in the letter. The significance of this exposure is more pronounced when compared to the intentionally veiled disclosures of Forten-Ada in her "An Appeal to Woman" (see chapter 5). Although her actual name remains hidden until revealed by her publisher and family, Forten nonetheless intentionally comes out from behind the ambiguity of the Ada persona to address white American women as an African American woman. Forten's slight pseudonymous lapse strengthens the cultural position and proposition of that writing, whereas, in the case of 2 Peter, such a lapse weakens the author's position. It raises more questions than it answers regarding trustworthiness and deception, particularly for modern readers shaped by Western conceptions of authenticity, reliability, and accuracy.

The pseudonymity of 2 Peter was recognized in antiquity. For instance, in the first extant systematic, ecumenical history (fourth century), Eusebius refers to the questionable status of this writing: "Of Peter, one epistle, that which is called his first, is admitted, and the ancient presbyters used this in their own writings as unquestioned, but the so-called second Epistle we have not received as canonical"; that is, it is not recognized as an undisputed work of the apostle, "but nevertheless it has appeared useful to many, and has been studied with other Scriptures" (Eusebius, *Hist eccl.* 3.10–4.3 [Lake, LCL]). In spite of its pseudonymity, the letter is still recognized as a valid extension of the Petrine tradition and Christian teaching.

Pseudonymity in 2 Peter as Credibility and Literary Extension

Whatever its origin, 2 Peter consistently invokes Peter's authority, witness, and literary legacy and goes to great lengths to attach its authorship to the historical Peter. Second Peter 1:12–15, for instance, participates in the well-known tradition that Jesus disclosed Peter's death to him: "Knowing that the taking off of my tent is soon, as our Lord Jesus Christ made clear to me" (compare John 13:36–37; 21:18–19; Acts of Peter 35; Acts of Peter and Paul 81–82). Following this, the letter retells the transfiguration story (2 Pet 1:16–18), though the retelling also includes elements of Jesus's baptism story as recounted in the Gospel of Matthew (see Matt 3:17). In both cases, the authors of 2 Peter underline the strong eyewitness character of the historical Peter, as if that needed to be reasserted.

Such rhetorical emphasis has led some scholars to suggest that the letter was written to defend the Petrine tradition.[6] Certainly, diversity was a common theme in the literary attestations of early Christianity. Christianness was multiple and, in turn, constantly under negotiation and adjudication. For example, in one of the earliest writings included in the New Testament, 1 Corinthians, Paul acknowledges rival apostolic traditions with which believers identify and assign value: "For it has been reported to me by Chloe's people that there are quarrels among you, my brothers and sisters. What I mean is that each of you says, 'I belong to Paul,' or 'I belong to Apollos,' or 'I belong to Cephas' [that is, Peter],[7] or 'I belong to Christ'" (1 Cor 1:11–12). Here, both Paul and Peter are referenced as sites of partisanship among the members. Likewise, the story about the Jerusalem Council meeting in Acts 15 portrays Paul and Peter as joint adjudicators of competing community teachings and perspectives.[8] Acts positions the two men on the same side of a debate regarding the inclusion of non-Israelite believers in the Christian community. Paul's account of the event in the letter of Galatians similarly places both men on the side of inclusion. However, Paul's account contains hints that some form of marginalization, difference, and distance existed between the two. According to Paul, the ranks of the apostolic circle were colored by prejudice that supposedly Peter succumbed to and Paul did not (Gal 2). The Acts account presents a process for negotiating between the community's diverse demographics, including non-Israelite messianic believers, while the Galatians account conveys a moment of confronta-

---

6. Robert Grant, *Heresy and Criticism: The Search for Authenticity in Early Christian Literature* (Louisville: Westminster John Knox, 1993), 4, 89–90; Edgar Krentz, "Peter: Confessor, Denier, Proclaimer, Validator of Proclomation—A Study in Diversity," *CurTM* 37.4 (2010): 330–31.

7. Here Peter is referred to in the Aramaic form of the Greek name, which is a common Pauline tendency; see 1 Cor 3:22; 9:5; 15:5.

8. Here Peter is referenced in both the Greek and Semitic forms of his name; see Acts 15:7 for *Petros* and 15:14 for *Symeōn*.

tion rather than conciliation. But neither denies that a diverse Christian constituency exists.

The heterogeneity of Christianness is also represented in later early Christian traditions. For example, at the turn toward the second century, 1 Clement recalls the history of rival traditions in 1 Corinthians as a mechanism for addressing intragroup rivalry in the current generation's community: "Truly he wrote to you in the Spirit about himself and Cephas and Apollos, because even then you had split into factions. Yet that splitting into factions brought less sin upon you, for you were partisans of highly reputed apostles and of a man approved by them" (1 Clem. 47:3–4; [trans. Holmes]). Diverse communities of Christianness relate separately to Paul and Peter as sites of authority and difference, but within the early tradition, the pair are understood to share a common teaching. For example, Irenaeus designates the pair a foundational unit in establishing the apostolic tradition and its succession while critiquing competing claims of apostolic authority. Like 2 Peter (2:1), Irenaeus dubs other Christian traditions heresies (*Haer.* 1.11.1; cf. 1.23.2; 1.28.1) as opposed to what they were, alternative—even "minoritized"[9]—Christian formulations: "Some of them declare themselves similar to Jesus; while others, still more mighty, maintain that they are superior to his disciples, such as Peter and Paul, and the rest of the apostles, whom they consider to be in no respect inferior to Jesus" (*Haer.* 1.25.2; cf. 3.3.2; adapted from *ANF* 1:350). Common across all these examples are the attestations of competing formulations of Christianness with not only Jesus but Peter and Paul as fixtures within the multiple traditions.

It would be easy, then, to assert that 2 Peter was intended to defend Petrine authority vis-à-vis Paul. This seems to be the case on first reading, for instance, the sixth or seventh-century pseudo-Petrine apocryphal Acts of Peter and Paul. The opening episode of the writing narrates diaspora

---

9. The term *minoritized* is used here to convey the "relation of domination and subordination, superiority and inferiority ... whereby one formation erects itself as dominant while casting others as minorities. Consequently, a minority formation is the product of a process of minoritization whereby that formation has been rendered minoritized by another" (Liew and Segovia, *Reading Biblical Texts Together*, xiii). The process of minoritization Liew and Segovia map as "at work in all axes of human identity" is evident in the discourse of 2 Peter and Irenaeus as they designate certain understandings Christian belief divergent by marking them heresies in need of ousting or eradication as opposed to mediation, conversation, and coexistence.

Hellenistic Jews petitioning Emperor Nero to forbid Paul's visit to Rome out of concerns that he will disrupt their communities with his claims about a Messiah. In response, the Roman communities of Christiannness, led by Peter, send a correspondence to Paul warning him of the danger:

> And while they were thus doing, some of those that had repented out of the nations, and that had been baptized at the preaching of Peter, sent elders to Paul with a letter to the following effect: Paul, dear servant of our Lord Jesus Christ, and brother of Peter, the first of the apostles, we have heard from the rabbis of the Jews that are in this Rome, the greatest of the cities, that they have asked Caesar to send into all of his govern-ments, in order that, wherever you may be found, you may be put to death. But we have believed, and do believe, that as God does not sepa-rate the two great lights which He has made, so He is not to part you from each other, that is neither Peter from Paul, nor Paul from Peter; but we positively believe in our Lord Jesus Christ, into whom we have been baptized, that we have become worthy also of your teaching. (adapted from *ANF* 8:477)

Closer analysis of the episode reveals the writing narrates a kind of soli-darity and apostolic partnership between Peter and Paul. In this text, Peter is not only an apostolic authority of emergent Christianness. He is also like Paul, an authoritative letter writer collaborating with his communi-ties to pen and circulate letters.[10] Dated centuries after the composition of 2 Peter, however, the apocryphal account renders more explicitly the tradition 2 Peter gestures toward in the mid-second century. Neither writ-ing appears to defend Petrine tradition as much as they assert a shared apostolic authority and literary endeavor between Peter and Paul. The two apostolic figures are not competitors, but compatriots.

Viewing the pseudonymous character of 2 Peter through the phenom-enon of African American women's moral discourse tilts the pendulum toward reading it as a rhetorical strategy of invocation rather than apol-ogetics. Among the nineteenth century women, biographical details are asserted, not defended. They are not intended to justify the authors' background or traditions. Rather, they are asserted to provide context to

---

10. Rather than a Peter-Paul conflict, the Acts of Peter and Paul narrates a Jew-Christian conflict. It raises concerns about emerging anti-Semitic rhetoric and con-ceptions in early Christian literature. Although not the focus of the discussion here, readers should be aware of this effect.

their words and assign gravity to their names. Their names alone carried no authority or influence, but coupled with details about their intersectional identities, their names disrupted popular sensibilities that African American women did not write with informed perspectives. Be they commendable or derogatory—the biographic details infuse the pseudonyms with significance and resonance. For example, the introductory label often accompanying Forten's pen name, Ada, describes her as "an intelligent colored Lady." This is not a defense; it is simply a statement associating Forten with African American communities and human capacities to acquire and apply knowledge. Similarly, Lee's titular label in her spiritual autobiography, "Jarena Lee, a colored woman," establishes the significance of her work because the name did not carry notoriety prior to the composition. The idea of an African American woman having a personal story of publishable quality and insight added authority and interest to Lee's story.

In contrast, the biblical letter did not have to assume a judicial strategy to defend Peter's authority because there was nothing to defend. The historic Peter's witness and literary contribution was a persistent stream in the tradition. There was no need to defend it. If the rhetorical endeavor of 2 Peter was an *apologia*, other traditions may be considered more influential and impressive and, thus, have a similar rhetorical impact as the biographical details Forten and Lee supplied to add a layer of distinction to their literary voices. Material that could provide greater distinction and proximate authority to Jesus might include Peter's commission experiences with Jesus (Matt 4:18–22; cf. Matt 28:16–20), his witness of Jesus walking on water (Matt 14:22–33; Mark 6:45–52), the healing of his mother-in-law (Mark 1:29–31), or any portion of the ascension stories (Luke 24:50–53). Second Peter mentions none of these. Peter's *apologia* speeches in Acts are yet another clue for what material might support a more compelling defense.[11] For example, Peter's defense of the Pentecost disruption references his participation in the group-witness of Jesus's resurrection, saying, "This Jesus God raised up, and of that all of us are witnesses" (Acts 2:32). In another defense speech, explaining the healing miracle of a man to temple authorities in Jerusalem, Peter references his eyewitness testimony of both Jesus's crucifixion and resurrection (4:10). Any one of these are potentially stronger biographical details for defending Peter's distinct apostolic witness than the

---

11. Kennedy, *New Testament Interpretation through Rhetorical Criticism*, 115.

ones found in 2 Peter.[12] Again, however, the letter did not need to appeal to any of these traditions. The authority of Peter was "beyond dispute."[13]

The authors of 2 Peter then are not deploying the name of Peter and the selection of biographical details to defend his apostolic legacy. Instead, Peter's legacy is borrowed to establish *the authors'* credibility and amplify the cultural influence of the letter's point of view and social intervention. The authors are no longer simply an isolated element of Christianness. Their words continue the stream of tradition dating back to the prophetic, wisdom, and apocalyptic discourses of Jewish scriptures; the gospels; and the influential teachings of Paul's letters.[14] Their letter becomes the *second* letter of the Petrine tradition.

In promoting the traditions of their community in the name of Peter, the writers not only hearken back to an apostolic figure but also skillfully contemporizes the figure. In the way that Forten borrowed and then reworked the Ada name into her embodiment, 2 Peter casts the historical Peter as an embodiment of the current Christian community, sharing the same expectations and experiencing the same challenges as the recipients of the letter. In doing so, the authors use Peter's face to recalibrate

---

12. The absence of the Acts material on Peter in the letter is striking. While Acts and 2 Peter appear closer together on the matter of Peter and Paul's alliance than earlier traditions like Gal 2, the nature of that relational harmony is different. The book of Acts depicts Peter and Paul as aligned on cultural and ethnic inclusion into the believing community (Acts 15). Even many of their speeches mirror each other in content and form (Acts 2:14–36 // 13:15–41). In contrast 2 Peter depicts their symmetry as influential writers of the tradition who espouse similar Christian positions in terms of belief and ways of life. This difference may signal that the authors of 2 Peter likely knew of the Acts tradition. Still, they either did not know it as well as other traditions, like the Synoptics or the Apocalypse of Peter, or they knowingly chose to cast a different Peter persona—namely, one resistant to cultural difference and diversity of thought within Christian communities.

13. Fornberg, *Early Church in a Pluralistic Society*, 15.

14. David G. Meade recalls J. Zmijewski's argument that "the heart of the matter is the relation of NT pseudonymity to Christian preaching, or, more precisely, to the preservation and propagation of apostolic tradition," even as he goes on to note that by "using the theme of 'reminder' in 2 Peter (1:12–15, 3:1f), he demonstrates the concern of the author for unfalsified tradition. Unfortunately, Zmijewski offers no mechanism for understanding how this extension of tradition could result in pseudonymity, other than a pneumatic *Werkzeug* concept like Aland" (Meade, *Pseudonymity and Canon*, 14). See also J. Zmijewski, "Apostolische Paradoxie und Pseudepigraphic im Neuen Testament 'Durch Erinnerung wachhalten' (2 Peter 1, 13; 3,1)," *BZ* 23 (1979): 161–71.

the original addressees to their status within the extensive network of Christianness. The letter's recipients do not represent a lesser, subordinate form of Christianness; rather, they are "equal in honorable quality as ours [Peter's] in bringing the justice of our God" (1:1). Second Peter's cultural rhetoric clarifies the implied readers' status and association with the tradition, challenging intracommunity ideals that might perceive the tradition as above or beyond the readers.[15] The letter recipients are members in equal measure with the apostles, teachers, and prophets whom they look to as models and guides (1:19; 2:1; 3:2). The Petrine face tasks the letter recipients to stop endeavoring to meet an apostolic level. They do not need to strive to embody some elevated disposition; instead, they should understand themselves to be equal contributors who extended apostolic authority already.

This strategy of esteem building is reminiscent of Wells's rationale for using the pseudonym, Iola. She initially deployed Iola as an insider name for speaking from, within, and to African American communities, not their white American counterparts. After she firmly established herself as a credible voice within her communities, her journalistic writings—particularly her investigative reporting of African American lynchings—moved into broader arenas, and Wells left the Iola name behind. Wells's name now carried the credibility and authority needed to influence her target audience toward the aims that inspired her to write in the first place—namely, nurturing an informed, free, and stable African American citizenry. It also extended her voice beyond the initially intended audience to a more global hearing. So, too, the authors and recipients of 2 Peter could move beyond the authority of the historical Peter to become apostles in their own right.

Pseudonymity in 2 Peter as Intra-Christian Witness

African American women writers used the rhetorical practice of pseudonymity to disrupt social norms. It was a means for them to contribute to American literary canons and participate in the public forums from which they had previously been excluded due to a lack of opportunities in education, citizenship, and fundamental human rights of agency, freedom, and voice. Pseudonymity was a vehicle for them to penetrate those barriers from the underside of societal and communal power. In contrast,

---

15. Martin, "Normative Biblical Motifs," 48.

the letter writers of 2 Peter were not excluded members who needed to use pseudonymity to be included. Whoever they were, they were already active participants of the community, able to not only participate fully in the cultural life of the community but also contribute to it vis-à-vis the creation of 2 Peter. The function of pseudonymity in the letter was not an attempt to secure a platform to be heard (as was the case with nineteenth-century African American women). It was an exercise in normalizing the power the authors already had.

Pseudonymity in 2 Peter sought to establish a singular normative way of believing, behaving, and even interpreting the lived experiences of its members and the outside world. As with other Christian communities, there was apparently a diversity of theological perspectives within the community and clashes between different segments of its membership: "But there were also false prophets among the people, as also there will be false teachers among your group. They will secretly bring in heresies producing destruction, even denying the Divine Enslaver who purchased them, bringing upon themselves swift destruction" (2 Pet 2:1). This verse signals that competing views about teachings and practices of Christianness clashed in the community—with much tension and contestation.

Under the face of Peter, these competing lived experiences and interpretations of Christianness were adjudicated and theological diversity was flattened. Unlike the literary traditions preceding it, 2 Peter did not attempt to mediate the situation so that multiple communal formulations could coexist. Rather, the writers rejected theological diversity and legitimized their form of Christianness as the most authentic manifestation of the social and religious beliefs and practices of the community, which they dubbed the sole "way of truth" (2:2) or "the way of justice" (2:21). Through the face of the historical Peter, the authors normalized a singular cultural community and identity of Christianness. Conformity was rewarded with inclusion (1:4), and nonconformity was penalized by expulsion (2:4–6).

The writers established two normalizing criteria in the name of the historical Peter. First, the writers invented a series of dichotomies, deploying a Sophistic device that flattens multiple iterations into either "this" or "that." For example, the letter distinguishes two conflicting images of peoplehood: (1) people of "religious habit" (*eusebian*; 1:3, 6–7; 3:11) versus "people lacking religious habit" (*asebēs*, 2:5; 3:7) and (2) people of "justice" (*dikaiosynē*, 1:1) versus people of "injustice" (*dikias*, 2:13). The rhetorical consequence is a rigid distinction that creates an "us" and "them" paradigm. Rather than calm and deescalate intragroup censure and influence,

2 Peter deploys Peter's authoritative face to ostracize and target groups with alternative perspectives.

Who were the historical antagonists to whom 2 Peter refers? Two scholarly propositions are typically posited to the historical riddle about the "false prophets" and "false teachers" of 2 Pet 2:1. Former scholarly assessments proposed the false teachers may have been an early gnostic or Marcionite sect who infiltrated the community and influenced others to subscribe to their version of Christianness.[16] A more recent perspective has debunked the gnostic notion by pointing to Epicureanism as a rival teaching. According to this perspective, 2 Peter's bad actors subscribed to Epicurean philosophical forms of thought, which opposed ideas about divine judgment, unfulfilled prophecy, injustice, and providence. They did not subscribe to the inevitable destruction of the world.[17] In either case, the outcome was, these scholars claimed, that the writers of 2 Peter responded with a standard form of polemic. This scholarly proposal presumes something nefarious on the part of the other group. It assigns the rhetorical polemics of 2 Peter's writers to the level of historical reporting, rather than to a rhetorical tactic of persuasion and cancellation. Focusing on whether the alternative teachers are gnostic teachers, subscribers to forms of Greco-Roman philosophical sensibilities, or a generic caricature of opponents, however, misses the significance of 2 Peter's cultural rhetoric.[18] It is clear from 2 Peter's rhetorical structure that the authors are

---

16. For an overturned argument for 2 Peter's opponents as gnostics, which dominates 2 Peter critical studies until the latter part of the twentieth century, see Käsemann, "Apologia for Primitive Christian Eschatology," 170–72; Walter Grundmann, *Der Brief des Judas und der zweite Brief des Petrus*, HKNT 15 (Berlin Evangelische Verlagsanstalt, 1974), 62–63. Bauckham explicitly rejects the traditional notion of gnostic opponents in 2 Peter, aligning himself to the positions of Neyrey and Fornberg. See Bauckham, *Jude, 2 Peter*, 156–57, cf. Fornberg, *Early Church in a Pluralistic Society*, 31–32, 119–26; Jerome H. Neyrey, "The Apologetic Use of the Transfiguration in 2 Peter 1:16–21," *CBQ* 42 (1980): 506.

17. Neyrey compares 2 Peter to Plutarch's *De sera numinis vindicta* and determines 2 Peter contends with forms of Epicureanism that include matters of cosmology, providence, freedom, and unfulfilled prophecy. See Jerome H. Neyrey, "The Form and Background of the Polemic in 2 Peter," *JBL* 99 (1980): 407–31; Witherington, *Socio-rhetorical Commentary on 1–2 Peter*, 278.

18. For a discussion about religious sensibilities among philosophical modes of thought, see Luke Timothy Johnson, *Among the Gentiles: Greco-Roman Religion and Christianity*, AYBRL (New Haven: Yale University Press, 2009).

skilled in the philosophical and cultural rhetorical art of polemics—from the use of dichotomies to the characterization of alternative teachings as false (2:1), immoral (2:2), and unjust (2:9). The point, however, is that they used these rhetorical skills to create a specific, monolithic version of Christianness.

Second Peter's rhetorical strategy was an attempt to authorize one version of Christian identity, thought, and practice relative to those offered by other Christians, whoever they may be. Buell argues that this polemics evinces "the rhetorical functions of ethnic reasoning." Describing the complexity of such intragroup clashes of Christianness, Buell states:

> As Christians sought to authorize their own versions of Christian thought and practice relative to those offered by other Christians, the rhetorical functions of ethnic reasoning unfolded in complex ways. An author might appeal to Christians as members of a people, but excoriate Christian rivals for just this rhetorical move. In these contexts, which are best known in so-called anti-gnostic polemic, the Christian rival may be portrayed as holding an overly narrow concept of "race," as insisting that innate characteristics determine one's possible inclusion in the ranks of Christians. For modern readers, this rhetoric echoes modern views of race sufficiently that we not only fail to see it as a rhetorical argument but also fail to see how other notions of race—as mutable, as formed in and through religious practices—undergird the Christian self-definitions posed in contrast to "gnostic" ones.[19]

Buell's description of the rhetorical function of ethnic reasoning at work among competing formulations of Christianness fits well the cultural rhetoric exhibited in 2 Peter. The letter pits one version of the cultural community of Christianness against another version. Rather than mediating between the two versions and advocating for unified belonging that does not require uniformity (as one might see Paul attempting to do in 1 Corinthians, for instance), the writers of 2 Peter reject the notion of pluralistic intra-Christian identities and communities. They champion intragroup reforms that embolden one group's legitimacy over another. The letter of 2 Peter is not seeking pluralism, even in its universalizing of Christianness. Forms of Christian identity are singular, not multiple, in the letter's logic.

---

19. Buell, "Rethinking the Relevance of Race," 474.

Other scholars argue that the false teachers are an invented foil used to espouse an orthodox teaching aligned to the apostolic tradition—indeed, one of the very figureheads of that tradition, Peter himself![20] From this perspective, it is orthodoxy rather than rivalry that is at work in the culture-making rhetoric of 2 Peter. Yet, the insistence that 2 Peter puts forward an orthodox teaching opens a Pandora's box of critical questions and concerns: What is orthodoxy in the early second century? Whose orthodoxy is 2 Peter reflecting? Even more disruptive, what does orthodoxy look like from the perspective of the other teachings 2 Peter targets? The question of orthodoxy or heterodoxy establishes a binary that privileges the historical winners over others that may have coexisted with them without critically asking whether the morals, behaviors, and attitudes of the winners are representative of a community modern readers want to be part of in the first place. However one answers these questions, 2 Peter's cultural rhetoric is clearly polemical. It uses conventional forms to attack a supposed antagonist group within the community. One wonders if the authors are once again inadvertently coming from behind the veil of the historic Peter. It is not the historic Peter readers see, but the authentic faces of people inclined to intolerance and anger from fear of what they may not fathom nor understand.

While the rhetoric is a standard strategy of antiquity, the authors may also be demonstrating a kind of interreligious illiteracy or, more accurately stated, a lack of inter-Christianness literacy. The insistence upon a single justice and truth stands in stark contrast to evidence from early Christian writings predating 2 Peter that repeatedly convey inter-Christian diversity

---

20. For some examples of the notion of rivals to so-called orthodox Christian teaching in 2 Peter, see Richard, *Reading 1 Peter, Jude, and 2 Peter*, 321; Nienhuis and Wall, *Reading the Epistles of James, Peter, John, and Jude as Scripture*, 131; Davids, *Letters of 2 Peter and Jude*. Exegetical discussions that establish binaries of orthodox and heterodox teaching are a persistent difficulty in critical 2 Peter studies because they consistently run the risk of simplifying the diverse and complicated environment of Christian expressions evident in the textual evidence. Such discussions are also a retention from earlier critical studies in 2 Peter, which were committed to pointing to 2 Peter as evidence for the increasing institutionalization of Christianity as a diminished iteration of the early Jesus movement: "From that has been said so far, it emerges that the epistle is a piece of documentation of the process of demarcation between right belief and heterodoxy; that, according to the almost unanimous verdict of criticism, it is the latest in date of all New Testament documents and in any event not written by the Apostle Peter" (Käsemann, "Apologia for Primitive Christian Eschatology," 172).

in beliefs, practices, and even lived experiences. Archived in the heterogenous Petrine literature, both in canonical and noncanonical Christian writings, the plurality of Christianness is undeniably present as a reality. It is not a possibility or fictive conjuration. Pluralistic inter-Christianness exists in the literature, and one can stay right within the various stories of Peter in the New Testament to see it, such as the story of Peter and Cornelius (Acts 10). This being the case, the strategy of the authors of 2 Peter seems oddly naïve about the realities of various formulations of Christianness. Moreover, they appear animated against it in a way that defies the lived experiences of Christianness.

Take, for instance, the spelling of Peter's name in the epistle: Symeōn Peter. In this formulation, the Semitic spelling *Symeōn* stands in first position before the Greek spelling *Petros*. The privileging of the Semitic name recalls the tradition of the Jerusalem Council in Acts 15, in which the apostle Peter appears as a Jewish-Christian proponent arguing for the full inclusion of gentile-Christian. At the council, the leader of the convened delegates, James, opens his affirmation of Peter's position with a reference to Peter's Semitic name: "*Symeon* has related how God first looked favorably on the Gentiles ..." (Acts 15:14, NRSV).[21] By using the Semitic name, James emphasizes Peter's connection to the Jewish element of the Christian community gathered there. Second Peter 1:1, on the other hand, hybridizes the dialectal name, rendering a Petrine image of two worlds: the Semitic-speaking and Greek-speaking worlds with their accompanying thought and behavior patterns. In other words, the letter activates a pluralistic image of Peter as a messianic Jew and a gentile ally. This pluralism is abandoned, however, in chapter 2 and following. It is as if the letter mentions the historic Peter's hybridity in order to flatten it into a monolithic identity.

The writers do the same with prophetic tradition. On the one hand, they formulate Christian teaching as an extension of the tradition of Israel's prophets and the Jesus movement's apostles: "In both, as a reminder, I awaken your group's sincere minds to remind you of the words having been previously spoken through the holy prophets and the commandment of the Lord and Savior also spoken through your apostles" (2 Pet 3:1b–2).

---

21. In the council, Peter was the first to speak on behalf of full inclusion of the gentile believers based on his experience at the household of Cornelius (Acts 10). The Peter-Cornelius-gentile cycle informs the Peter-James-Paul-apostolic cycle in Acts, where the Semitic form of Peter's name is evoked (Acts 15:7–11).

Again, the appeal echoes back to the portrayal of the Jerusalem Council leader, James, and his rhetorical strategy of appealing to the prophets. After affirming Peter's testimony of gentile inclusion (and implicitly the testimonies of Paul and Barnabas), James appeals to the prophetic tradition:

> [15] This agrees with the words of the prophets, as it is written,
> [16] "After this I will return,
> and I will rebuild the dwelling of David, which has fallen;
> from its ruins I will rebuild it,
> and I will set it up,
> [17] so that all other peoples may seek the Lord—
> even all the gentiles over whom my name has been called.
> Thus says the Lord, who has been making these things
> [18] known from long ago." [19] Therefore I have reached the decision that we should not trouble those gentiles who are turning to God, [20] but we should write to them. (Acts 15:15–20, NRSVue)

According to James, the prophetic tradition of Israel is an authoritative source for conciliating the matter of cross-cultural inclusion. The letter writers make a similar rhetorical move, appealing to the prophets as the foundational teaching of authority, except they do so to advocate for intragroup reforms that move toward homogeneity rather than a plurality. While Peter is the leading face of plurality and inclusion in Acts 15, he is the face of singularity and exclusion in 2 Peter. Two competing faces of Peter and uses of the prophetic tradition on matters of diversity and inclusion coexist in the New Testament's canonical traditions. As the latest composition among the writings, 2 Peter's version is not merely a continuation or extension of Peter's canonical legacy. The strategy of pseudonymity accentuates a different rhetorical intention. The writers employ pseudonymity in favor of intragroup reforms that move toward antipluralistic identities and away from earlier moderated forms of cross-cultural exchanges and mixed theological beliefs within the Jesus movement.

Reading 2 Peter through nineteenth-century African American women amplifies the distinct Petrine legacy cast in the letter. Each used pseudonyms to respond to their contexts and propose alternative cultural scripts for those inside the communities. Nineteenth-century African American women writers' struggled against racial prejudice and slavery. Wells and Forten employed alternative names to facilitate a thoroughgoing engagement with broader nineteenth-century public opinion and cultural scripts that mapped inferior, unteachable, uncivilized, godless, childlike, and other such pejorative and depreciatory labels onto African American bodies and communities. They used pseudonymity as a tool to display African Americans' social and intellectual capacity to meet their white counterparts on equal terms and to, thereby, achieve full inclusion in American culture and society.[22] Their oral performances, scribal writing, and print publications were "continuously intersecting and mutually reinforcing habits" that operated as "reciprocal acts" in the process of meaning-making for those positioned on the margins of American society.[23] Second Peter, on the other hand, was written from within and toward its insider cultural community. Rather than advocate for full acceptance and inclusion of its diverse membership and their varied perspectives and habits, the letter deploys pseudonymity to marginalize. Both kinds of literature used pseudonymity as a mechanism to respond to the contemporary agenda of their authors and offer instructions for the historical moments of their receiving, interpretive communities. Yet, where African American women used pseudonymity to challenge the minoritized status placed on them, 2 Peter's writers used pseudonymity to impose the status with such force that it might trigger group separation.

Conclusion

Examining pseudonymity in the cultural rhetoric of 2 Peter through its phenomenon in nineteenth-century African American women's writings surfaces the formative quality of the testamentary letter. Yes, it recalls a legendary figure in early Christian tradition between eighty and one hundred years after his likely execution in Rome under Nero. More than that, the testament genre also contemporizes his story and voice by having Peter again speak to communities of believers while signaling Peter's mortality. Peter is not the resurrected Jesus. He will die and, indeed, has already died, and the readers know it. There exists, however, an essential distinction between the pseudonymity of 2 Peter and the practice employed among African American women. Whereas the latter used pseudonymity to be seen, acknowledged, and endorsed publicly in the stories of their bodies and peoplehood, the pseudonymity of 2 Peter serves the purpose of con-

---

22. Kelley, "Talents Committed to Your Care," 38.
23. Mary Kelley, "'The Difference of Colour': Reading and Writing Abolitionism," *Social Dynamics* 45 (2019): 168.

cealing the identity and stories of the letter's actual composers. The Petrine figure becomes a veil that hides the faces and names of the text's original composers while they masquerade their writing as Peter's own.

The names that African American women like Wells and Forten adopted breached the literary boundary that rendered their endeavors rare. These women wielded pseudonymity to disrupt an American literary tradition that systematically excluded women, African Americans, and especially African American women. Conversely, pseudonymity in 2 Peter reinforced a previously established tradition while extending the borders of Petrine discourse, which was already heterogeneous in its constituent writings. By the latter part of the second century, traditions about Peter were archived in apocryphal gospels (the Gospel of Peter), apocalypses (the Apocalypse of Peter), acts (the Acts of Peter and the Twelve Apostles), and letters (1 Peter, the Letter of Peter to Philip). Now it appeared in a hybrid genre form, the testament letter (2 Peter).[24]

Whereas African American women used pseudonymity to correct, critique, and expand a tradition and thereby take the tradition elsewhere, the writers of 2 Peter employed the strategy to situate itself inside a pre-existing tradition and establish their perspectives as the norm. Despite these two rhetorical intentions and outcomes, both kinds of literature put forward a transparent literary fiction in order to cultivate what they held as most significant—the existential challenges of their communities, both inside and outside their ranks. Their artful deployment of pseudonymity as a mechanism for social response departs from the traditional debates about authenticity and pseudonymity, raising matters related to the culture making and intercultural possibilities and challenges of the discourse.

---

24. For a survey of Petrine discourse, see Fred Lapham, *Peter: The Myth, the Man, and the Writings: A Study of Early Petrine Text and Traditions*, JSNTSup 239 (London: Sheffield Academic, 2003). Jorg Frëy acknowledges the heterogenous creation of a Petrine discourse to which Peter's name and face are attached: "Second Peter could enter a wider 'Petrine discourse,' adding a number of new aspects to an already existing variety of Petrine images. Thus, 2 Peter's image of Peter and its contributions to the discourse are not totally new but draw on various aspects of Peter's message as transmitted in earlier 'Petrine' writings, while modifying and occasionally correcting them" (Frey, "Second Peter in New Perspective," 23).

Part 4
Practices of Biblical Citation and Interpretation

7
Interpreting Biblical Traditions in African American Women's Reforms

The previous chapters focused on how practices in African American women's moral discourses can shed light on specific topics within 2 Peter studies. Matters related to the translation of *dikaiosynē* as either "justice" or "righteousness" shape how we understand the letter's social-religious point of view (chapters 3–4). Pseudonymous attribution reveals how the letter leverages the authoritative face of the historical Peter to establish a particular form of Christianness (chapters 5–6). In effect, both the nineteenth century women and the letter writers composed compelling theological positions from the legacies and occasions that informed their community's beliefs and practices. This chapter and the next shall look more closely at how these writers use specific biblical traditions as a source for their cultural rhetoric.

Christian Interpretive Practices

Wilda C. Gafney's description of rabbinic midrash supplies a generative heuristic to examine how 2 Peter and nineteenth-century African American women writers resourced common biblical traditions. Gafney describes rabbinic midrash as "religious readings" that "discern value in texts, words, and letters, as potential revelatory spaces." As a set of Jewish exegetical "approaches to the literal texts of the Scriptures," midrashic translations and interpretations serve religious readers. They reimagine "dominant narrative readings while crafting new ones to stand along-side—not replace—former readings."[1] Using some of the same biblical

---

1. Gafney, *Womanist Midrash*, 2–3; James L. Bailey and Lyle D. Vander Broek, *Literary Forms in the New Testament: A Handbook* (Louisville: Westminster John Knox, 1992), 42–49.

traditions from the Septuagint and other early Christian writings, the authors of 2 Peter and nineteenth-century women interpreters penned antithetical narrative readings that contribute to different culture-making modes of persuasion.[2] The rhetorical effect the women biblical interpreters sought to achieve in their readings included expanding the Christian community in American social life, politics, arrangement, and citizenship. In contrast, the rhetorical effect of 2 Peter's reading of biblical texts contracted Christian communities under its influence down to a single form. The authors of 2 Peter appropriate rhetorical effect to meet their endeavor to profile, dissuade, and dishonor alternative Christian teachings among their membership. However, both leverage traditions inherited from Jewish, Christian, and other cultural forms to create their own unique model of Christianness.

Gafney does not conflate rabbinic midrash with Christian forms of biblical interpretation. She acknowledges that a close similarity exists between the two traditions due to the genealogy of one as the progenitor of the other. But she cautions against labeling Christian interpretations (or reinterpretations) of Jewish Scriptures as explicitly midrashic.

> Christian biblical exegesis from the patristic fathers to contemporary lay and specialized biblical interpretation holds much in common with traditional rabbinic midrash. Indeed, the writings of Christian mystics from the desert mothers and fathers to contemporary poets and preachers are as creative, insightful, and revelatory as classic midrash. Christian and rabbinic fathers share allegorical and metaphorical readings of the text, in many cases coming to surprisingly similar conclusions—for example, the tendency to read the Song of Songs as an allegory about the relationship between God (or Christ) and people (Israel or church-as-new-Israel). In some cases, biblical interpreters from different traditions come to the same conclusion about a text; in others, interpreters from the same tradition come to wildly differing conclusions about the same text.[3]

Gafney nuances the relationship between rabbinic midrash and Christian forms of biblical interpretation and acknowledges their similarities without compromising their integrity as separate traditions with distinct

---

2. Gafney, *Womanist Midrash*, 2–3; Bailey and Vander Broek, *Literary Forms in the New Testament*, 42–43.

3. Gafney, *Womanist Midrash*, 5.

reception histories. Her approach is instructive for this chapter. Although the writers of 2 Peter and African American women's literature participate in traditions of scriptural readings and reinterpretations, they do not produce Christian forms of rabbinic midrash. Rather, they generate their own form of interpretation that leverages the literary legacies of the past to benefit the present.

Contemporizing Biblical Traditions for Social Response in the Nineteenth Century

The Christian canon was the authoritative source of religious tradition in nineteenth-century America and the lingua franca of American political discourse. The Christian Bible thus supplied nineteenth-century African American women interpreters with rich material for their cultural interventions. African American women interpreters used these sources to argue that freedom, equality, voice, and citizenship across cultural and racial divides are both Christian and civil imperatives. They used biblical interpretation to respond to polemical attacks directed at them from outside and within their local communities. Their interpretive readings cultivated, in turn, cultural rhetoric attentive to religious and societal matters. The result was socially responsive and compelling literary productions fashioned from biblical discourses and language.

The Witness of Transfiguration

The transfiguration story is a Christian biblical tradition that frequently *NB* occurs in nineteenth-century African American women's writings. Although rarely identified explicitly as the transfiguration, the tradition is recognizable in specific details such as references to a mountain, the changing of Jesus's clothes miraculously, or a divine voice from heaven.[4] Those details help hearers and readers retrieve the story from memory and

---

4. The transfiguration story occurs in the Synoptic Gospels (Matt 17:1–9; Mark 9:2–10; Luke 9:28–37), and elements appear in the Gospel of John as Jesus interprets his death as prelude to the farewell discourse (12:28–30), though not in the form of the stories from the Synoptics. Some of the common details are: mountain: Matt 17:1 // Mark 9:2 // Luke 9:28; miraculous attire change: Matt 17:2 // Mark 9:3 // Luke 9:29; voice sounding from an overshadowing cloud: Matt 17:5 // Mark 9:7 // Luke 9:34–35; cf. voice from heaven in John 12:28.

bring it forward into the present rhetorical moment, connecting it to what is current by remembering the past.

For example, Charlotte Forten Grimké (1837–1914) was a renowned African American abolitionist, poet, and teacher from two prominently known abolitionist families, the Fortens of Philadelphia and the Grimkés of Washington, DC. In the 1860s, Grimké volunteered to serve as the first African American teacher in the Port Royal Experiment. "Union soldiers had captured the South Carolina Sea Islands," which mainly consisted of a large plantation.[5] At that site, the Union established a school for the newly freed people of the region, and Grimké served as one of its teachers. Grimké wrote correspondences to family and friends describing the natural environment and documenting the political conditions during the Civil War in South Carolina. In 1864, the *Atlantic Monthly* journal printed a series of these correspondences.

In "Life on the Sea Islands," Grimké describes the island's landscape as a welcome contrast to the destruction of enslavement the land had known. Threaded through her correspondence are accounts about ongoing conflict with "rebels" in the region fighting to regain control from the Union and reinstate enslavement. She uses imagery from the transfiguration story to elucidate the natural beauty of Port Royal Island and balance her accounting of conflict and violence:

> Then we entered a by-way leading to the plantation, where we found the Cherokee rose in all its glory. The hedges were *white* with it; it canopied the trees, and hung from their branches its long sprays of *snowy* blossoms and dark, *shining* leaves, forming perfect arches, and bowers which seemed fitting places for fairies to dwell in. How it gladdened our eyes and hearts! It was as if all the dark shadows that have so long hung over this Southern land had flitted away, and, in this *garment of purest white*, it *shone forth transfigured*, beautified, forevermore.[6]

Grimké describes both the physical and social environment of the islands using imagery from accounts of the transfiguration in the KJV. For example, her reference to "purest white" coupled with "shone forth transfigured"

---

5. Hollis Robbins and Henry Louis Gates Jr., "Charlotte Forten Grimké (1837–1914)," in Robbins and Gates, *The Portable Nineteenth-Century African American Women Writers*, 129.

6. Charlotte Grimké, "Life on the Sea Islands" (1864), in Robbins and Gates, *Portable Nineteenth-Century African American Women Writers*, 155, emphasis added.

borrows the imagery of miraculous transformation and brilliance found in passages such as Mark 9:2b–3: "and he was transfigured before them. And his raiment became shining, exceeding white as snow; so as no fuller on earth can white them." Grimké's coupling of the color white with illumination suggests that the transfiguration account taken from the KJV Gospel of Matthew may also be a source for her, with its recollection of Jesus's raiment in its transfigured form as "white as the light" (Matt 17:2). Grimké blends the imagery of Jesus's transfiguration as recorded across the gospels to describe a current physical and social reality. In so doing, she brings the transfiguration moment forward, using it to point to current realities. The gospel transfiguration supplies her with language to describe the natural beauty of Port Royal Island and convey the struggles for social transformation during the Civil War. She recalls and recontextualizes the gospel witness of transfiguration for her community's current reality.

In contrast, the itinerant preacher and women's rights activist Zilpha Elaw (1790–1873) deploys elements of the transfiguration story from Mark 9 as she recounts a personal religious experience:[7]

> About this time it happened that I was from home a few weeks on a visit; and as I was sitting in the house of God, I was caught up in spirit, away from and far above all *sublunary* things; and appeared to be *standing on a very elevated place* in the midst of tens of thousands, who were all seated around, clothed in *white*; my own complexion and *raiment* were also *white*, and I was employed in addressing this immense concourse: it was such a scene as had never before entered into my conceptions; and presently it disappeared, and I found myself again in the chapel.[8]

Like Grimké, Elaw leverages the imagery of light and the color white. She also deploys the word "raiment" and recounts experiences of divine

---

7. Most of what is known about Zilpha Elaw comes from her autobiography, *Memoirs of the Life* (1846). According to her autobiography, Elaw was born to free African American parents in Pennsylvania, and she joined the Methodist church as a teenager. She is one of the trailblazing African American women preachers (like Jarena Lee and Julia A. J. Foote), traveling the globe in the nineteenth century, preaching at revivals, tent services, churches, and conferences about God's Spirit, salvation, fellowship, and liberty for all God's people and creation. Mitzi J. Smith, "'Unbossed and Unbought': Zilpha Elaw and Old Elizabeth and a Political Discourse of Origins," *Black Theology* 9.3 (2011): 287–311.

8. Elaw, *Memoirs of the Life*, 82, emphasis added.

elevation and vision (cf. Mark 9:3–4; Matt 17:3; Luke 9:29).[9] Jesus's trans-figuration story, as translated in the KJV, is not only an authoritative reference for Elaw. It also is a compelling image that legitimates her call story to preach the gospel publicly as a woman to mixed-gender audiences. "I pondered this wonderful vision over in my mind, and concluded that it was given to me as a token that the Lord had destined me for enlarged and more elevated spheres of effort; and the Christian friends to whom I related it, also thought it a prelude to my future ministerial work."[10] Elaw suggests her experience is comparable to the biblical accounting of Jesus's commissioning on the mountain of transfiguration, and her womanhood does not diminish its quality. Her reading of the transfiguration opens space for the inclusion of other identities in religious leadership. It is a rhe-torical mechanism for expanding Christian cultures to include women's voices and revelations under God's divine decision-making authority.

Another biblical interpreter, Sarah Jane Woodson Early (1825–1907), speaks about the successes and necessities of the African American wom-an's club movement in her 1894 address, "The Organized Efforts of the Colored Women of the South to Improve Their Condition." Early was an educator, temperance activist, and women's club movement pioneer. In the first paragraph of her essay, she defends the necessity of the club movement among African American women, using details from the transfiguration to designate the movement as an extension of God's divine interventions.

> In this age of development and advancement all the forces which have been accumulating for centuries past seem to be concentrated in one grand effort to raise mankind to that degree of intellectual and moral excellence which a wise and beneficent Creator designed that he should enjoy. No class of persons is exempt from this great impulse. The most unlettered, the most remote and obscure, as well as the most refined and erudite seem to have felt the touch of an unseen power, and to have *heard a mysterious voice calling them to ascend higher* in the scale of being. It is not a strange coincidence, then, that in this period of restlessness and activity the women of all lands should simultaneously see the necessity of taking a more *exalted position*, and of seeking a more effective way of

---

9. Mitzi J. Smith, "Zilpha Elaw," in *Handbook of Women Biblical Interpreters: A Historical and Biographical Guide*, ed. Marion Taylor (Grand Rapids: Baker Academic, 2012), 185–87.

10. Elaw, *Memoirs of the Life*, 82, emphasis added.

ascending to the same plane, and assuming the more responsible duties of life with her favored brother.[11]

Early's repetition of words for ascension and reference to an unseen voice captures the religious experience of a commission or calling story. She deploys the imagery of a theophany, particularly a glorified "mountain-top" experience, to reenvision the experience of being God's agent in the current moment. Her aim is to promote women's collective participation and action in uplifting African American communities within a society that seeks their oppression or removal. She accomplishes her rhetorical task by crafting a judicial appeal with undertones of transfiguration and commissioning stories like Moses and the burning bush. Women like Early, Elaw, and Grimké embrace such stories as images of African American people's religious and social inheritance. Rather than disinherited people, they identify their communities as an extension of divine imperatives and legitimacy and bring the biblical experience forward into their present moment.

The Commissioning of the Prophetic Call

The prophetic tradition of the Bible is as prominent in the moral discourses of African American women as the transfiguration. As one scholar states, these women consistently turned "to scripture for literary material" as "an attempt to position themselves as inheritors of the prophetic mantle."[12] As already seen above, Elaw and Early used elements of the transfiguration account to establish women's right to lead and preach in religious and civic spaces. African American women also activated prophetic echoes from other commission stories in the Christian Bible. For example, Elizabeth (1766–1867), "a preaching contemporary" of Zilpha Elaw and Jarena Lee, describes her commissioning story in a form reminiscent of Jeremiah's story. Just as God asks Jeremiah the same question multiple times ("what do you see?"; Jer 1:11, 13), so too does God pose multiple forms of a question to Elizabeth at her call moment, "Art though willing to be saved?"[13]

---

11. Sarah J. Early, "The Organized Efforts of the Colored Women of the South to Improve their Condition" (1894), in Robbins and Gates, *Portable Nineteenth-Century African American Women Writers*, 380, emphasis added.
12. Bassard, *Transforming Scriptures*, 12.
13. Riggs, *Can I Get a Witness*, 4.

Similarly, Jarena Lee appeals to Mary Magdalene's divine commission to proclaim Jesus's resurrection (John 20:11–18; Matt 28:1–10) as a prophetic task her own preaching endeavor replicates: "Did not Mary first preach the risen Saviour, and is not the doctrine of the resurrection the very climax of Christianity.... Then did not Mary, a woman, preach the gospel? For she preached the resurrection of the crucified Son of God."[14] Other prophetic commission stories the women writers frequently reference include those of Moses (Exod 3:1–2; see Frances Watkins Harper); Jonah (1:1–2; 3:1–3; see Zilpha Elaw), or the Galilean fishermen turned Jesus's disciples (Mark 1:16–20; see Jarena Lee).[15] They intentionally link their callings and writings to the work of biblical prophets and apostles (2 Pet 3:2).[16]

Jarena Lee, for example, explicitly resources the biblical prophetic call stories to legitimize her right as a woman to preach and lead within her Christian communities and beyond as an American citizen. The epigraph for Lee's autobiography, *The Life and Religious Experience and Journal*, is a selection taken from the Jewish prophet, Joel 2:28: "And it shall come to pass ... that I will pour out my Spirit upon all flesh; and your sons, and your *daughters* shall prophesy."[17] Lee uses the prophetic source to link her position as an itinerant preacher and activist to the voice of the prophets. The prophetic tradition Lee draws on is not general but specific. She leverages a particular prophetic stream of thought that includes women to counteract sexism within and outside her African American Christian communities. She underscores that link further by exercising a standard translation strategy in biblical interpretation, emphasizing Joel's reference to women in italics. The biblical commission story form supplied a struc-

---

14. Riggs, *Can I Get a Witness*, 7.

15. Riggs, *Can I Get a Witness*, 7, 17, 60.

16. Also referenced in African American women's moral discourses, explicitly or implicitly, is the commissioning of Mary (Luke 1:26–38) and Paul (Acts 9; 22:3–21) (Bailey and Vander Broek, *Literary Forms in the New Testament*, 144–46).

17. Emphasis added by Lee. "Indeed, the cross of sexism often seemed to loom over every technical decision the writer made. For example, it was common to preface the narrative with a scripture that established the theme. Jarena Lee chose as her epigraph a selection that linked her with the line of prophets from the Old Testament on, but one that specifically includes women in that tradition. And Lee emphasized that connection by italicizing the reference to women. Both *The Life and Religious Experience* and *Religious Experience and Journal* begin with the following quotation from Joel (2:28): 'And it shall come to pass ... that I will pour out my Spirit upon all flesh; and your sons, and your daughters shall prophesy'" (Foster, *Written by Herself*, 72).

ture for the women to enunciate their religious experiences. It also gave them authoritative proof to assert their authority as agents of God and service to humanity.

The Wisdom Tradition of the Proverb

Another standard feature of the moral discourses of African American women is the use of the proverb. Whether drawing upon wisdom sayings from the Bible or from their African American and indigenous heritages, these women used proverbs to rationalize the moral necessity of moving people from the margins to the center of Christian cultural communities and society.

For example, in her 1892 essay "The Negro as Presented in American Literature," Anna Julia Cooper uses a proverb to elevate the importance of African American perceptions of their European American neighbors. She engages the proverb as a rhetorical maneuver to shift the site of perception. For her, the question is not merely what white Americans think of their African American neighbors, but rather what African Americans think of their white Christian neighbors.

> What I hope to see before I die is a black man honestly and appreciatively portraying both the Negro as he is, and the white man, occasionally, as seen from the Negro's standpoint.
>
> There is an old proverb "The devil is always painted black—by white painters." And what is needed perhaps, to reverse the picture of the lordly man slaying the lion, is for the lion to turn painter.
>
> Then too we need the calm clear judgment of ourselves and of others born of a disenchantment similar to that of a little girl I know in the South, who was once being laboriously held up over the shoulders of a surging throng to catch her first glimpse of a real live president. "Why Nunny," she cried half reproachfully, as she strained her little neck to see—"It's nuffin but a man!"[18]

Cooper deploys the proverb as a wisdom teaching from her community to reveal something about the inner workings of society. Her proverb is an instrument of reflection and exposure. It reveals society's normalizing of the white American gaze at the expense of ignoring African American experiences and insights, which are also a part of America's cultural

---

18. Cooper, *Voice of Anna Julia Cooper*, 159.

fabric. Although society is structured to prioritize European American perceptions of African Americans, Cooper's proverb installs a different assessment value—African American opinion is also important. Moreover, her proverb invites the reflective practice of switching places with others to see and experience the world as someone else and to encourage a vantage point that is other than the dominant one—namely, the minoritized view. Ultimately, Cooper uses the proverb to instigate a change toward greater inclusion and moral consideration. Her proverb amplifies the social honor and significance of African American experience. She uses it to assign credit and voice to her community in a larger society intent on exploiting them as voiceless and imperceptive people.

The Language of Spirit-Filled Inspiration

Language about the presence and activity of spirit also saturates the moral discourses of African American women. For example, Elaw's autobiography opens with a brief rehearsal of her childhood where she recounts the death of her father: "It pleased God to remove my dear father to the world of spirits."[19] In narrating her conversion and call stories, she also uses the language of "spirit" and "spirits," proclaiming, "The hardest hearts are melted into tenderness; the driest eyes overflow with tears, and the loftiest spirits bow down: the Creator's works are gazed upon, and His near presence felt around."[20] Similarly, she rehearses the directives of her spirit-led commission: "It was revealed to me by the Holy Spirit, that like another Phoebe, or the matrons of the apostolic societies, I must employ myself in visiting families, and in speaking personally to the members thereof, of the salvation and eternal interests of their souls, visit the sick, and attend upon other of the errands and services of the Lord."[21] For Elaw, the created world—both seen and unseen—is full of spirit activity.[22] Her writings depict authentic religious experience as dynamic exchanges between the Divine Spirit (which she often identifies as the "Holy Spirit") and the spirits

---

19. William L. Andrews, *Sisters of the Spirit: Three Black Women's Autobiographies of the Nineteenth Century* (Bloomington: Indiana University Press, 1986), 53.

20. Riggs, *Can I Get a Witness*, 11.

21. Riggs, *Can I Get a Witness*, 14.

22. See Shively T. J. Smith, "Zilpha Elaw and the 'Spirit,'" in *1–2 Peter and Jude*, ed. Pheme Perkins, Eloise Rosenblatt, and Patricia McDonald, Wisdom Commentary 56 (Collegeville, MN: Liturgical Press, 2022), 29–32.

of individuals, ancestors, creation, and even antagonistic spirits, which she often brands with the moniker "Satan." Moreover, Elaw's notion of Spirit carries expectations of revelation and interpretation. She sees the work of the Spirit as the work of inspired insight and meaning and an extension of prophetic activity.

The Tradition of Balaam and the Dumb Donkey

Lee's spiritual autobiography supplies another example of biblical retelling. Her autobiography accounts for "her call to preach the Gospel" (as the subtitle states) and establishes women's legitimate right to preach and assume religious leadership through it. To this end, Lee deploys the story of Balaam and the donkey to underscore the absurdity of denying women's right to speak on behalf of God.

> I met with many troubles on my journey, especially from the elder, who like many others, was averse to a woman's preaching. And here let me tell that elder, if he has not gone to heaven, that I have heard that as far back as Adam Clarke's time, his objections to female preaching was met by the answer—"If an ass reproved Balaam, and a barn-door fowl reproved Peter, why should not a woman reprove sin?" I do not introduce this for its complimentary classification of women with donkeys and fowls, but to give the reply of a poor woman, who had once been a slave. To the first companion she said—"May be a speaking woman is like an ass—but I can tell you one thing, the ass seen the angel when Balaam didn't."[23]

Lee's reading of the Balaam story champions the place and voice of women within her religious communities. According to her biblical reasoning, the scriptures attest that even nonspeech-oriented animals have been employed in God's service. If even animals can speak, why shouldn't women be given a voice?

The trope of the talking donkey in the Num 22 account supplies more than simply imagery to address sexism and patriarchy broadly. The use of this biblical trope in nineteenth-century African American women's literature provides materials for them to tell their personal stories.[24] Lee,

23. Jarena Lee, "Religious Experience and Journal of Mrs. Jarena Lee," in *Spiritual Narratives*, Schomburg Library of Nineteenth-Century Black Women Writers (New York: Oxford University Press, 1988), 23.

24. Bassard, *Transforming Scriptures*, 6, 8–10.

for example, not only uses the story of the talking donkey to talk about women's right to voice broadly, but she deploys it as evidence for her own religious experiences in the form of otherworldly visions.

visions = true words

> The following day I walked fourteen miles to a meeting, where also we were greatly favored with the presence of God. Soon after this, I thought of going home to Philadelphia. I got about three miles on foot, when an apparent voice said, "If thou goest home thou wilt die." I paused for a moment, and not comprehending what it meant, pursued my journey. Again I was startled by something like a tapping on my shoulder, but, on turning round, I found myself alone, which two circumstances created a singular feeling I could not understand. I thought of Balaam when met by the angel in the way. I was taken sick and it seemed I should die in the road. I said I will go back, and walked about four miles to Bridgeport.[25]

Lee uses the experience of divine intervention and encounter narrated in the Balaam account as biblical precedence for her divine encounter and response of reversal. She was going one way, and intuition warned her against continuing. Lee, in response, reversed course on the road. The Balaam story supplies her with wisdom proof. Its citation helps her rationalize the experience and articulate it to others, so they too comprehend its significance.

Lee also uses the story as biblical proof to withstand prejudice against women. In the same paragraph in which she mentions the Balaam story, she talks about how Christian male leadership treated her in Bridgeport: "On Wednesday night I spoke to the people at Trenton Bridge, and notwithstanding the opposition I had met with from brother Samuel R—, then on the circuit, the Lord supported the 'woman preacher' and my soul was cheered. On Thursday I walked fourteen miles, when the friends applied to the elder to let me talk for them, but his prejudices also, against women preaching were very strong, and tried hard to disaffect the minds of the people."[26] Lee was not accepted by a man at Trenton Bridge or an elder in a nearby town. She could have become disheartened, but she persevered. The Lord supported her, as evidenced in her Balaam-like encounter, and her "soul was cheered." Lee used "the Balaam story as a trope" to establish her "own agency and discourse."[27] Whereas Lee's use and interpretation of the Balaam story served her rhetorical aim to expand the imaginations

25. Lee, "Religious Experience and Journal," 33.
26. Lee, "Religious Experience and Journal," 33–34.
27. Bassard, *Transforming Scriptures*, 10.

of Christian communities about the role of women in religious leadership and influence, the next chapter will demonstrate how 2 Peter used the same story as a weapon to cultivate and deepen prejudices.

Conclusion

Biblical traditions helped African American women plot new social possibilities and cultural scripts. Their interaction with biblical texts created a dialectic between the Bible's canonical authority and the authority of their own lived experiences. They "read" the scripts and trends of their lives while reading the stories of biblical figures and their worlds and put the two in conversation. The Bible's voice did not eclipse their stories. Rather, these women used biblical witnesses to provide their personal and community anecdotes with more texture and to rebrand themselves and their communities as "the people of God." Biblical citation and interpretation, therefore, was both a source and pathway for deepening the epistemological and spiritual resources the women already possessed. They used the Bible as a sourcebook for language, stories, and images familiar in nineteenth-century ecclesial and civic contexts to address unfamiliar and unnamed circumstances characterizing the intersectional realities of those who are women, Americans, and people of African descent.[28]

Having sampled the rhetorical value of the stories of Jesus's transfiguration, prophetic commissioning accounts, the literary forms of proverbs, spirit-filled inspiration, and the tradition of Balaam among some African American women biblical interpreters, the next chapter examines how 2 Peter interprets the same traditions. This examination is not exhaustive but selective. It represents a sampling of the biblical traditions they share and emphasizes how their readings are distinct. Due to space, the book does not explore all possibilities for interpretive comparisons, such as their different treatments of biblical traditions like Noah and the flood or Sodom and Gomorrah.[29] The selected examples, however, demonstrate

---

28. To speak of "intersectional realities" is to analyze "the complexity in the world, in people, and in human experiences." Intersectionality means observing and describing "the events and conditions of social and political life and the self" as "shaped by many factors in diverse and mutually influencing ways" (Collins and Bilge, *Intersectionality*, 2, 193).

29. Other traditions include "Just Lot," the stories of angels trafficking between heaven and earth, and even the apocalyptic traditions of the Day of Judgment. The

what a phenomenological exegesis yields in the exegesis of early Christian literature, especially 2 Peter.

---

chapter highlights some traditions that tend to be eclipsed in traditional treatments about the histories of interpretation and reception history within 2 Peter with the hopes of signaling other opportunities for study.

8

Contemporizing Biblical Traditions in 2 Peter

Like the nineteenth-century African American women writers centuries and worlds later, the letter of 2 Peter repurposes Jewish and Christian traditions. In doing so, the letter redefines the possibilities of these traditions in ways that serve the purpose of the letter writers: to enforce conformity by eliminating alternative perspectives of Christianity.

Second Peter's Interpretive Practices

A hallmark of 2 Peter's rhetorical effect is its recollection and retelling of specific authoritative traditions from its Jewish and Christian traditions. The letter contains two explicit quotations from the Septuagint: one in 2 Pet 2:22 (cf. Prov 26:11) and one in 2 Pet 3:13 (Isa 66:22). It also incorporates a series of biblical retellings that include Noah and the flood, Sodom and Gomorrah, stories about angels, and the Balaam and donkey account. Second Peter also sources and interprets authoritative traditions from the Jesus movement. The letter's catalog of specifically Christian traditions blends traditions about the apostles, spirit-filled inspiration, Jesus's transfiguration, and a baptism saying. The authors of 2 Peter select a range of artificial proofs in the form of personal eyewitness testimonies, quotations of scriptural passages, and forms of propositions (*logoi*), examples, and arguments.[1] Such repurposing reimagines familiar Jewish and Christian traditions, updating or contemporizing them for the current moment.

---

1. Duane Watson, "The Epistolary Rhetoric of 1 Peter, 2 Peter, and Jude," in *Reading 1–2 Peter and Jude: A Resource for Students*, ed. Eric F. Mason and Troy W. Martin, RBS 77 (Atlanta: Society of Biblical Literature, 2014), 50.

Like the rabbis, the authors of 2 Peter interpret these inherited "Scriptural Writings" (3:16) to create new dominant readings that stand alongside traditional interpretations and shape the community's attitudes about itself in the present moment. Like the African American women, the letter writers recall Jewish and Christian stories as proofs of the authors' contemporary endeavor of communal reform. Moreover, like their nineteenth-century counterparts, the authors of 2 Peter embed an implicit reformist endeavor within an animating prophetic mode. The letter seeks to calibrate its readership to prophetic knowledge by appealing to its community stories (1:12; 3:1–2), divine things (3:10–12), and holy people (3:2), and they seek to elevate their rank and status within the broader global Jesus movement (1:1) by appealing to their prophetic calling. Indeed, the letter repeatedly insists that it is only through proper comprehension of their prophetic place in God's unfolding drama that the recipients can counter and dismiss false teachers and teaching (3:14–18) as well as false prophets and prophecies (1:19–2:1; 3:3–7)—all of which the letter locates as active among the membership. Unlike their nineteenth-century counterparts, however, 2 Peter cites these stories as a mechanism for sifting its membership into enfranchised conformists and disenfranchised Others. Through its testament-letter form, the letter advances a Christian manner of life defined by homogeneity and conformity as opposed to hospitality, mediation, and coexistence.

Contemporizing Biblical Traditions in 2 Peter

The Witness of Transfiguration

As demonstrated in chapter 7, elements from the transfiguration story recur throughout the writings of nineteenth-century African American women. The biblical story of transfiguration supplied these writers with language, imagery, and source material for detailing social transformations that involve greater inclusion and equity (as is the case with Charlotte Forten Grimké's account of the South Carolina Sea Islands at the turn of the Civil War). It also supplied them with an honorific exemplar of prophetic installation and experience that affirmed their calls as preachers (as is the case with Zilpha Elaw) or their collective calls to women's movements focused on education and community uplift (as is the case with Sarah Jane Woodson Early). As a popular gospel tradition, the transfiguration accounts accorded social and religious gravity to the culture-making tenor of the women's literature.

Likewise, 2 Pet 1:16–18 leverages the gospel tradition as an authorizing tradition. In 2 Peter, readers stand alongside Peter as he narrates, in short form, what happened on the mountain of transfiguration. It is a bit like standing with one of the ghosts from the classic story of Scrooge, watching the reel play on a past scene so the audience can reflect on it. In this analogy, the ghost is the apostolic figure, Peter. In addition to using the transfiguration account to legitimize Peter's voice, the letter writers also deploy the story as a tool to forge their conformist criteria. They interpret the transfiguration to validate expelling alternative formulations of Christian understanding, which they designate "cleverly devised myths" (*sesophismenois mythois*, 1:16). To this end, 2 Peter's version of the transfiguration includes details not included in the gospel tradition.

The New Testament gospels contain three versions of the transfiguration account: Mark 9:2–8; Matt 17:1–8; Luke 9:28–36.[2] Second Peter recycles the Synoptic accounts in abbreviated form. It omits several details that are consistent across the tradition while retaining others in modified form. The omitted details are: (1) the presence of Moses and Elijah; (2) Peter's suggestion to construct three tents and Jesus's response; (3) the names and the number of the disciples present with Peter; (4) reference to their fear; and (5) the overshadowing cloud.[3] Despite the absence of these narrative features, the transfiguration story remains identifiable in 2 Peter because of the details it retains in modified form.

First, the general setting of the transfiguration in the letter remains the mountain. Whereas the gospel tradition describes the mountain as high or elevated (Mark 9:2; Matt 17:1; Luke 9:28), the writers of 2 Peter

---

2. The glorification moment in John 12:27–33 contains the element of a heavenly voice, but the voice proclaims something entirely different from the Synoptic versions of transfiguration and even baptism (cf. Matt 3:13–17): "I have glorified it [God's name] and I will glorify it again."

3. Moses and Elijah: Mark 9:4; Matt 17:3; Luke 9:30; three tents (*skēnē*): Matt 17:4; Mark 9:5; Luke 9:33; Jesus's response: Mark 9:6 and Matt 17:7; present disciples: Mark 9:2; Matt 17:1; Luke 9:28; fear: Mark 9:6; Matt 17:7; Luke 9:34; cloud: Mark 9:7; Matt 17:5; Luke 9:34.

describe it as "holy" (1:18).[4] Second, in the letter, a divine voice is still integral to the event. However, 2 Peter depicts the divine voice as resounding from heaven (cf. John 12:28), as opposed to the Synoptic tradition's locating it in a "cloud" (Mark 9:7; Matt 17:5; Luke 9:35). In these two modifications, 2 Peter appears to preserve another version of the transfiguration account found in the Ethiopic version of the Apocalypse of Peter (vv. 15–17). Scholars traditionally argued the Apocalypse borrowed its material from 2 Peter.[5] However, as demonstrated throughout this book, 2 Peter leverages traditions and legacies of all forms. What initially appears to be innovation is frequently imitation (albeit with calculated modifications) in 2 Peter. It is therefore likely that the letter writers are not inventing these unique details. Rather, they borrow them from the Apocalypse of Peter, combining its details with those of the Synoptic tradition to create their own authoritative version repurposed for their Christian brand.

Second Peter also retains the phrase "honor and glory" from the Apocalypse of Peter as another repurposed textual affinity.

2 Pet 1:17a: For he received from the God–Father social *honor and* divine *glory* when a voice was carried by the magnificent glory to him.

Apoc. Pet. 15–17: "[And] you have seen the patriarchs, and like this (is) that which is their rest.' And I rejoiced and believed that this (will be) "the *honour and glory* of those who pursued my righteousness."[6]

---

4. The language of *hagios horos* (holy mountain) is a Greek phrase that occurs in some pseudepigraphical writings, especially Enoch and Ezekiel, occurring within five words of each other; however, it is not a phrase occurring in the New Testament. See references: 1 En. 26.2; Apoc. Ezek. 3.9; Liv. Pro. 2.15. It also occurs one time in Josephus, *B.J.* 3.7.32. It also occurs one time in the apocryphal Apocalypse of Paul (9) and one time in the apostolic fathers (Barn. 11.3: "Is my holy mountain Sinai a desert rock? For you shall be as the fledglings of a bird that flutter about when they are taken away from the nest").

5. Bauckham, *Jude, 2 Peter*, 157–58.

6. Quoted in Paul Foster, "Does the *Apocalypse of Peter* Help to Determine the Date of 2 Peter?," in *2 Peter and the Apocalypse of Peter: Towards a New Perspective*, ed. Jörg Frey, Matthijs den Dulk, and Jan G. van der Watt (Leiden: Brill, 2019), 240, emphases added. Foster used the translation of Dennis Buchholz, *Your Eyes Will Be Opened: A Study of the Greek (Ethiopic) Apocalypse of Peter*, SBLDS 97 (Atlanta: Scholars Press, 1988), 232–44. Beck follows a different versification schema for this verse, denoting the same passage as 16.5 (Beck, *Justice and Mercy in the Apocalypse of Peter*,

In the Apocalypse of Peter, the phrase is spoken by Peter, who quotes the words of "my Lord and God Jesus Christ" at the transfiguration moment.[7] That is, Jesus first employs the phrase "honor and glory," and the Peter narrator then recalls it for readers. Similarly, the Peter narrator of the letter of 2 Peter deploys the phrase "honor and glory," but there is no indication that Jesus spoke it first. In the letter, Peter deploys the phrase as a descriptor of Jesus's prophetic and christological role (1:16–18). It is nomenclature for marking the status and function of Jesus, not his direct speech.

By explicitly combining "honor" (*timē*) and "glory" (*doxa*), the letter writers add a foundational element from the Mediterranean social world that is present elsewhere in the New Testament (and the Apocalypse of Peter) but absent from the Synoptic transfiguration accounts. In the New Testament, the language of *timē* is frequently used to characterize human forms of honor (1 Pet 1:7; 2:7, 17; 1 Cor 12:23–24; John 4:44) while *doxa* often characterizes divine forms of honor associated with God and Jesus (John 5:44; 7:18; 8:50; 1 Cor 2:8).[8] None of the transfiguration accounts from the Synoptics use the language and social value of *timē* explicitly, and the language of *doxa* occurs only in the Gospel of Luke, which adopts the language of *doxa* in its description of Jesus's exchange with Moses and Elijah. The text says Moses and Elijah appeared in glory (*doxa*) and were speaking of his departure (*exodus*, Luke 9:31). In this *doxa* occurrence, honor functions as an ascribed quality. Moses and Elijah inherently hold the status of divine—even prophetic—honor connoted as glory (*doxa*). It is preestablished from their family membership and their prophetic roles and histories.[9] In contrast, Luke seems to bestow honor upon Jesus by

---

73). Beck also translates the passage slightly different from Foster and Buchholz: "And I rejoiced and believed such will be 'the honour and glory for those who were persecuted for my righteousness.'"

7. Apoc. Pet 15–17 in Foster, "Does the *Apocalypse of Peter* Help," 240; in contrast to Beck's translation of "Lord, Jesus Christ" for the same passage, which he identifies as 16.6 (Beck, *Justice and Mercy in the Apocalypse of Peter*, 73).

8. There are some exceptions in which *dox*-honor characterizes human honor in the ordinary sense of honor, fame, and repute (John 5:44; 7:18; 8:50; 1 Thess 2:6), but the dominant trend in rhetorical deployment and semantic usage occurs in the rhetorical logic of 2 Peter. An informative source on the social value of honor and shame in New Testament studies is Richard L. Rohrbaugh, ed., *The Social Sciences and New Testament Interpretation* (Grand Rapids: Baker Academic, 1996), 19–40.

9. Prophet Moses references: Luke 16:29, 31; 20:37; 24:27, 44; prophet Elijah references: Luke 1:17; 4:25–26; 9:8, 19.

saying the apostles "saw Jesus's *doxa* and the two men who stood with him" (Luke 9:32). The language presupposes that the apostolic witnesses had not recognized the *doxa*-honor before that moment in the gospel and that Jesus may not even have had it before that moment.[10] Jesus's *doxa* appears more acquired by his prophetic company and proximity than ascribed by his association with the divine.

Both ascribed and acquired forms of *doxa* operate in Luke's account, but 2 Peter picks up on the subtle form of acquired honor and amplifies it by using two different terms for honor instead of just one: *doxa* (divinely glorified honor) and *timē* (human honor). As noted above, standard grammatical studies of koine Greek connote *timē* as a human form of honor and material valuation, whereas *doxa* is defined as a divine form. The letter of 2 Peter reflects this convention.[11] By using two different terms instead of just one, as in the Gospel of Luke, the letter's discourse not only positions Jesus in the prophetic role (*timē*), but also signals his connection to the divine (*doxa*). Both forms of honor are bestowed from heaven, by the God-Parent who himself holds "Majestic *doxa*" (1:17). The reference to God as Parent suggests that the act of bestowal is not only heavenly but occurs within a heavenly household where wisdom is also acquired.

Another detail 2 Peter retains from the Synoptic tradition is the divine pronouncement: "This is my Son, my Beloved, in whom I am well pleased" (1:17b). Synoptic versions of the transfiguration pronouncement vary slightly, with both Mark and Matthew including a final imperative "Listen to him" (Mark 9:7; Matt 17:5) and Luke's account using the title "my Chosen" instead of "the Beloved" (Luke 9:35). Matthew's baptism account (Matt 3:17), however, preserves the divine pronouncement most like 2 Peter's version in form and language. The only difference is that the letter uses the possessive form "my" before "beloved" and Matthew does not.

Matt 3:17: This is my Son, *the* Beloved, with whom I am well pleased.

---

10. The Gospel of Luke does not explicitly use *doxa* as a characteristic of Jesus until the transfiguration account. For example, in the temptation account, the devil appears to offer Jesus *doxa*, indicating that, according to the storyline, it is not yet bestowed (Luke 4:6) and recognizable by others until Luke 9.

11. BDAG, s.v. "τιμή"; s.v. "δόξα"; J. Schneider, "τιμή," *TDNT* 8:1181–83; Gerhard Kittel, "δόξα," *TDNT* 2:178–81.

2 Pet 1:17b: This is my Son, *my* Beloved, in whom I am well pleased.

The reference to "tents" or "tabernacles" found in Synoptic versions is also retained in 2 Peter. It is not located within its rehearsal of the transfiguration, however, and a different Greek form is deployed. The gospels use the term to narrate Peter's failed response at the moment of revealed divine commission: he proposed to build three "tents" (*skēnas*) in honor of Jesus's transfigured moment, one for Jesus, one for Moses, and one for Elijah (Mark 9:5; Matt 17:4; Luke 9:33). The letter writers deploy imagery of tents or dwellings, not at the transfiguration, but earlier in the preceding unit as a feature in the prediction of Peter's death (1:12–15). There, the imagery of the tent (*skēnōma*, 2 Pet 1:13) is reconfigured as the bodily dwelling of the apostle Peter, rather than an external dwelling that marks the presence of Elijah and Moses. Although the letter uses a different word for tent, *skēnōma* instead of *skēnas*, the same root (*skēn-*) connects the two traditions. The letter writers modify the Greek term to intentionally shift readers' visualization of where the prophets of God dwell. Rather than dwelling in human-made edifices, the writers locate prophetic activity and spirit-filled prophecy and interpretation in God-made bodies—in this case, the bodily legacy of the apostle Peter.

The letter version of the transfiguration depicts Peter's character differently from the gospel tradition. Whereas Synoptic accounts portray Peter as one who misunderstood the significance of the moment, saying, "he did not know what he said" (Luke 9:34; cf. Mark 9:6, 10), the letter portrays Peter as one with not only comprehension but prophetic insight and revelation: "And we have made firm the prophetic word" (2 Pet 1:19). Peter personifies a reliable witness to the activities of Jesus and God. In the letter, Peter does not claim complete comprehension of the transfiguration at the event's time. Instead, the writers leave the passage of time unexplained. Peter witnesses the transfiguration, and then, at some unexplained later date, he understands the nature of prophetic revelation. The letter's transfiguration version rewrites history—specifically, it rewrites Peter.[12] It recasts the protagonist and story following the rhetorical strategy of *prosopopoeia*, narrating the transfiguration account in Peter's voice, face, and authority. By leveraging Peter's authority, they also fasten in place the work of the Holy Spirit in prophetic communication, which is their

---

12. Neyrey, *2 Peter, Jude,* 172.

subsequent point: "no prophetic writing is a matter of personal interpretation. For not at any time was a prophecy brought by the will of human beings, but people spoke from God who were being carried along by the Holy Spirit" (2 Pet 1:20–31).

The details the letter retains from both the Synoptic tradition and the Apocalypse of Peter serve two rhetorical functions. First, they make the story recognizable to letter readers, who were insiders of Christianness and, therefore, likely aware of the gospel tradition of transfiguration (2 Pet 1:12–15). Second, the narrative details are helpful for advancing the letter's social agenda. The letter's transfiguration account is wielded rhetorically as a form of witness attestation. It verifies Peter's apostolic identity as the writer (1:1; 1:12–15). In turn, the constructed apostolic character and face of the letter are strengthened. It also fuses apostolic witness with prophetic messages. The transfiguration story in 2 Peter brands Peter as a prophetic figure comparable to Moses and Elijah. The message of the apostolic tradition, with Peter as the representative steward, becomes aligned with prophetic discourse. The story renews the apostolic authority and, in turn, affirms the community's identity and social role in the drama of the Jesus movement. Their experience is not an anomaly, and their witness is not a diminished form of the apostolic witness. Second Peter presents the traditions of the apostles, the prophets, and the current social-cultural realities of the community as unified strands of the same religious habit, sensibility, and ethnoreligious identity.

The Commissioning of the Apostolic Prophet

African American women frequently drew upon prophetic traditions in their personal commission stories as an authoritative source, as attested in the Jarena Lee instance referenced in chapter 7. They threaded the biblical tradition of prophets and prophecies throughout their spiritual autobiographies and intertwined it with their own personal experiences. The tradition supplied them with the literary forms and religious details to authenticate their experiences and tell stories of community influence, civic service, and social position. Extending biblical prophetic traditions, African American women became agents of God. Their activities extend biblical endeavors to change social dynamics both within and outside their respective local Christian communities.

In contrast, 2 Peter portrays God's apostolic agent, Peter, in the line of apostles and prophets to shape social dynamics *within* the community.

The letter writers link Peter to the traditions of the apostles and prophets as an artful rhetorical calculation. The opening title describes Peter as an apostle, and the transfiguration story places him among the inner circle of apostolic witnesses accompanying Jesus on the holy mountain (2 Pet 1:18), namely, Peter, James, and John (Mark 9:2). The letter writers also add Paul to its apostolic roster in 3:15–16, conveying allegiance and alignment between Peter and Paul. Together, Peter, James, John, and Paul represent an apostolic extension of the prophetic tradition, both in their activities and, more importantly, in their literary works and interpretations (2 Pet 1:19–21; 3:1–2). Another early Christian writing, Clement of Alexandria's *Stromateis*, preserves a similar tradition. Where 2 Peter is subtle, this early Christian writing is more direct: "But they preserved the true tradition of the blessed doctrine in direct line from Peter, James, John, and Paul, the holy apostles, child [*pais*] inheriting from father (only a few are like [*homoios*] their fathers) and came with God's help to plant in us those seeds of their apostolic progenitors" (*Strom.* 1.11.3).[13] A near contemporary composition to 2 Peter, Clement's *Stromateis* maps the exact succession of apostolic personages that 2 Peter arranges in its discourse. Both texts imagine a direct line between the biblical prophets, the apostolic circle, and the early Christian community.

The letter writers are not the historical Peter, but they use the traditions associated with Peter to disarm their readers. They use traditions that carry legitimacy to champion one Christian attitude and behavior over other formulations. The letter writers interpreted apostolic and prophetic traditions to support a cultural version of Christianness that espouses unity without variety. In contrast, African American women writers employed the same tactic to espouse Christian unity across diversity. The same material is construed persuasively toward divergent social and cultural ends.

Contemporary readers of 2 Peter should struggle with the letter's historical reality. The authors chose to deploy influential sources to divide its membership. In doing so, they chose an interpretive strategy that was not predetermined but set by their cultural imaginations and parameters. The traditions of the apostles and prophets are not predisposed to Christian notions of unity without variety. Instead, the position is a cultural outcome imposed by those interpreting the tradition in their current moments according to their cultural and social agendas. Recognizing this

---

13. Quoted by Buell, *Making Christians*, 84.

raises questions about the canonical significance of 2 Peter. Does the letter's canonical status skew authoritative traditions toward divisive ends, or is it a warning about what derogatory, dehumanizing, and intolerant interpretive maneuvers produce?

The Wisdom Tradition of the Proverb

As discussed in chapter 7, nineteenth-century African American women used proverbs to shift perceptions about African Americans in their society. Writers like Anna Julia Cooper used proverbs to encourage inclusion and mutual respect. In contrast, the wisdom sayings in 2 Peter amplify social dishonor and shame to exclude and expel community members. The letter writers deploy the literary form as a tool to discredit and erase certain people.

The letter deploys two proverbs in one verse to authorize its derogatory portrayal of its opponents:

2 Pet 2:22a: A dog having returned to its own vomit
2 Pet 2:22b: A sow having been washed only to wallow in the mud

This double proverb depicts how false teachers return to teachings outside of Christ's followership: the false teachers are like dogs or swine, their previous lifestyle like vomit or mud. Here, the writers leverage Jewish wisdom traditions, such as Prov 26:11, which references a dog that finds its vomit enticing enough to return repeatedly. Similarly, they echo Synoptic wisdom sayings that reference dogs and pigs. For example, Matt 7:6 says, "Don't give holy things to dogs, and don't throw your pearls in front of pigs. They will stomp on the pearls, then turn around and attack you" (CEB). This gospel tradition pairs dogs and pigs together as amoral contrasts to the morality of the Jesus movement. This Synoptic stream of wisdom discourse is itself closely related to priestly discourse from Jewish tradition. In talking about "holy things," the discourse not only recalls the Israelite consecration of rituals but also exhibits familiarity with the stories and rhetoric of the Torah. For example, it echoes Exod 29:33: "They alone should eat the food that was used to purify them, to ordain them, and to make them holy. No one else should eat it because it is holy." The teachings that attack the false teachers, then, are not merely false; they are unholy.

With its appeal to the natural habits of dogs and swine, the authors of 2 Peter address portions of their Christian membership as animals. They use a rhetorical mechanism for isolating one group from others and installing rigid formulations of Christian identity and practice with those who remained. Dismissing this as a mere polemical tactic modeled from philosophical discourse undermines the cultural-making force of this rhetoric and its social implications. Compared to Cooper, who used an African American proverb to break down barriers between people, 2 Peter's rhetorical decision appears violently divisive. The authors of 2 Peter deploy the literary form of proverbs in one verse to push certain members within the group to the margins and even outside the community.

The Language of Spirit-Filled Inspiration

Nineteenth-century biblical interpreters such as Zilpha Elaw valued Spirit-filled interpretation. They believed interpretation involves multiple actors, divine *and* human, sacred and secular. These interpreters characterized existence as a spiritual and worldly entanglement in which God's Spirit generates prophetic utterance and action. Therefore, women like Elaw rehearsed the activities of God's spirit in their callings and lived experiences to validate their personhood and place within their Christian communities and the larger so-called Christian American society.

In contrast, 2 Peter connects the workings of the Spirit to inspired interpretation and prophetic speech to delegitimate the personhood, credibility, and place of a particular set of religious ideas, interpretations, *and* people within its Christian communities. Direct language about the Spirit occurs only once in 2 Peter, where the letter addresses the matter of inspired interpretation: "For not at any time was a prophecy brought by the will of human beings, but people spoke from God who were being carried along by the Holy Spirit" (1:21). According to the logic of the letter, the primary realm of God's Spirit activity is in the process of meaning-making and prophetic action. This statement, however, occurs directly before one of the most explicit statements about the operation of diverse ideologies, interpretations, and divine authority in the discourse (2 Pet 2:1): "But there were also false prophets among the people, as also there will be false teachers among your group. They will secretly bring in heresies producing destruction, even denying the divine enslaver who purchased them, bringing upon themselves swift destruction." The origin and directional flow of prophecy are essential. What is the origin of prophecy? Who speaks credibly and on whose behalf? If a prophetic utterance stems from humans and serves humans, it is a false prophecy. If it stems from God and serves God's community, it is true prophecy. At the center is the acknowledgment that

Spirit activity, orchestrated by God through designated agents, is the only legitimate activity.

Here, the letter writers seek to establish how their communities understood the prophetic word, oral and written. While the apostles and leaders of the Jesus movement make the prophetic word clear, members of the movement do not automatically embrace those views (see 2:2). Indeed, 1:19 is an exhortation encouraging the readers to pay attention to the prophetic word, insinuating there is a danger they have not done so in the past. Similarly, 1:20–21 and 2:1–3 indicate that the letter's recipients must sift between various interpretations to discern those who are credible and those who are not. The letter writers suggest that interpretation is of various sorts, but the legitimatizing element is prophecy that stems from the work of the Holy Spirit. The letter designates the Spirit as the arbiter of religious ideas and interpretations rather than the apostles or the prophets.

According to the rhetorical logic of 2 Peter, the purpose of Christian prophecy is to speak on behalf of the God-Parent with the Holy Spirit operating as the animating force within human agents. As 1:20–21 state, prophetic writing is not produced by "personal interpretation" but by the Holy Spirit's "carrying them along." Relationally speaking, this section's discourse intends to develop a collaborative enterprise, not individual and personal initiative. The letter disparages individuality, written or oral, in the prophetic production of God's will.

The Tradition of Balaam as Wisdom Discourse on Conformity

Nineteenth-century African American women used the story of Balaam to legitimate women's right to preach and lead their religious community. Lee, for instance, contrasts women's intellectual speech acts against that of nonhuman creations. If an animal can speak God's will, why not a woman?

In contrast, 2 Peter uses the same story as a weapon to cultivate and deepen prejudices. Second Peter deploys a particular version of the Balaam tradition to demonize alternative Christian understanding within the community (2 Pet 2:15–16). The book of Numbers portrays Balaam in a positive light as someone who refused to curse Israel (see Num 22:22–38). More popular Jewish tradition, as found in the book of Joshua and the book Nehemiah, presents him as one who constantly accepts bribes to draw Israel into idolatry (see Deut 23:4; Josh 24:9–10; Neh 13:2). This more common cycle is what 2 Peter resources when describing its opponents: "They went off course, forsaking a straight way, having followed the way of Balaam, the son of Bosor, who loved the wages of injustice" (2 Pet 2:15). The letter writers blend the defamatory Balaam tradition with the tradition that casts him in a more commendable light after following the guidance of the donkey that possesses prophetic sight. Much in the same way as the letter writers blend the transfiguration account with Matthew's baptismal pronouncement saying (see above), here they blend two different traditions to further diminish the quality of Balaam's so-called prophetic status. His donkey, a nonspeaking and irrational animal, acts rationally and even prophetically by verbally warning the prophet of the dangers ahead on the road: "But Balaam was censured for his wrongdoing: a speechless donkey having spoken in a man's voice put a stop to the prophet's madness" (2 Pet 2:16 // Num 22:27-30). The donkey speaks in service to preserving life. It observes and responds appropriately to God's revelations (Num 22:31-33). The letter's opponents, by contrast, act more animalistic than animals themselves (2 Pet 2:12).

The authors interpret the Balaam cycle within a larger discourse that defines Christian wisdom as one of unity without variety. The authors do this by juxtaposing the phrase "way of truth" (2:2) to the "way of Balaam" (2:15). In Greco-Roman world, the language of "way" carries the meaning of moral and wisdom teaching. The authors of 2 Peter use this language to craft a set of wisdom teachings for the conforming constituents of its in-group.

> Wisdom Teaching 1 (2 Pet 2:2): "way of truth" (*hodos tēs alētheias*)
> Wisdom Teaching 2 (2 Pet 2:15): "way of Balaam" (*hodō tou Balaam*)
> Wisdom Teaching 3 (2 Pet 2:21): "way of justice" (*hodon tēs dikaiosynēs*)

The first wisdom teaching, encapsulated in the phrase "way of truth," functions as antiteaching. From verses 3-14, the letter writers narrate the consequence of choosing not to go the way of truth and, in turn, paint a picture from the contrary position. The second wisdom teaching, the "way of Balaam" (2:15-19), extends the series of anecdotes and traditions rehearsed in the previous verses by providing a more storied reference. It functions as a centerpiece model, enumerating the consequences of Balaam-type actions and the effects of rejecting the singular way of truth practiced within the community. The last unit of wisdom teaching, represented by the phrase "way of justice," occurs in verses 20-22. This culminating statement rehearses the inevitable end of those who refuse to follow the way of the community: expulsion. The Balaam cycle, as recounted in 2 Peter, is not only relevant for understanding how its cultural rhetoric caricatures rival Christian formulations. It also highlights how a conceptual device can be used to conceal forced defection. The Balaam story is not a recurring topic in early Christian literature, particularly among the twenty-seven writings of the New Testament. It occurs explicitly in only two other places, Rev 2:14 and Jude 11. There does not appear to be a strong connection between 2 Peter and Rev 2:14, but an intertextual ripple occurs between 2 Pet 2:15 and Jude 11.

> Jude 11: Woe to them! For they go the way of Cain, and abandon themselves to Balaam's error for the sake of gain, and perish in Korah's rebellion.

> 2 Pet 2:15: They went off course, forsaking a straight path, having followed the path of Balaam, the son of Bosor, who loved the wages of injustice.

Both writings activate Jewish discourses of wisdom and prophecy through their references to Balaam and, in turn, the false prophets of Israelite tradition. The Balaam story functions as an exemplar of the popular stereotype of Israel's false prophets, who are caricatured as people of deceit (Deut 4:19; 13:6; Isa 19:14; Jer 23:13; Ezek 14:11), impure motives (Zech 13:2; Mark 3:30), and trickery (Num 25:18: Isa 53:9; Acts 13:10).[14] The Balaam tradition signals attitudes about in-group and out-group dynamics. It pits its members against each other, dividing them into separate paths. The antagonists are not located outside the communities; both Jude and 2 Peter address members within the community.

Another indicator that the writers of 2 Peter are forcing their rivals' defection while launching a series of rhetorical maneuvers to conceal *their motives* is the unique use of language for flight. The verb for fleeing or escaping, *apopheugō*, occurs three times in 2 Peter (1:4; 2:18, 20). This compound form for flight, combining the root word *pheugo* and the prefix *apo-*, does not appear elsewhere among the writings of the New Testament, not even in the infancy account found in Matt 2, where the root *pheugo* is used without the prefix to describe the flight of Jesus's family to Egypt (Matt 2:13).[15] In the Septuagint, however, the compound occurs

---

14. Bruce J. Malina and John J. Pilch, *Social-Science Commentary on the Letters of Paul* (Minneapolis: Fortress, 2006), Kindle loc. 623–24. See note for 2:3–4.

15. Shively T. J. Smith, "One More Time with Assata on My Mind: A Womanist

once. In the wisdom discourse of Sir 22:22, the compound word form for flight, *apopheugō*, is used in a wisdom saying to describe a forced separation between parties: "If you open your mouth against a friend, be not concerned, for reconciliation is possible—with the exception of reproach and arrogance and revealing a secret and a treacherous blow—in these cases any friend will flee [*apopheugō*]" (NETS). In both 2 Peter and Sirach, *apopheugō* is used to describe the separation of two parties who were once on amicable, even close, terms. Sirach counsels readers toward acts of reconciliation in response to verbal altercations that produce relational ruptures in friendship; 2 Peter, on the other hand, is penned to perform the act of rupture—namely, to speak against "friends" within the Christian in-group. The letter indicates no commitments to reconciliation or mediation. Indeed, it appears that the writers are acting on the Sirach teaching with the express purpose of dealing such a "treacherous blow" in order to force the flight of their opponents.

Conclusion

The letter of 2 Peter and African American women's literature share some common biblical traditions, but they interpret them religiously and socially towards different ends. In the nineteenth century, African American women find the traditions of the transfiguration, commission stories, wisdom, spiritual inspiration, and Balaam useful for their messages about liberation, inclusion, citizenship, and access. The authors of Peter similarly find them useful. However, 2 Peter's interpretive engagement with these various strands opposes pluralistic reform. It does not recount polemical attacks directed at the community but models how to practice such tactics within the community. The letter's polemical style, as expressed through its interpretive practices, is a mechanism for forcing conformity to or flight from the Christian communities under its influence.

Rereading of the Escape to Egypt (Matt 2:13–23) in Dialogue with an African American Woman Fugitive Narrative," in *Womanist Interpretations of the Bible: Expanding the Discourse*, ed. Gay L. Byron and Vanessa Lovelace, SemeiaSt 85 (Atlanta: SBL Press, 2016), 139–64.

Conclusion:
The Reception of 2 Peter in African American Women's Moral Discourses

Across Jewish and early Christian literature, the prophetic tradition supplies literary form, themes, language, and imagery for describing the acts of God's agents—be they biblical prophets and apostles or African American women prophets and writers. The letter of 2 Peter uses prophetic tradition to convey its message, but the letter does not, in turn, become a source for African American women who looked to do the same. While African American women seem to pull from similar Jewish and early Christian traditions as the letter, they do not explicitly employ the letter of 2 Peter in their literary tasks and social responses. One can only wonder why 2 Peter is not a source of religious readings for African American women's moral discourse. Perhaps that is the optimal question to ask at this point in the book—namely, is there something about the cultural rhetoric of 2 Peter that made it unappealing to African American women biblical interpreters of the nineteenth century?

Silencing 2 Peter

In stark contrast to their use of biblical citations and language from the gospels and Acts, Paul's letters and the letters of James and Jude, writings such as Hebrews or Revelation, and even a few references to 1 Peter, reference to 2 Peter in African American women's moral discourse is virtually nonexistent. Among the primary sources reviewed, Broughton, a Baptist women's suffragist, is the only woman in the canon to reference 2 Peter explicitly. She briefly cites 2 Pet 3:18 in her Bible study guide called "Bible Authority for Women's Work," in which she uses the verse to advocate for women's equal leadership within her southern African American Baptist fellowships. However, she does not reference 2 Peter in her autobiography nor supply any extended exposition on the letter.[1]

The general silence of African American women about 2 Peter stands out when one considers their adoption of other biblical texts. Broughton, for instance, both references and interprets 1 Pet 2:9 in her guide on "Women's Work," saying, "When God called out a peculiar people for himself, he made choice of the MOTHER of Israel."[2] Here, Broughton follows the agenda of 1 Peter by reflecting on the relationship between the identity of believers—especially those most vulnerable and exposed in the world—and the proclamation of Jesus's suffering and death. She follows 1 Peter's ethnic reasoning and asserts Christianity constitutes a new people while she makes the bold interpretive decision in the nineteenth century to connect God to a divinely-installed mother figure of Israel.

In other instances, readers encounter these women engaging biblical imagery to address their current strivings for human freedom, dignity, and prosperity. In addition to the numerous examples discussed in chapter 7, for instance, nineteenth-century African American women gesture frequently toward the New Testament domestic codes (Col 3:18–4:1; Eph 5:21–6:9; 1 Tim 2:8–15; 5:1–2; 6:1–2; Titus 2:1–10; 3:1–7; 1 Pet 2:18–3:7; 5:1–5). In doing so, these women directly challenge, if not outright discard, the enslavement commands in these household codes. For example, Frances Ellen Watkins Harper (1825–1911), an essayist and poet, was an abolitionist speaker for anti-slavery societies in New England. Her writings advocated for the improved conditions of enslaved or newly emancipated people of African descent in America. She wrote a poem titled "Bible Defense of Slavery" in the mid-nineteenth century. In the 1855 version of the poem, she critiques the interpretive work of white American Christian preachers in the pulpit who use the Bible to conceal the immorality of the institution of slavery and thereby lie about what God intended for people.

> For the fiercest wrong that ever rose
> Since Sodom's fearful cry,

---

1. Virginia Broughton, *Twenty Years' Experience of a Missionary in Spiritual Narratives*, intro. Sue E. Houchins (New York: Oxford University Press, 1988), 130–40. To review Broughton's Bible studies portions, consult Riggs, *Can I Get a Witness*, 40–41.

2. Capitalization of "mother" is Broughton's own literary decision ("Woman's Work," 408).

The word of life has been unclos'd
To give your God the lie.[3]

Here, similar to 2 Pet 2:6, Watkins Harper deploys the Sodom reference as an example of a people's awareness of the punitive response of God to their misdeeds. Using this reference, she conveys that the Bible's language about slavery is not the problem; rather, the problem is the dominant American Christian reading and use of that discourse to justify contemporary forms of enslavement as righteous and even necessary. Watkins Harper designates the use of the Bible for justifying enslavement the epitome of interpretive dishonesty veiled behind the banner of Christian identity and biblical witness: "An infidel could do no more / To hide his country's guilty blot, / Than spread God's holy record o'er/ The loathesome leprous spot."[4] Consistently across their moral writings, African American women read the biblical record as aligned to their position of liberation and equality as human beings made in the image of God, rather than as a witness to their humanity as something less.

These women were not, however, equally aligned in their readings of the gendered household roles prescribed and narrated across the Bible. Women like Broughton, for instance, espouse women's equal rights to American citizenship. However, she designates the home as the primary site of women's agency and contribution through catering to children, husbands, and the community. Affirming the exodus story as God's preference for emancipation, she adopts the position that women's primary divine role is as wife and mother by saying:

> In the deliverance of Israel from Egyptian bondage, it was the love and wisdom of woman that preserved, nourished and trained the man child that God called to be the leader, judge and priest for his people. Just here, as the care and training of children is preeminently the work of woman, we pause to say a few words concerning the influence and duty of women to children.[5]

Broughton reads the biblical perspective of womanhood and its descriptions of women's roles as coordinates for women's infinite agency and

3. Frances Ellen Watkins Harper, "Bible Defense of Slavery" (version 2), in Robbins and Gates, *The Portable Nineteenth-Century African American Women Writers*, 302–3.

4. Watkins Harper, "Bible Defense of Slavery," 303.

5. Broughton, "Woman's Work, 408.

influence. Rather than setting limits on women's activities and voice, women's place in the home for Broughton is the starting point of their agency, but not the exclusive site. "Did I say woman more needed [*sic*] in your cabinet than as an errand girl? Yes, brethren, you will find her of service upon your Executive Boards, both State and National. She'll do you good everywhere, all the days of your life; for God has said, 'It is not good that man should be alone.'"[6] Broughton understands women's agency as extending beyond the patriarchal social arrangement proposed in the biblical texts. But she does not abandon notions that women's fundamental role is as partner to husbands, mother to children, and care tender for their larger communities.[7]

In contrast, Sojourner Truth more readily sets women's agency outside the household, assigning the larger civic and political arenas as a potential first site for African American women's voices and activities. One perhaps could even say she thought women's leadership in the public sphere could improve the geopolitical landscape for the world when she says:

> Why children, if you have woman's rights give it to her and you will feel better. You will have your own rights, and they wont be so much trouble.… I have heard the bible and have learned that Eve caused man to sin. Well if woman upset the world, do give her a chance to set it right side up again. The Lady has spoken about Jesus, how he never spurned woman from him, and she was right. When Lazarus died, Mary and Martha came to him with faith and love and besought him to raise their brother. And Jesus wept—and Lazarus came forth. And how came Jesus into the world? Through God who created him and woman who bore him. Man, where is your part? But the women are coming up blessed

---

6. Broughton continues her thought about women's contribution by, nonetheless, circling back to conventional household roles of mother and wife, reaffirming its significance as in accordance with scripture by saying: "God help us to examine this subject in the light of his Word! Do it for the sake of the children, who need the united wisdom of men and women to guard their wayward feet in the path of righteousness; do it for the sake of our homes, where we want love, order, peace and purity; but know we cannot have them unless husband and wife work and plan together. Let us do it for the sake of our country, where good and just laws are so much needed for the protection and encouragement of both man and woman; and above all for the sake of the Lord Jesus, who has prayed the Father that we might be one even as he and his Father were one; that the World might believe he was sent of the Father" (Broughton, "Woman's Work," 412).

7. Broughton, "Women's Work," 407–13.

by God and a few of the men are coming up with them. But man is in a
tight place, the poor slave is on him, woman is coming on him, and he is
surely between a hawk and a buzzard.[8]

Similar to Truth, Julie A. J. Foote (1823–1900) emphasizes women's
leadership in the ecclesial and public spheres as opposed to the household.
She critiques male pastors who interpret the Bible for their own freedom,
while continuing to use it to maintain the subordination, even silence, of
women's agency and voice. Reporting her disapproval for how the Bible
is used to support the idea that women are unfit to lead, preach, or speak
publicly about matters of faith and civic duty within African American
Christian communions she says: "To this, Minister Monroe and another
man—I had almost said a fiend in human shape—answered that they did
not believe in women's preaching, and would not admit one in the church,
striving hard to justify themselves from the Bible, which one of them
held in his unholy hands."[9] Like Watkins Harper, Foote highlighted the
interpretive practices of Christian leaders as the chief problem in how the
Bible's social codes empower some while disempowering others. For some
African American women writing in the nineteenth century, the Bible's
social arrangements are a starting point but not an ending point for African Americans and women's social place. For others, the problem of the
Bible's prescriptions of social caste and descriptions of social location falls
on the shoulders of the interpretive actors who choose to emphasize that
as the Christian message in the first place.

These women, then, had a complicated relationship with biblical texts.
They resourced the tradition—using various biblical passages as materials—in different ways and to different ends. But the overall canonical
influence of the Christian Bible on these women is undeniable. Many of
them learned to read and write by studying the Bible, and they taught
others in their communities using the Bible as the textbook. Maria Stewart, a Boston abolitionist orator and contemplative writer, attests to the
Bible's function as a source of learning and faith:

---

8. Sojourner Truth, "Speech Delivered to Women's Rights Convention in Akron
Ohio" (1851), in Robbins and Gates, *The Portable Nineteenth-Century African American Women Writers* (New York: Penguin, 2017), 7–8.
    9. Julia A. J. Foote, "Selections from A Brand Plucked from the Fire" (1870),
in Robbins and Gates, *The Portable Nineteenth-Century African American Women
Writers*, 198.

> I have borrowed much of my language from the Holy Bible. During the years of childhood and youth it was the book that I mostly studied; and now, while my hands are toiling for their daily sustenance, my heart is most generally meditating upon its divine truths. I am more and more convinced that the cause of Christ will never be built up, Satan's kingdom will never be destroyed, the chains of slavery and ignorance will never burst, and morality and virtue will never flourish, till ... the professing followers of Christ arise and shine forth, and prove to the world that there is a reality in religion, and a beauty in the fear of the Lord.[10]

Stewart's reflection attests that the language and stories of the Bible were essential cultural materials for African American rhetorical communities, be they Christian identified or not. The reason for this was that, from the time of the Puritan colonial settlers of New England through the Civil War era, the public speech and political theology of America reflected biblical discourses, conceptions, and literary forms (see chapter 3). Not surprisingly, African Americans adopted biblical rhetoric as their own, bending it toward their constructive task of making and remaking a people in a strange land that they now called home. African American women's exercises in biblical interpretation in the nineteenth century served the purpose of articulating the self-awareness, spirituality, and social critique they held with or without the Christian claim. Because of this, their overwhelming collective silence and nonuse of 2 Peter stands out. Thus, this book emphasizes the phenomenon of discursive interpretation, citational techniques, and rhetorical strategy in the women's writings, as opposed to tracing how they interpreted the letter (i.e., the women's particular readings and meaning-making of 2 Peter).

Still, it is helpful at this point to consider why 2 Peter was not a germane conversation partner for nineteenth century African American women. Second Peter's absence from these women's writings suggests that its textual construction of Christian behavior and attitudes was not conducive to their rhetorical aims. The rhetoric of 2 Peter was dangerously like the moral suasions characterizing white, Eurocentric formulations of Christianness in America. The letter expresses Christian rhetoric that calls its people dogs and pigs without consciousness (2:22). It espouses an ethnic Christian identity construction that made group

---

10. Maria W. Stewart, *Meditations from the Pen of Mrs. Maria W. Stewart* (Washington, DC: Enterprise, 1879).

spaces inhospitable (2:1–3) and inhumane (2:4, 9) for those deemed other.[11] There is no restraint in the rhetoric of 2 Peter nor remorse. It carries no sense that mediation is an appropriate communal response to intracommunal differences. Moreover, the letter writers assume the normativity of their position while targeting alternative expressions as aberrations in need, ultimately, of suppression and removal. There was no place for 2 Peter's moral position and persuasive effect in the reception history of nineteenth-century African American women.

The letter's canonical voice recounts the circumstances that suited its writers' positions. They assert that those who left defected voluntarily without acknowledging the lack of Christian welcome the letter extends to those who tried to live among them as their kinspeople. What traditional biblical scholarship dubs as heretical opponents, unorthodox rivals, gnostic-teaching retentions, or Epicurean philosophical notions of providence, nineteenth-century African American women viewed differently (see chapters 2 and 6). Rather than identifying 2 Peter's opponents as analogous to their hegemonic white opponents, the women appear to have perceived the *entire* discourse of 2 Peter as the problem.

Nineteenth-century African American women modeled an approach to 2 Peter that not only exercised a selective rejection of its epistolary theology but that, perhaps, also invited those committed to the doctrine of inspiration to reevaluate the letter's position as both authoritative and canonical. Influenced by the women's limited use of 2 Peter, contemporary interpreters can question if 2 Peter's authority depends on its social theology of God's justice—which the letter links to the traditions of the apostles, the prophets, and Jesus's transfiguration. Interpreters can also ponder the letter's use of the apostle Peter's name and its theological frame

---

11. Second Peter's violent rhetorical strategy and tone is not unique within the New Testament. It participates in a canonical trail of invective that targets Others based on ethnicity, belief, practice, etc. For example, Gay L. Byron describes the rhetoric of Titus 1:10–16 as abusive and ethnically prejudicial: "The key to understanding ethno-political rhetorics is to explore how these rhetorics function as political invective for the purpose of advancing certain teachings within early Christian communities. In the brief letter to Titus, the ethnic slur directed against the Cretans is an example of an ethno-political rhetoric…. The Cretans in this text are part of a larger discourse of political invective. The author used this ethnic group to slander certain groups who were not representing the prescribed teachings, values, and beliefs of the dominant voices within the community" (Byron, *Symbolic Blackness and Ethnic Difference in Early Christian Literature*, 2–3).

of justice. The letters writers couple a hybridized version of the apostle's name with the Greek word for "justice" to install measures of exclusion, censure, homogeneity, and disinheritance, all while calling their activities "the way of truth" (2:2). Nineteenth-century African American women might supply a throughway by which to reconsider such exhortations simply by the absence of 2 Peter in their moral writings.

By selectively avoiding the use of 2 Peter, African American women writers showcase the range of meanings attached to biblical authority, canon, inspiration, and literalism.[12] They represent a cautionary tale for contemporary Bible readers, advising against confusing the authority of scripture with the need to adjudicate the cultural implications of biblical rhetoric in existentially current moments. What these women demonstrate is that just because a writing like 2 Peter is scripture does not mean that its use in contemporary contexts and societies is automatically good or moral. Indeed, their limited use of 2 Peter models an interpretive sensibility that takes from the Bible what is revelatory and constructive for the work of collective peoplehood and identity while leaving behind those things that are counterproductive to the (re)creation of God's people in the current moment.

Interpreting 2 Peter through
African American Women's Moral Discourse

Viewed through the phenomenon of nineteenth-century African American women's moral discourses, the cultural rhetoric of 2 Peter appears intolerant. The letter participates in polemical name calling (e.g., 2 Pet 2:22), it lacks standard Christian language of hospitality (cf. 1 Pet 4:9; Heb 13:2; Rom 12:13), and there are no signs of mediation across differences (cf. Acts 15; Jas 4:11; 1 Cor 11:17–22). It does not strive for diverse inclusion nor stimulate considerations about alternative group compositions. The letter writers draw from the pluralism of their Mediterranean environment while intentionally denying it as a value of Christian identity and a distinction of Christian behavior.

Bearing this point in mind, I concede that my approach is unique. Nineteenth-century African American women's writings are not the conventional point of departure for examining the rhetorical character of

---

12. Noll, *America's God*, 367–85.

2 Peter or its reception history in early Christian literature and history. Moreover, it is not lost on me that for some within biblical studies and early Christian literature, it is jarring to find analysis of 2 Peter delayed as the second step in critical exegesis and historical reconstruction. This book, however, intentionally models a different kind of interaction with early Christian literature. Buell's approach to historical investigation and reconstruction of early Christianity as an ethnic identity offers a generative path for delineating the approach of this project. Describing how one should trace the identity formations of ancient Greekness, Buell leverages Greek historian Simon Goldhill's assertion that "the historian's narration has to go back and forth between present and past, like a weaver's shuttle, to make up a picture."[13] This book models interpretation at the nexus point between two historical phenomena of discursive religious writing, interpretation, and culture-making rhetoric: nineteenth-century African American women's moral discourses and 2 Peter's epistolary discourse. Without collapsing their historical differences, the book renders the early Christian discourse of 2 Peter knowable in a new form, using African American women's writing as an instrument for completing the picture of the testament letter.

Three features distinguish my approach and shape the interpretive play between text and context modeled in earlier chapters: (1) I am a biblical interpreter and a historian of early Christianity, meaning my primary aim is to account for early Christian literature in its cultural rhetorical contexts, although I do so from a different epistemological trajectory. This project's chief task is reexamining 2 Peter, not nineteenth-century writings per se. (2) I focus thematically on representing common topics extant in scholarly conversations about 2 Peter. As such, 2 Peter studies set the agenda for what I analyze in African American women's moral discourses, and it is 2 Peter to which I return again and again. For example, I explore how analyzing the rhetorical phenomenon of pseudonymity in the writings of nineteenth-century African American women (ch. 5) can inform descriptions of 2 Peter's pseudonymous character (ch. 6). Such an approach has the potential to change the nature of critical conversations about pseudonymity and the New Testament in general, as well as in Petrine studies. (3) I intend my approach to serve as an intervention in interpretive his-

---

13. Quoted in Buell, *Why This New Race*; Simon Goldhill, *Who Needs Greek? Contests in the Cultural History of Hellenism* (Cambridge: Cambridge University Press, 2002), 11. Emphasis in original.

tory, which traditionally has kept African American women from being at the table of critical biblical studies. I resource their discursive strategies, citational techniques, and treatments of biblical themes as materials for exegeting 2 Peter. Recent scholarly endeavors have shifted to systematically recover and catalog African American biblical interpretive activities in conversation with early Christian writings.[14] Participating in this effort, albeit with modified focus, I also aim to expand the annals of American interpretive histories of the New Testament by resourcing African American literature in literary, historical, and existential approaches to biblical interpretation.

I label my interpretive approach phenomenological exegesis. This reading strategy engages in comparative analysis of similar phenomena in rhetorical strategy and cultural influence.[15] A phenomenological approach analyzes the cultural rhetoric and discursive phenomena of one historical community to sensitize interpreters to the spectrum of meaning potentials and histories related to biblical writings and their ancient contexts and

---

14. While I was completing this book, for example, Lisa Bowens published her magisterial work: *African American Readings of Paul*; see Shively T. J. Smith, review of *African American Readings of Paul*, by Lisa Bowens, *Theological Studies* 83.2 (2022): 319–20. Other similar historical accountings of African American interpretive traditions include Emerson B. Powery, "Under the Gaze of the Empire: Who Is My Neighbor?," *Int* 62 (2008): 134–44; Emerson B. Powery and Rodney Steven Sadler, *The Genesis of Liberation: Biblical Interpretation in the Antebellum Narratives of the Enslaved* (Louisville: Westminster John Knox, 2016); Mitzi J. Smith, *Womanist Sass and Talk Back: Social (In)justice, Intersectionality, and Biblical Interpretation* (Eugene, OR: Cascade, 2018); Randall C. Bailey, ed., *Yet with a Steady Beat: Contemporary U.S. Afrocentric Biblical Interpretation*, SemeiaSt 42 (Atlanta: Society of Biblical Literature, 2003); Herbert Robinson Marbury, *Pillars of Cloud and Fire: The Politics of Exodus in African American Biblical Interpretation*, Religion and Social Transformation (New York: New York University Press, 2015); Vincent L. Wimbush, *The Bible and African Americans: A Brief History*, Facets (Minneapolis: Fortress, 2003); and Jeremy Punt, *Postcolonial Biblical Interpretation: Reframing Paul* (Ledien: Brill, 2015); Callahan, *Talking Book*.

15. Amos N. Wilder signals the phenomenological aspects of biblical rhetorical analysis. In the latter part of the twentieth century, he spotlights the relationship-making qualities of New Testament writings and literary forms such as the parables, but he does not go as far as talking about it as a culture-making endeavor within the varieties of early Christian culture-making activities evident across the diverse early Christian writings in and beyond the canon. See, for example, Amos N. Wilder, *The New Voice: Religion, Literature, Hermeneutics* (New York: Herder & Herder, 1969); Wilder, *Jesus' Parables and the War of Myths: Essays on Imagination in the Scriptures*, ed. James Breech (Philadelphia: Fortress, 1982).

rhetorical aims. Phenomenological exegesis is not limited to only drawing on other Bible-receiving interpretive communities. Although not modeled in this book, a phenomenological approach can function as a strategy for interreligious comparison. It can resource other historical contexts, social moments, and peoplehood. The underlying presupposition of phenomenological exegesis is that no interpreter is a blank slate, functioning as an entirely objective reader. No one can block out everything. Instead of pretending such bias is avoidable, a phenomenological approach to interpretation critically leverages the reality of bias. The interpreter chooses to work her way through biblical writings and histories from a particular location of reception history and lived experience.[16] In this book, I have aimed to draw on (or to use as a resource) the cultural rhetoric of African American women's moral discourses to interpret 2 Peter in a way, heretofore, not taken.

Proposing an Alternative Genealogy for Biblical Studies

This study takes a different path in tracing reception history and considering the rhetorical afterlife of 2 Peter. While acknowledging the sources of early Christian traditions evident in 2 Peter, the book does not limit the study to the periods of Clement, Eusebius, Tertullian, Athanasius, and even Calvin or Luther. Instead, this study attends to the interpretive practices of nineteenth-century African American women who, like the male figures listed above, resourced biblical imagery, rhetoric, and thought worlds to critique and advocate for new social arrangements, religious definitions, and cultural particularities. In some ways, this book rejects the notion that the most noteworthy reception of 2 Peter—or any early Christian writing, canonical or noncanonical—stops in the so-called patristic and reformation periods. Moreover, it does not presuppose that the most exemplary historical readings and usages of early Christian writings exist chiefly within Euro-Western histories, frameworks, and social responses to the changing tides of societies.

Second Peter and the other writings of early Christianity had many lives of reception, interpretation, and usage. These different moments of receipt offer insight into the potential meanings and dimensions of social rhetoric and historics. Privileging one genealogical history of early

---

16. Punt, "Inhabiting the World in Front of the Text," 207–24.

Christian writings over others or ignoring the legitimacy and interpretive opportunities of other engagements is a form of scholarly suppression.[17] Such omissions and silences impoverish the field of critical biblical studies and histories and inhibit the full significance of early Christian literature from being realized.

Of course, no project accounts for all the tracks of reception history that any single early Christian writing has to its credit because the historical endeavor is always selective. In this case, I select the moral discourses of nineteenth-century African American women as the interpretive path, though I could have surveyed its reception history across all nineteenth-century African American literature. Alternatively, I could have veered away from the nineteenth century altogether and centered my interpretive lens on the twentieth century or even the more recent histories of the twenty-first century. This examination could have considered 2 Peter's reception history and rhetorical lineage among literary interpretive communities in South Africa, Botswana, or Asian regions like India or South Korea.[18] All of these are viable paths of investigation; however, I established the limits of this study from the fabric of my curiosities and scholarly interests in nineteenth-century African American women writers. As my silent teachers, hidden from view in the biblical academy, these women teach me that my interpretive voice and maneuvers matter, even as the narrow terrain of academia tells me that successful navigation of its landscape hinges on my ability to accept the status quo silently. I choose the interpretive community that—while unacknowledged by mainstream academia—has

---

17. Unpublished essay by Luis Menéndez-Antuña, "Whiteness and the Dismissal of Emancipatory Hermeneutics in Biblical Studies: A Decolonial Genealogy" (paper presented at a Wabash Group session at Boston University School of Theology, Boston, 20 October 2022).

18. For other approaches emphasizing social location of the author, see Tat-siong Benny Liew and Fernando F. Segovia, eds., *Reading Biblical Texts Together: Pursuing Minoritized Biblical Criticism*, SemeiaSt 98 (Atlanta: SBL Press, 2022); Tat-siong Benny Liew, *What Is Asian American Biblical Hermeneutics? Reading the New Testament* (Honolulu: University of Hawi'i Press, 2008); R. S. Sugirtharajah, *Voices from the Margin: Interpreting the Bible in the Third World*, 25th anniv. ed. (Maryknoll, NY: Orbis, 2016); Tat-siong Benny Liew, ed., *Postcolonial Interventions: Essays in Honor of R. S. Sugirtharajah*, Bible in the Modern World (Sheffield: Sheffield Phoenix, 2009); Mary F. Foskett and Jeffrey K. Kuan, *Ways of Being, Ways of Reading: Asian American Biblical Interpretation* (St. Louis: Chalice, 2006); Kwok Pui-lan, *Discovering the Bible in the Non-biblical World*, Bible & Liberation (Eugene, OR: Wipf & Stock, 2003).

always journeyed with me, demonstrating critical biblical engagement that addresses current matters of social exclusion and inequality. Bringing them out of their hiding place, this examination places nineteenth-century African American women writers where they belong—next to Clement, Justin Martyr, Augustine, Martin Luther, Albert Schweitzer, Howard Thurman, and others who read early Christian writings not only to convey something about them but also to convey something *with* them.

Nineteenth-century African American women modeled a principled approach by choosing not to use 2 Peter in their context because of what the letter carries out rhetorically, as well as how it achieves its end. Although these women exercised an interpretive decision of disregard in their context, I am unconvinced that sidestepping 2 Peter is the most appropriate approach for contemporary contexts. Silence and circumvention, as they relate to 2 Peter, cannot be permitted today because it allows a particular brand of Christian moral suasion to go unchecked as legitimate, godly, and just. Such strands of Christian discourse tout justice so that it can do the most unjust things—dehumanize others, discourage community across differences, marginalize some and extradite others. The letter of 2 Peter reminds us how un-Christian people of Christianity can be when we let opposing understandings about God's activities, timing, and possibilities shade our view of what it means to be, first and foremost, truly "equal in honorable quality ... in bringing the justice of our God" (2 Pet 1:1) within our local and global communities. Modern-day biblical scholars must wrestle with two tough questions. First, do we avoid 2 Peter because it contradicts many early Christian writings, particularly in the New Testament, that offer encouragement to share all things in common (Acts 2:44; 4:32), extend hospitality to each other and strangers (Matt 10:11; Mark 6:10; Luke 9:4; 10:7–8), greet each other with mutuality and love (1 Pet 3:8), and proclaim the good news so that captives are set free (Luke 4:14–21)? Second, do we turn a blind eye to 2 Peter because it supports the ideas of those who want to assert only one Christian identity, practice, and embodiment?

African American women's moral discourses tutor us now that a choice is necessary. We learn that close readers of biblical texts such as 2 Peter determine the kinds of societies, communities, and religious imperatives to which they subscribe and reinscribe as they sift meanings from the past and interpret them for current realities. The ends to which readers interpret 2 Peter may be more a reflection of our current human commitments and strivings than of the letter's ancient meaning. Interpreting 2 Peter today holds up a mirror for the attitudes and behaviors of religious communities when they address each other pejoratively, seek each other's cursed destruction, and champion the exclusion of neighbors simply because they share a difference of opinion or living pattern. Reading 2 Peter for its cultural rhetoric forces us to ask, *Are these the people we want to be now?*

Bibliography

Biblical Studies and Early Christian Literature

Bailey, James L., and Lyle D. Vander Broek. *Literary Forms in the New Testament: A Handbook.* Louisville: Westminster John Knox, 1992.

Bailey, Randall C., ed. *Yet with a Steady Beat: Contemporary U.S. Afrocentric Biblical Interpretation.* SemeiaSt 42. Atlanta: Society of Biblical Literature, 2003.

Baird, William. *History of New Testament Research.* 3 vols. Minneapolis: Fortress, 1992–2013.

Barbara Aland, Kurt Aland, Iōan D Karavidopoulos, Carlo Maria Martini, and Bruce M Metzger, eds. *The Greek New Testament.* 5th rev. ed. Stuttgart: Deutsche Bibelgesellschaft/United Bible Societies, 2014.

Bauckham, Richard J. "2 Peter and the Apocalypse of Peter Revisited: A Response to Jörg Frey." Pages 261–81 in *2 Peter and the Apocalypse of Peter: Towards a New Perspective.* Edited by Jörg Frey, Matthijs den Dulk, and Jan G. van der Watt. Leiden: Brill, 2019.

———. *Jude, 2 Peter.* WBC 50. Nashville: Thomas Nelson, 2003.

Beavis, Mary Ann. *The First Christian Slave: Onesimus in Context.* Eugene, OR: Wipf & Stock, 2021.

Beck, Eric J. *Justice and Mercy in the Apocalypse of Peter : A New Translation and Analysis of the Purpose of the Text.* WUNT 427. Tübingen: Mohr Siebeck, 2019.

Bell, Daniel. *The Cultural Contradictions of Capitalism.* New York: Basic Books, 1976.

Berger Peter, and Thomas Luckmann. *The Social Construction of Reality: A Treatise in the Sociology of Knowledge.* Garden City, NY: Doubleday, 1967.

Bigg, Charles A. *Critical and Exegetical Commentary on the Epistles of St. Peter and St. Jude.* ICC. Repr., Edinburgh: T&T Clark, 1978.

Black, C. Clifton. "Rhetorical Criticism." Pages 256–77 in *Hearing the New Testament: Strategies for Interpretation*. Edited by Joel B. Green. Grand Rapids: Eerdmans, 1995.

Blasi, Anthony J. Paul-André Turcotte, and Jean Duhaime. *Handbook of Early Christianity: Social Science Approaches*. Walnut Creek, CA: AltaMira, 2002.

Bloch, Marc. *The Historian's Craft*. Manchester, UK: Manchester University Press, 1954.

Blount, Brian K. *Cultural Interpretation: Reorienting New Testament Criticism*. Minneapolis: Fortress, 1995.

Bowens, Lisa. *African American Readings of Paul: Reception, Resistance and Transformation*. Grand Rapids: Eerdmans, 2020.

Bremmer, Jan N. "Orphic, Roman, Jewish and Christian Tours of Hell: Observations on the Apocalypse of Peter." Pages 305–22 in *Other Worlds and Their Relation to This World: Early Jewish and Ancient Christian Traditions*. Edited by Erik M. M. Eynikel, Florentino Garcia Martinez, Joseph Verheyden, and Tobias Nicklas. JSJSup 143. Leiden: Brill, 2010.

Buchholz, Dennis. *Your Eyes Will Be Opened: A Study of the Greek (Ethiopic) Apocalypse of Peter*. SBLDS 97. Atlanta: Scholars Press, 1988.

Buell, Denise Kimber. *Making Christians: Clement of Alexandria and the Rhetoric of Legitimacy*. Princeton, NJ: Princeton University Press, 1999.

———. "Rethinking the Relevance of Race for Early Christian Self-Definition." *HTR* 94 (2001): 449–76.

———. *Why This New Race: Ethnic Reasoning in Early Christianity*. New York: Columbia University Press, 2008.

Byron, Gay L. *Symbolic Blackness and Ethnic Difference in Early Christian Literature*. New York: Routledge, 2002.

Byron, Gay L., and Hugh R. Page Jr., eds. *Black Scholars Matter: Visions, Struggles, and Hopes in Africana Biblical Studies*. RBS 100. Atlanta: SBL Press, 2022.

Callahan, Allen Dwight. *The Talking Book: African Americans and the Bible*. New Haven: Yale University Press, 2006.

Callan, Terrance. *Acknowledging the Divine Benefactor: The Second Letter of Peter*. Eugene, OR: Pickwick, 2014.

Cameron, Averil. *Christianity and the Rhetoric of Empire: The Development of Christian Discourse*. Sather Classical Lectures. Berkeley: University of California Press, 1991.

Carter, Warren. *The Roman Empire and the New Testament: An Essential Guide*. Nashville: Abingdon, 2006.

Collins, Patricia Hill, and Sirma Bilge. *Intersectionality. Key Concepts*. Malden, MA: Polity Press, 2016.

Counet, Patrick Chatelion. "Pseudepigraphy and the Petrine School: Spirit and Tradition in 1 and 2 Peter and Jude." *HvTSt* 62 (2006): 403–24.

Davids, Peter H. *The Letters of 2 Peter and Jude*. Pillar New Testament Commentary. Grand Rapids: Eerdmans, 2006.

De Wet, Chris L. *The Unbound God: Slavery and the Formation of Early Christian Thought*. Routledge Studies in the Early Christian World. New York: Routledge, 2018.

———. *Preaching Bondage: John Chrysostom and the Discourse of Slavery in Early Christianity*. Oakland: University of California Press, 2015.

Donelson, Lewis R. *1 and 2 Peter and Jude: A Commentary*. NTL. Louisville: Westminster John Knox, 2010.

Dube, Musa. "Intercultural Biblical Interpretations." *Swedish Missiological Themes* 98.3 (2010): 361–88.

———. *Other Ways of Reading: African Women and the Bible*. GBPS 7. Atlanta: Society of Biblical Literature, 2001.

———. "Reading for Decolonization (John 4.1–42)." Pages 51–75 in *John and Postcolonialism: Travel, Space, and Power*. Edited by Musa W. Dube and Jeffrey L. Staley. London: Sheffield Academic, 2002.

Duling, Dennis. *The New Testament: History, Literature, and Social Context*. 4th ed. Belmont, CA: Wadsworth, 2003.

Elliott, John H. *A Home for the Homeless: A Social-Scientific Criticism of 1 Peter, Its Situation and Strategy*. 2nd ed. Eugene, OR: Wipf & Stock, 2005.

Elliott, Robert C. *The Literary Persona*. Chicago: University of Chicago Press, 1982.

Epistle to Diognetus. English translation by Bart D. Ehrman. LCL 25. Cambridge: Harvard University Press, 2003.

Eusebius. *The Ecclesiastical History*. English translation by Kirsopp Lake. LCL 153. Cambridge: Harvard University Press, 1926.

FitzGerald, Frances. *The Evangelicals: The Struggle to Shape America*. New York: Simon & Schuster, 2017.

Fitzmyer, Joseph A. "The Name Simon." *HTR* 56 (1963): 105–112.

Fornberg, Tord. *An Early Church in a Pluralistic Society: A Study of 2 Peter*. ConBNT 9. Lund: Gleerup, 1977.

Foskett, Mary F., and Jeffrey K. Kuan. *Ways of Being, Ways of Reading: Asian American Biblical Interpretation*. St. Louis: Chalice, 2006.

Foster, Paul. "Does the *Apocalypse of Peter* Help to Determine the Date of 2 Peter?" Pages 217–60 in *2 Peter and the Apocalypse of Peter: Towards a New Perspective*. Edited by Jörg Frey, Matthijs den Dulk, and Jan G. van der Watt. Leiden: Brill, 2019.

Fredriksen, Paula. *Paul, the Pagan's Apostle*. New Haven: Yale University Press, 2017.

Frey, Jörg. *The Letter of Jude and the Second Letter of Peter: A Theological Commentary*. Translated by Kathleen Ess. Waco, TX: Baylor University Press, 2018.

———. "Second Peter in New Perspective." Pages 7–74 in *2 Peter and the Apocalypse of Peter: Towards a New Perspective*. Edited by Jörg Frey, Matthijs den Dulk, and Jan G. van der Watt. Leiden: Brill, 2019.

Gadamer, Hans-Georg. *Truth and Method*. Translated by Joel Weinsheimer and Donald G. Marshall. 2nd ed. New York: Crossroad/Continuum, 2004.

Gafney, Wilda C. *Womanist Midrash: A Reintroduction to the Women of the Torah and the Throne*. Westminster John Knox, 2017.

Gager, John. *Kingdom and Community: The Social World of Early Christianity*. Englewood Cliffs, NJ: Prentice-Hall, 1975.

Gilmour, Michael J. *The Significance of Parallels between 2 Peter and Other Early Christian Literature*. AcBib 10. Atlanta: Society of Biblical Literature, 2002.

Goldhill, Simon. *Who Needs Greek? Contests in the Cultural History of Hellenism*. Cambridge: Cambridge University Press, 2002.

Gorman, Michael J. *Elements of Biblical Exegesis: A Basic Guide for Students and Ministers*. Rev. and exp. ed. Grand Rapids: Baker Academic, 2010.

Grant, Jacquelyn. "Black Theology and the Black Woman." Pages 418–33 in *Black Theology: A Documentary History, 1966–1979*. Edited by Gayraud S. Wilmore and James H. Cone. Maryknoll, NY: Orbis, 1979.

Grant, Robert. *Heresy and Criticism: The Search for Authenticity in Early Christian Literature*. Louisville: Westminster John Knox, 1993.

Grundmann, Walter. *Der Brief des Judas und der zweite Brief des Petrus*. Theologischer HKNT 15. Berlin: Evangelische Verlagsanstalt, 1974.

Grünstäudl, Wolfgang. *Petrus Alexandrinus: Studien zum historischen und theologischen Ort des Zweiten Petrusbriefes*. WUNT 2/315. Tübingen: Mohr Siebeck, 2013.

Harrill, J. Albert. *The Manumission of Slaves in Early Christianity*. Tübingen: Mohr Siebeck, 1995.

Harrington, Daniel J. "Jude and 2 Peter." Pages 159–299 in *1 Peter, Jude and 2 Peter*, edited by Donald P. Senior and Daniel J. Harrington. SP 15. Collegeville, MN: Liturgical Press, 2003.

———. *Jude and 2 Peter*. SP. Collegeville, MN: Liturgical Press, 2003.

Hayes, John H. *Dictionary of Biblical Interpretation*. 2 vols. Nashville: Abingdon, 1999.

Henning, Meghan R. *Hell Hath No Fury: Gender, Disability, and the Invention of Damned Bodies in Early Christian Literature*. AYBRL. New Haven: Yale University Press, 2021.

———. *Educating Early Christians through the Rhetoric of Hell: "Weeping and Gnashing of Teeth" as Paideia in Matthew and the Early Church*. WUNT 382. Tübingen: Mohr Siebeck, 2014.

Hills, Margaret Thorndike. *A Ready-Reference History of the English Bible*. New York: American Bible Society, 1971.

Hockey, Katherine M., and David Horrell. *Ethnicity, Race, Religion: Identities and Ideologies in Early Jewish and Christian Texts, and in Modern Biblical Interpretation*. New York: Bloomsbury Academic, 2018.

Holmes, Michael W., ed. *Apostolic Fathers*. 3rd ed. Accordance version. Grand Rapids: Baker, 2007.

Horrell, David G. "The Product of a Petrine Circle? A Reassessment of the Origin and Character of 1 Peter." *JSNT* 86 (2002): 29–60.

———. "'Race,' 'Nation,' 'People': Ethnic Identity-Construction in 1 Peter 2.9." *NTS* 58 (2012): 123–43.

Horsley, R. A. "The Slave Systems of Classical Antiquity and Their Reluctant Recognition by Modern Scholars." *Semeia* 83–84 (1998): 19–66.

———. *Sociology and the Jesus Movement*. 2nd ed. New York: Crossroad, 1994.

Hughes, Richard T. *Myths America Lives By: White Supremacy and the Stories That Give Us Meaning*. 2nd ed. Urbana: University of Illinois Press, 2018.

Jakab, Attila. "The Reception of the Apocalypse of Peter in Ancient Christianity." Pages 174–86 in *The Apocalypse of Peter*. Edited by Jan N. Bremmer and István Czachesz. Studies in Early Christian Apocrypha 7. Leuven: Peeters, 2003.

Johnson, Luke Timothy *Among the Gentiles: Greco-Roman Religion and Christianity*. AYBRL. New Haven: Yale University Press, 2009.

———. "The New Testament's Anti-Jewish Slander and the Conventions of Ancient Polemic." *JBL* 108 (1989): 419–41.

Johnson, Sylvester. *The Myth of Ham in Nineteenth-Century American Christianity: Race, Heathens, and the People of God.* New York: Palgrave, 2004.

Kaaluund, Jennifer T. *Reading Hebrews and 1 Peter with the African American Great Migration: Diaspora, Place and Identity.* LNTS 598. London: T&T Clark, 2020.

Kahl, Brigitte. *Galatians Re-imagined: Reading with the Eyes of the Vanquished* (Minneapolis: Fortress, 2010.

Kartzow, Marianne Bjelland. *The Slave Metaphor and Gendered Enslavement in Early Christian Discourse: Double Trouble Embodied.* New York: Routledge, 2018.

Käsemann, Ernst. "An Apologia for Primitive Christian Eschatology." Pages 169–95 in *Essays on New Testament Themes.* Translated by W. J. Montague. SBT 41. Naperville, IL: Allenson, 1964.

Kennedy, George A., ed. *Progymnasmata: Greek Textbooks of Prose Composition and Rhetoric.* WGRW 10. Atlanta: Society of Biblical Literature, 2003.

———. *New Testament Interpretation through Rhetorical Criticism.* Studies in Religion. Chapel Hill: University of North Carolina Press, 1984.

King, Karen L. *What Is Gnosticism?* Cambridge: Harvard University Press, 2003.

———. "Translating History: Reframing Gnosticism in Postmodernity." Pages 264–77 in *Tradition und Translation: Zum Problem der Interkulturellen Übersetzbarkeit religiöser Phänomene; Festschrift für Carsten Colpe zum 65. Geburstag.* Edited by Christoph Elsas et al. Berlin: De Gruyter, 1994.

———. "Which Early Christianity?" Pages 66–84 in *The Oxford Handbook of Early Christian Studies.* Edited by Susan Ashbrook Harvey and David G. Hunter. New York: Oxford University Press, 2010.

Klauck, Hans-Josef, and Daniel P. Bailey. *Ancient Letters and the New Testament: A Guide to Context and Exegesis.* Waco, TX: Baylor University Press, 2006.

Knight, Jonathan. *2 Peter and Jude.* New Testament Guides. Sheffield: Sheffield Academic, 1995.

Koch, Klaus. "Pseudonymous Writing." *IDBSup* 712–14.

Krentz, Edgar. "Peter: Confessor, Denier, Proclaimer, Validator of Proclomation—A Study in Diversity." *CurTM* 37.4 (2010): 320–33.

Kucicki, Janusz. *The Function of the Speeches in the Acts of the Apostles.* BibInt 158. Leiden: Brill, 2018.

Küster, Volker. "The Project of an Intercultural Theology." *Swedish Missiological Themes* 93.3 (2005): 417–32.

Kwok Pui-lan. *Discovering the Bible in the Non-biblical World.* Bible & Liberation. Eugene, OR: Wipf & Stock, 2003.

Lapham, Fred. *Peter: The Myth, the Man and the Writings: A Study of Early Petrine Text and Tradition.* JSNTSup 239. London: Sheffield Academic, 2003.

Lieu, Judith M. "The Forging of Christian Identity and the *Letter to Diognetus.*" Pages 171–89 in *Neither Jew nor Greek? Constructing Early Christianity.* London: T&T Clark, 2002.

———. "Identity Games in Early Christian Texts: The Letter to Diognetus." Pages 59–71 in *Identities and Ideologies in Early Jewish and Christian Texts, and in Modern Biblical Interpretation.* Edited by Katherine M. Hockey and David G. Horrell. London: T&T Clark, 2018.

Liew, Tat-siong Benny. *Postcolonial Interventions: Essays in Honor of R.S. Sugirtharajah.* Bible in the Modern World. Sheffield: Sheffield Phoenix, 2009.

———. *What Is Asian American Biblical Hermeneutics? Reading the New Testament.* Honolulu: University of Hawi'i Press, 2008.

Liew, Tat-siong Benny, and Fernando F. Segovia, eds. *Reading Biblical Texts Together: Pursuing Minoritized Biblical Criticism.* SemeiaSt 98. Atlanta: SBL Press, 2022.

Lim, Sung Uk. "Race and Ethnicity Discourse in Biblical Studies and Beyond." *Journal for the Study of Religions and Ideologies* 15.45 (2016): 120–42.

Malina, Bruce J. "Understanding New Testament Persons." Pages 41–61 in *The Social Sciences and New Testament Interpretation.* Edited by Richard Rohrbaugh. Grand Rapids: Baker Academic, 1996.

Malina, Bruce J., and John J. Pilch. *Social-Science Commentary on the Letters of Paul.* Minneapolis: Fortress, 2006.

Marbury, Herbert Robinson. *Pillars of Cloud and Fire: The Politics of Exodus in African American Biblical Interpretation.* Religion and Social Transformation. New York: New York University Press, 2015.

Martin, Clarice J. "Normative Biblical Motifs in African American Women's Moral Discourse: Maria Stewart's Autobiography as a Resource for Nurturing Leadership From the Black Church Tradition." Pages 47–72 in *The Stones That the Builders Rejected: The Development of Leader-*

ship from the Black Church Tradition. Edited by Walter E. Fluker. Harrisburg, PA: Trinity Press International, 1998.

Masenya, Madipoane J. "African Womanist Hermeneutics: A Suppressed Voice from South Africa Speaks." *JFSR* 11.1 (1995): 149–55.

Mbuvi, Andrew M. *Jude and 2 Peter.* New Covenant Commentary Series. Eugene, OR: Cascade, 2015.

McKim, Donald K. *Historical Handbook of Major Biblical Interpreters.* Downers Grove, IL: InterVarsity, 1998.

Meade, David G. *Pseudonymity and Canon: An Investigation into the Relationship of Authorship and Authority in Jewish and Earliest Christian Tradition.* Grand Rapids: Eerdmans, 1987.

Menéndez-Antuña, Luis. "Of Social Death and Solitary Confinement: The Political Life of a Gerasene (Luke 8:26–39)." *JBL* 138 (2019): 643–64.

———. "Whiteness and the Dismissal of Emancipatory Hermeneutics in Biblical Studies: A Decolonial Genealogy." Paper presented at a Wabash Group session at Boston University School of Theology, Boston, MA. 20 October 2022.

Mitchell, Margaret M. Review of *Rhetorical Criticism of the Bible: A Comprehensive Bibliography with Notes on History and Method,* by Duane F. Watson and Alan J. Hauser. *CBQ* 57 (1995): 615–16.

———. "Rhetorical and New Literary Criticism." Pages 615–33 in *The Oxford Handbook of Biblical Studies.* Edited by Judith M. Lieu and J. W. Rogerson. Oxford: Oxford University Press, 2008.

Mitchell, Stephen. *Anatolia: Land, Men, and Gods in Asia Minor.* 2 vols. Oxford: Clarendon, 1993.

Mosala, Itumeleng J. *Biblical Hermeneutics and Black Theology in South Africa.* Grand Rapids: Eerdmans, 1989.

Nasrallah, Laura, and Elisabeth Schüssler Fiorenza, eds. *Prejudice and Christian Beginnings: Investigating Race, Gender, and Ethnicity in Early Christian Studies.* Minneapolis: Fortress, 2009.

Neufeld, Dietmar, and Richard E. DeMaris. *Understanding the Social World of the New Testament.* New York: Routledge, 2010.

Neyrey, Jerome H. *2 Peter, Jude.* AB 37C. New York: Doubleday, 1993.

———. "The Apologetic Use of the Transfiguration in 2 Peter 1:16–21." *CBQ* 42 (1980): 504–19.

———. "The Form and Background of the Polemic in 2 Peter." *JBL* 99 (1980): 407–31.

———. "The Form and Background of the Polemic in 2 Peter." PhD. diss., Yale University, 1977.

Neyrey, Jerome H., and Eric C. Stewart. *The Social World of the New Testament: Insights and Models*. Grand Rapids: Baker Academic, 2008.

Nicnhuis, David R., and Robert W. Wall. *Reading the Epistles of James, Peter, John and Jude as Scripture*. Grand Rapids: Eerdmans, 2013.

Origen. *Commentary on the Epistle to the Romans: Books 1–5*. Edited by Thomas P. Scheck. Washington, DC: Catholic University of America Press, 2001.

Park, Wongi. "The Blessing of Whiteness in the Curse of Ham: Reading Gen 9:18–29 in the Antebellum South." *Religions* 12.11 (2021): 1–18.

———. *The Politics of Race and Ethnicity in Matthew's Passion Narrative*. Cham, Switzerland: Palgrave, 2019.

Pliny the Younger. *Letters and Panegyricus*. Translated by Betty Radice. 2 vols. LCL 59. Cambridge: Harvard University Press, 1969.

Potter, Jonathan. *Representing Reality: Discourse, Rhetoric and Social Construction*. Thousand Oaks, CA: Sage, 1996.

Powery, Emerson B. "'Lost in Translation: Ethnic Conflict in Bibles'—The Gospels, 'Race,' and the Common English Bible: An Introductory and Exploratory Conversation." *Ex Auditu* 31 (2015): 154–68.

———. "Under the Gaze of the Empire: Who Is My Neighbor?" *Int* 62 (2008): 134–44.

Powery, Emerson B., and Rodney Sadler. *The Genesis of Liberation: Biblical Interpretation in the Antebellum Narratives of the Enslaved*. Louisville: Westminster John Knox, 2016.

Punt, Jeremy. "Inhabiting the World in Front of the Text: The New Testament and Reception Studies." *Neot* 34.1 (2000): 207–24.

———. *Postcolonial Biblical Interpretation: Reframing Paul*. Leiden: Brill, 2015.

Reese, Ruth Anne. *2 Peter and Jude*. Two Horizons New Testament Commentary. Grand Rapids: Eerdmans, 2007.

Reicke, Bo. *The Epistles of James, Peter, and Jude*. AB 37. Garden City, NY: Doubleday, 1964.

Reinhartz, Adele. "The Hermeneutics of Chutzpah: A Disquisition on the Value/s of 'Critical Investigation of the Bible.'" *JBL* 140 (2021): 8–30.

Richard, Earl. *Reading 1 Peter, Jude, and 2 Peter: A Literary and Theological Commentary*. Macon, GA: Smyth & Helwys, 2000.

Richards, E. Randolph. *Paul and First-Century Letter Writing: Secretaries, Composition, and Collection*. Downers Grove, IL: InterVarsity Press, 2004.

Richards, E. Randolph, and Kevin J. Boyle, "Did Ancients Know the Testaments Were Pseudepigraphic? Implications for 2 Peter." *BBR* 30 (2020): 403–23.

Robbins, Vernon K. *Exploring the Texture of Texts: A Guide to Socio-rhetorical Interpretation*. Valley Forge, PA: Trinity Press International, 1996.

———. *The Tapestry of Early Christian Discourse: Rhetoric, Society and Ideology*. New York: Routledge, 1996.

Rogers, Richard A. "From Cultural Exchange to Transculturation: A Review and Reconceptualization of Cultural Appropriation." *Communication Theory* 16 (2006): 474–503.

Rohrbaugh, Richard L., ed. *The Social Sciences and New Testament Interpretation*. Grand Rapids: Baker Academic, 1996.

Sanders, E. P. *Paul and Palestinian Judaism: A Comparison of Patterns of Religion*. Philadelphia: Augsburg, 1977.

Schaff, Philip, and Henry Wace, ed. *Church Fathers: The Nicene and Post-Nicene Fathers*. Second Series. Accordance version. Edinburgh: T&T Clark.

Schüssler Fiorenza, Elisabeth. *Rhetoric and Ethic: The Politics of Biblical Studies*. Minneapolis: Fortress, 1999.

———. *Searching the Scriptures: A Feminist Commentary*. Vol. 2. New York: Crossroad, 1994.

———. *Searching the Scriptures: A Feminist Introduction*. Vol. 1. New York: Crossroad, 1993.

Smelser, Neil J. "Culture: Coherent or Incoherent." Pges 3–28 in *Theory of Culture*. Edited by Richard Münch and Neil J. Smelser. Berkeley: University of California Press, 1992.

Smith, Mitzi J. "'Unbossed and Unbought': Zilpha Elaw and Old Elizabeth and a Political Discourse of Origins." *Black Theology* 9.3 (2011): 287–311.

———. *Womanist Sass and Talk Back: Social (In)justice, Intersectionality, and Biblical Interpretation*. Eugene, OR: Cascade, 2018.

———. "Zilpha Elaw." Pages 185–87 in *Handbook of Women Biblical Interpreters: A Historical and Biographical Guide*. Edited by Marion Taylor. Grand Rapids: Baker Academic, 2012.

Smith, Shively T. J. "Historical Criticism: Methods." Pages 37–54 in *The New Cambridge Companion to Biblical Interpretation*. Edited by Ian Boxall and Bradley C. Gregory. Cambridge: Cambridge University Press, 2023.

——. "One More Time with Assata on My Mind: A Womanist Rereading of the Escape to Egypt (Matt 2:13–23) in Dialogue with an African American Woman Fugitive Narrative." Pages 139–64 in *Womanist Interpretations of the Bible: Expanding the Discourse*. Edited by Gay L. Byron and Vanessa Lovelace. SemeiaSt 85. Atlanta: SBL Press, 2016.

——. "Preliminary Thoughts: The Hermeneutical Dilemmas of the Allies, Colleagues, and Guild of African American Biblical Scholar-Teachers." Pages 39–45 in *Black Scholars Matter: Visions, Struggles, and Hopes in Africana Biblical Studies*. Edited by Gay L. Byron and Hugh R. Page Jr. RBS 100. Atlanta: SBL Press, 2022.

——. Review of *African American Readings of Paul*, by Lisa Bowens. *Theological Studies* 83.2 (2022): 319–20.

——. "Witnessing Jesus Hang: Reading Mary Magdalene's View of Crucifixion through Ida B. Wells's Chronicles of Lynching." Pages 296–323 in *Stony the Road We Trod: African American Biblical Interpretation*. Edited by Cain Hope Felder. 30th anniv. exp. ed. Minneapolis: Fortress, 2021.

——. "Zilpha Elaw and the 'Spirit.'" Pages 29–32 in *1–2 Peter and Jude*. Edited by Pheme Perkins, Eloise Rosenblatt, and Patricia McDonald. Wisdom Commentary 56. Collegeville, MN: Liturgical Press, 2022.

Soards, Marion L. *The Speeches in Acts: Their Content, Context, and Concerns*. Louisville: Westminster John Knox, 1994.

Starr, James M. *Sharers in Divine Nature: 2 Peter 1:4 in Its Hellenistic Context*. ConBNT 33. Stockholm: Almqvist & Wiksell, 2000.

Stowers, Stanley. *Letter Writing in Greco-Roman Antiquity*. LEC 5. Philadelphia: Westminster, 1986.

Stringfellow, Thornton. "The Bible Argument: Or, Slavery in the Light of Divine Revelation." Pages 459–522 in *Cotton Is King and Pro-Slavery Arguments: Comprising the Writings of Hammond, Harper, Christy, Stringfellow, Hodge, Bledsoe, and Cartwright on This Important Subject*. Edited by E. N. Elliott. Augusta, GA: Pritchard, Abbott & Loomis, 1860.

Sugirtharajah, R. S. *Voices from the Margin: Interpreting the Bible in the Third World*. 25th anniv. ed. Maryknoll, NY: Orbis, 2016.

Taylor, Marion Ann. "Celebrating 125 Years of Women in the Society of Biblical Literature (1894–2019)." Pages 1–44 in *Woman and the Society of Biblical Literature*. Edited by Nicole L. Tilford. BSNA 29. Atlanta: SBL Press, 2019.

Taylor, Marion Ann, and Agnes Choi, eds. *Handbook of Women Biblical Interpreters: A Historical and Biographical Guide*. Grand Rapids: Baker Academic, 2012.

Trimiew, Darryl M. "The Social Gospel Movement and the Question of Race." Pages 17–37 in *The Social Gospel Today*. Edited by Christopher H. Evans. Louisville: Westminster John Knox, 2001.

Vinson, Richard B., Richard F. Wilson, and Watson E. Mills. *1 and 2 Peter, Jude*. Smyth & Hewys Bible Commentary. Macon, GA: Smyth & Helwys, 2010.

Voth, Steven. "Justice vs. Righteousness: A Contextualized Analysis of 'tsedeq' in the KJV(English) and the RVR(Spanish)." *Journal of Biblical Text Research* 20 (2007): 279–310.

Watson, Duane F. "The Epistolary Rhetoric of 1 Peter, 2 Peter, and Jude." Pages 47–62 in *Reading 1–2 Peter and Jude: A Resource for Students*. Edited by Eric F. Mason and Troy W. Martin. RBS 77. Atlanta: Society of Biblical Literature, 2014.

Watson, Duane F., Terrance D. Callan, Mikeal Parsons, and Charles Talbert. *First and Second Peter*. Paideia. Grand Rapids: Baker Academic 2012.

Weems, Renita. "Reading Her Way through the Struggle: African American Women and the Bible." Pages 31–50 in *The Bible and Liberation: Political and Social Hermeneutics*. Edited by Norman K. Gottwald and Richard A. Horsey. Maryknoll, NY: Orbis, 1993.

———. "Womanist Reflections on Biblical Hermeneutics." Pages 216–24 in *1980–1992*. Vol. 2 of *Black Theology: A Documentary History*. Edited by James H. Cone and Gayraud S. Wilmore. Maryknoll, NY: Orbis, 1999.

West, Gerald O., and Musa W. Dube Shomanah. *The Bible in Africa: Transactions, Trajectories, and Trends*. Leiden: Brill, 2000.

Westphal, Merold. "The Philosophical/Theological View." In *Biblical Heremeneutics: Five Views*. Edited by Stanley E. Porter and Beth M. Stovell. Downers Grove, IL: InterVarsity Press, 2012.

Wilder, Amos N. *Jesus' Parables and the War of Myths: Essays on Imagination in the Scriptures*. Edited by James Breech. Philadelphia: Fortress, 1982.

———. *The New Voice: Religion, Literature, Hermeneutics*. New York: Herder & Herder, 1969.

Wilson, Bryan R. "A Typology of Sects." Pages 361–83 in *Sociology of Religion: Selected Readings*. Edited by Roland Robertson. Baltimore: Penguin, 1969.

Wimbush, Vincent L. *The Bible and African Americans: A Brief History*. Facets. Minneapolis: Fortress, 2003.

———. "Interpreters—Enslaving/Enslaved/Runagate." *JBL* 130 (2011): 5–24.

———. *Refractions of the Scriptural: Critical Orientation as Transgression*. Routledge Studies in Religion. New York: Routledge, 2016.

———. *White Men's Magic: Scripturalization as Slavery*. New York: Oxford University Press, 2011.

Winn, Adam, ed. *An Introduction to Empire in the New Testament*. RBS 84. Atlanta: SBL Press, 2016.

Witherington III, Ben. *A Socio-rhetorical Commentary on 1–2 Peter*. Vol. 2 of *Letters and Homilies for Hellenized Christians*. Downers Grove, IL: InterVarsity Press, 2007.

Zmijewski, J. "Apostolische Paradosis und Pseudepigraphie im Neuen Testament 'Durch Erinnerung wachhalten' (2 Petr 1, 13; 3,1)." *BZ* 23 (1979): 161–71.

African American History and Literature

Andrews, William L. *Sisters of the Spirit: Three Black Women's Autobiographies of the Nineteenth Century*. Bloomington: Indiana University Press, 1986.

Asante, Molefi Kete. *Language, Communication, and Rhetoric in Black America*. New York: Harper & Row, 1972.

———. *Race, Rhetoric, and Identity: The Architecton of Soul*. Amherst, NY: Humanity Books, 2005.

Asante, Molefi Kete, and Rosemary Chai. "Nkrabea and Yuan in Akan and Chinese: Cultural Intersections and Communication Implications in an African and an Asian Society." *Journal of Black Studies* 44.2 (2013): 119–36.

Bassard, Katherine Clay. *Transforming Scriptures: African American Women Writers and the Bible*. Athens: University of Georgia Press, 2010.

Bracks, Lean'tin L., ed. *African American Almanac: Four Hundred Years of Triumph, Courage and Excellence*. Canton, MI: Visible Ink, 2012.

Broughton, Virginia. *Twenty Years' Experience of a Missionary in Spiritual Narratives*. Introduction by Sue E. Houchins. New York: Oxford University Press, 1988.

———. "Women's Work." Pages 407–13 in *The Portable Nineteenth-Century African American Women Writers*. Edited by Hollis Robbins and Henry Louis Gates Jr. New York: Penguin, 2017.

Bruce, Dickson D. *Black American Writing from the Nadir: The Evolution of a Literary Tradition, 1877–1915*. Baton Rouge: Louisiana State University Press, 1989.

Carter, George E., et al., eds. *The Black Abolitionist Papers, 1830–1865*. Microfilm ed. 17 reels. Sanford, NC: Microfilming Corporation of America, 1981.

Carter, Jennie. *A Black Journalist of the Early West*. Edited by Eric Gardner. Margaret Walker Alexander Series in African American Studies. Jackson: University Press of Mississippi, 2007.

Cima, Gay Gibson. "Black and Unmarked: Phillis Wheatley, Mercy Otis Warren, and the Limits of Strategic Anonymity." *Theatre Journal* 52.4 (2000): 465–95.

Cook, Mary V. "Women's Place in the Work of the Denomination." Pages 464–82 in *The Portable Nineteenth-Century African American Women Writers*. Edited by Hollis Robbins and Henry Louis Gates Jr. New York: Penguin, 2017.

Cooper, Anna J. *The Voice of Anna Julia Cooper*. Edited by Charles Lemert and Esme Bhan. Legacies of Social Thought Series. Lanham, MD: Rowman & Littlefield, 1998.

Cooper, Brittney. "Ain't I a Lady? Race Women, Michelle Obama, and the Ever-Expanding Democratic Imagination." *MELUS* 35.4 (2010): 39–57.

Early, Sarah J. "The Organized Efforts of the Colored Women of the South to Improve their Condition." 380–85 in *The Portable Nineteenth-Century African American Women Writers*. Edited by Hollis Robbins and Henry Louis Gates Jr. New York: Penguin, 2017.

Elaw, Zilpha. *Memoirs of the Life, Religious Experience, Ministerial Travels, and Labours of Mrs. Elaw*. Edited by Kimberly D. Blockett. Regenerations. Morgantown: West Virginia University Press, 2021.

Ernest, John. "From Mysteries to Histories: Cultural Pedagogy in Frances E. W. Harper's Iola Leroy." *American Literature* 64.3 (1992): 497–518.

Equal Justice Initiative. *Lynching in America: Confronting the Legacy of Racial Terror*. 3rd ed. Equal Justice Initiative, 2017.

"Exposing the 'Thread-Bare Lie': How Ida B. Wells Used Investigative Journalism to Uncover the Truth about Lynching." *Chicago Stories*. WTTW. https://tinyurl.com/SBL4533c.

Fanon, Franz. *Black Skin, White Masks*. Translated by Richard Philcox. Repr., New York: Grove Press, 2008.

Foner, Eric. *Reconstruction: America's Unfinished Revolution, 1863–1877*. New American Nation Series. New York: Harper & Row, 1988.

Foote, Julia A. J. "Selections from A Brand Plucked from the Fire." Page 189–99 in *The Portable Nineteenth-Century African American Women Writers*. Edited by Hollis Robbins and Henry Louis Gates Jr. New York: Penguin, 2017.

Forten, Sarah Louise. "Hours of Childhood." The *Liberator*. December 15, 1833. https://blackfreedom.proquest.com/hours-of-childhood/.

———. "A Mother's Grief." The *Liberator*. July 7, 1832. https://blackfreedom.proquest.com/a-mothers-grief/.

———. "To the Hibernia." The *Liberator*. May, 1833. https://blackfreedom.proquest.com/to-the-hibernia/.

———. "The Slave." The *Liberator*. 1831. https://blackfreedom.proquest.com/the-slave/.

Foster, Frances Smith. *Written by Herself: Literary Production by African American Women, 1746–1892*. Bloomington: Indiana University Press, 1993.

Gates, Henry Louis, Jr. *Stony the Road: Reconstruction, White Supremacy, and the Rise of Jim Crow*. New York: Penguin, 2019.

Gernes, Todd S. "Poetic Justice: Sarah Forten, Eliza Earle, and the Paradox of Intellectual Property." *New England Quarterly* 71.2 (1998): 229–65.

Goffman, Erving. "Stigma and Social Identity." Pages 256–65 in *Understanding Deviance: Connecting Classical and Contemporary Perspectives*. Edited by Tammy L. Anderson. New York: Taylor & Frances, 2014.

Grimké, Charlotte. "Life on the Sea Islands." Pages 130–64 in *The Portable Nineteenth-Century African American Women Writers*. Edited by Hollis Robbins and Henry Louis Gates Jr. New York: Penguin, 2017.

Hanson, Joyce A. "The Making of a Race Woman." Pages 11–55 in *Mary Mcleod Bethune and Black Women's Political Activism*. Columbia: University of Missouri Press, 2003.

Higginbotham, Evelyn Brooks. "Baptist Church." Pages 84–88 in *Black Women in America: An Historical Encyclopedia*. Edited by Darlene

Clark Hine, Elsa Barkley Brown, and Rosalyn Terborg-Penn. Vol. 1. Bloomington: Indiana University Press, 1993.

Insko, Jeffrey. "Anachronistic Imaginings: 'Hope Leslie's Challenge to Historicism." *American Literary History* 16.2 (2004): 179–207.

Jones, Charles Colcock. *The Religious Instruction of the Negroes in the United States.* N.p.: 1842.

Kelley, Mary. "'The Difference of Colour': Reading and Writing Abolitionism." *Social Dynamics* 45 (2019): 156–73.

———. "Talents Committed to Your Care': Reading and Writing Radical Abolitionism in Antebellum America." *New England Quarterly* 88.1 (2015): 37–72.

Lee, Jarena. "Religious Experience and Journal of Mrs. Jarena Lee." Pages 3–87 in *Spiritual Narratives.* Schomburg Library of Nineteenth-Century Black Women Writers. New York: Oxford University Press, 1988.

———. *Religious Experience and Journal of Mrs. Jarena Lee: Giving an Account of Her Call to Preach the Gospel; Revised and Corrected from the Original Manuscript Written by Herself.* Repr., Philadelphia, 1849.

Lindhorst, Marie. "Politics in a Box: Sarah Mapps Douglass and the Female Literary Association, 1831–1833." *Pennsylvania History* 60 (1998): 263–78.

Logan, Rayford Whittingham. *The Betrayal of the Negro, from Rutherford B. Hayes to Woodrow Wilson.* New York: Collier, 1965.

Miltenberger, Scott A. "Forten, James." Pages 36–38 In *Encyclopedia of African American History, 1619–1895: From the Colonial Period to the Age of Frederick Douglass.* New York: Oxford University Press, 2006.

Noll, Mark A. *America's God: From Jonathan Edwards to Abraham Lincoln.* Oxford: Oxford University Press, 2002.

———. "The Image of the United States as a Biblical Nation, 1776–1865." Pages 39–58 in *The Bible in America: Essays in Cultural History.* Edited by Nathan O. Hatch and Mark A. Noll. New York: Oxford University Press, 1982.

Page, Yolanda Williams, ed. *Encyclopedia of African American Women Writers.* 2 vols. Westport, CT: Greenwood Press, 2005.

Paquet, Sandra Puchet. "Prince, Mary." Page 599 in *The Oxford Companion to African American Literature.* Edited by William L. Andrews, Frances Smith Foster, and Trudier Harris. New York: Oxford University Press, 1997.

Pinn, Anthony B. *Understanding and Transforming the Black Church.* Eugene, OR: Cascade, 2010.

Pinn, Anne H., and Anthony B. Pinn. *Fortress Introduction to Black Church History*. Minneapolis: Fortress, 2002.

Prince, Mary. "Excerpt from *The History of Mary Prince, a West Indian Slave*." Pages 13–24 in *The Portable Nineteenth-Century African American Women Writers*. Edited by Hollis Robbins and Henry Louis Gates Jr. New York: Penguin, 2017.

Purvis, Sarah Forten. "The Abuse of Liberty." Page 253 in *The Portable Nineteenth-Century African American Women Writers*. Edited by Hollis Robbins and Henry Louis Gates Jr. New York: Penguin, 2017.

Reed, Ashley. *Heaven's Interpreters: Women Writers and Religious Agency in Nineteenth-Century America*. Ithaca: Cornell University Press, 2020.

Richardson Elaine B., and Ronald L. Jackson II, eds. *African American Rhetoric(s): Interdisciplinary Perspectives*. Carbondale: Southern Illinois University Press, 2007.

———. *Understanding African American Rhetoric: Classical Origins to Contemporary Innovations*. London: Taylor & Francis, 2003.

Riggs, Marcia. *Can I Get a Witness? Prophetic Religious Voices of African American Women: An Anthology*. Maryknoll, NY: Orbis, 1997.

———. *Plenty Good Room: Women versus Male Power in the Black Church*. Cleveland: Pilgrim, 2003.

Robbins, Hollis, and Henry Louis Gates Jr., eds. *The Portable Nineteenth-Century African American Women Writers*. New York: Penguin, 2017.

Sedgwick, Catharine M. *Hope Leslie; or Early Times in Massachusetts*. New York: White, Gallaher, & White, 1827.

Sellman, James Clyde. "Walker, David." Pages 989–90 in *Africana: The Encyclopedia of the African and African American Experience*. Edited by Kwame Anthony Appiah and Henry Louis Gates Jr. New York: Basic Civitas Books, 1999.

Sterling, Dorothy, ed. *We Are Your Sisters: Black Women in the Nineteenth Century*. New York: Norton, 1984.

———. *Meditations from the Pen of Mrs. Maria W. Stewart*. Washington, DC: Enterprise, 1879.

Stewart, Maria A. "An Address: African Rights and Liberty." February 27, 1833, African Masonic Hall, Boston. Iowa State University Archives of Women's Political Communication. https://tinyurl.com/SBL4533b.

———. "An Address Delivered at the African Masonic Hall." Pages 30–37 in *The Portable Nineteenth-Century African American Women Writers*. Edited by Hollis Robbins and Henry Louis Gates Jr. New York: Penguin, 2017.

———. "Address Delivered before the Afric-American Female Intelligence Society of Boston." April 28, 1832. Iowa State University Archives of Women's Political Communication. https://tinyurl.com/SBL4533a.

———. *Meditations from the Pen of Mrs. Maria W. Stewart*. Washington: Enterprise Publishing Company, 1879.

———. "Religion and the Pure Principles of Morality, the Sure Foundation on Which We Must Build." Pages 28–42 in *America's First Black Woman Political Writer*. Edited by Marilyn Richardson. Bloomington: University of Indiana Press, 1987.

Stout, Harry S. "Word and Order in Colonial New England." Pages 19–38 in *The Bible in America: Essays in Cultural History*. Edited by Nathan O. Hatch and Mark A. Noll. New York: Oxford University Press, 1982.

Truth, Sojourner. "Speech Delivered to Women's Rights Convention in Akron Ohio." Page 7 in *The Portable Nineteenth-Century African American Women Writers*. Edited by Hollis Robbins and Henry Louis Gates Jr. New York: Penguin, 2017.

Watkins Harper, Frances Ellen. "Bible Defense of Slavery." Pages 302–3 in *The Portable Nineteenth-Century African American Women Writers*. Edited by Hollis Robbins and Henry Louis Gates Jr. New York: Penguin, 2017.

Wells, Ida B. *Crusade for Justice: The Autobiography of Ida B. Wells*. 2nd ed. Negro American Biographies and Autobiographies. Chicago: University of Chicago Press, 2020.

Wilkerson, Isabel. *Caste: The Origins of Our Discontent*. New York: Random House, 2020.

Williams, Fannie Barrier. "The Intellectual Progress of the Colored Woman of the United States since the Emancipation Proclamation." Pages 394–405 in *The Portable Nineteenth-Century African American Women Writers*. Edited by Hollis Robbins and Henry Louis Gates Jr. New York: Penguin, 2017.

Williams, Yolanda, ed. *Encyclopedia of African American Women Writers*. Vols. 1–2. Westport, CT: Greenwood Press, 2007.

Winch, Julie. "'You Have Talents—Only Cultivate Them': Philadelphia's Black Female Literary Societies and the Abolitionist Crusade." Pages 101–18 in *The Abolitionist Sisterhood: Women's Political Culture in Antebellum America*. Edited by Jean Fagan Yellin and John C. Van Hornes. Ithaca, NY: Cornell University Press, 1994.

Ancient Sources Index

Modern Authors Index

Subject Index

Printed in the USA
CPSIA information can be obtained
at www.ICGtesting.com
LVHW090631110923
757122LV00009B/58